Joseph Jones

Major Jones's travels

Joseph Jones

Major Jones's travels

ISBN/EAN: 9783337208172

Printed in Europe, USA, Canada, Australia, Japan

Cover: Foto ©Andreas Hilbeck / pixelio.de

More available books at **www.hansebooks.com**

Major Jones's Travels.

WITH EIGHT ILLUSTRATIONS.

By Major Joseph Jones,
(OF PINEVILLE, GEORGIA.)

AUTHOR OF

"Major Jones's Courtship," "Major Jones's Georgia Scenes,"
"Rancy Cottem's Courtship," etc.

PHILADELPHIA:
T. B. PETERSON & BROTHERS.

PRICE 75 CENTS.

MAJOR JONES'S COURTSHIP

WITH 21 FULL PAGE ILLUSTRATIONS.

BY MAJOR JOSEPH JONES.
(OF *PINEVILLE, GEORGIA.*)

Author of *"Rancy Cottem's Courtship," "Major Jones's Chronicles of Pineville," "Major Jones's Sketches of Travel,"* etc.

"By this time the galls was holt of my coat-tail, hollerin as hard as they could."—*Page* 188.

ONE VOLUME, SQUARE 12mo., PAPER COVER. PRICE 75 CENTS

☞ *Major Jones's Courtship is for sale by all Booksellers and News Agents, or copies of it will be sent to any one, at once, post-paid, on remitting Seventy-five cents in a letter to the publisher*

T. B. PETERSON & BROTHERS, Philadelphia, Pa.

"When I was reddy to start, I went to the door to see my trunks put on the waggon, and when I cum back, thar he stood in the same place, deaf and dum, with his hands down by his side, and his head up, looking me rite in the face."—*Letter* x. *p.* 95.

MAJOR JONES'S TRAVELS.

MAJOR JONES.

PHILADELPHIA:
T. B. PETERSON & BROTHERS;
306 CHESTNUT STREET.

MAJOR JONES'S TRAVELS.

DETAILING HIS

Adventures, Humorous Scenes, and Incidents,

WHILE ON HIS

TOUR FROM GEORGIA TO CANADA.

BY MAJOR JOSEPH JONES.
(Of Pineville, Georgia.)
AUTHOR OF "MAJOR JONES'S COURTSHIP," "RANCY COTTEM'S COURTSHIP," "MAJOR JONES'S GEORGIA SCENES," ETC.

With Eight Illustrations by Darley.

PHILADELPHIA:
T. B. PETERSON & BROTHERS;
306 CHESTNUT STREET.

COPYRIGHT:
T. B. PETERSON & BROTHERS.
1880.

MAJOR JONES'S COURTSHIP.

Major Jones's Courtship. *Author's New, Enlarged, and Rewritten Edition.* Detailed in a Series of Letters, with Humorous Scenes, Incidents, and Adventures. By Major Joseph Jones, of Pineville, Georgia, author of "Rancy Cottem's Courtship," "Major Jones's Travels," "Major Jones's Georgia Scenes," etc. With Twenty-One Full Page Illustrations, on Tinted Plate Paper, by Darley and Cary. One volume, square 12mo., uniform with this volume, price 75 cents.

MAJOR JONES'S TRAVELS.

Major Jones's Travels. Detailing his Adventures, Humorous Scenes, and Incidents that happened, in each town he visited, while on his tour from Georgia to Canada. By Major Joseph Jones, of Pineville, Georgia, author of "Major Jones's Courtship," "Rancy Cottem's Courtship," "Major Jones's Georgia Scenes," etc. With Eight Full Page Illustrations on Tinted Plate Paper, by Darley. One volume, square 12mo., uniform with this volume, price 75 cents.

MAJOR JONES'S GEORGIA SCENES.

Major Jones's Georgia Scenes. Comprising his celebrated Sketches of Georgia Scenes, with his Adventures, Incidents and Characters he met. By Major Joseph Jones, of Pineville, Georgia, author of "Major Jones's Courtship," "Rancy Cottem's Courtship," "Major Jones's Travels," etc. With Twelve Full Page Illustrations, on Tinted Plate Paper, by Darley. One volume, 12mo., uniform with this volume, price 75 cents.

RANCY COTTEM'S COURTSHIP.

Rancy Cottem's Courtship. *Author's Edition.* Detailed with Other Humorous Sketches and Adventures. By Major Joseph Jones, of Pineville, Georgia, author of "Major Jones's Courtship," "Major Jones's Travels," "Major Jones's Georgia Scenes," etc. With Eight Full Page Illustrations, on Tinted Plate Paper, by Cary. One volume, square 12mo., uniform with this volume, price 50 cents.

PREFACE.

Reader, do you feel like gwine on a jurny to the north! If you do, jest take a seat with me, and I'll carry you from Pineville to Quebeck, and back agin in a little or no time. I don't know as I can offer quite sich inducements to travelers, as is offered by some of the pop'lar *writers* of the day; but if I can't promise you sich elegant style nor sich instructive and entertainin gossip by the way, I can carry you over the route as cheap as most of 'em, and with as little danger to your *morals*.

We will travel in steamboats, ralerodes, stage-coaches, and canal-boats, over rivers, lakes and mountains. We will visit cities, towns, and country, and see every kind of scenery, and make the acquaintance of all sorts of people; but if the trip should prove dull and uninterestin to you, you can sleep over the long stretches, and if you should git cumpletely out of patience with your auther, you can stop on the way and git aboard of the next *book* that cums along.

But in sober yearnest: this little sketch of my perrygrinations among the big cities of the northern states, was rit with no higher aim than to amuse the idle hours of my frends, and if it fails to do that, its a spilt job. If I had made a bigger book, I'd tuck up too much of the reader's time with sich unprofitable nonsense, and the strait jacket imposed on me by the limits of my volume, made it difficult for me to accomplish what I sot out to do. To git over so much ground even by the shortest route I could find, tuck a good deal of room, and if I stopped to introduce a incident or describe a interestin scene now and then, I found my letters gittin so long that my book wouldn't hold 'em.

I don't want to be understood, though, as makin a apology for my book—not by no means. Sich as it is, I'm responsible for it. But with this brief explanation, them what waste the time to read what I have rit about my travels, will understand why these pages aint no more deservin the compliment they thus pay to

Ther frend til deth,

Jos. Jones.

ILLUSTRATIONS.

Portrait of Major Joseph Jones on his travels ....*Title Cut.*

" Old Moma was sittin' in the door when Major Jones went to her, and she raised her old dim eyes, almost white with age, and looked at him. 'Why, Massa Joe, God bless you; you gwine away widout tellin pore old Moma good by?'" ....*Page* 34.

"Then cum the kissin bisness. I took the worst job fust, and kissed old Miss Stallins and mother, and then kissed the galls two or three times a piece, all round." ....*Page* 35.

"It tuck the breth clean out of me, my tongue felt as if it was full of needles, and I drapped the glass and spurted the rest out of my mouth quicker'n lightnin, but before I could git breth to speak to the chap, he ax'd me if I wasn't well." ....*Page* 87.

"With that, the little ragged cuss sot up a big laugh, and put his thumb on his nose and wiggled his fingers at me. 'Do you see anything green?' ses he, 'eh, hoss?'" ....*Page* 91.

" When I was reddy to start, I went to the door to see my trunks put on the waggon, and when I cum back thar he stood in the same place, deaf and dum, with his hands down by his side, and his hed up, lookin me rite in the face." ....*Page* 95.

"Says she to Major Jones, I'm a poor woman, my husban's sick, won't you hold this bundle for me till I go in the drug-store for some medicin'. I did so, got tired of waiting, and walked down to the lamp-post to see what it was. 'It was a live baby,' and the sweat poured out of me, I tell you, in a stream." ....*Page* 128.

"I soon seed what she was up to, and so I started to go, but the fust thing I know'd she had the yarn round my neck, and the next minit 'bout five hundred of 'em was pullin at me, all singin, 'Cum with me, my dear.'"
Page 148.

MAJOR JONES'S TRAVELS.

LETTER I.

Pineville, Geo., May 5, 1845.

To Mr. Thompson:—*Dear Sir*—I have almost gin up writin intirely, sense you quit editin the Southern Miscellany; but I spose I'm like other peeple what's got the *kakoethis skribendy*, as they call it, and never will git cumpletely cured of it as long as I live. Dr. Mountgomery ses it depends a grate deal how peeple take it, whether they ever git over it or not; sumtimes, he ses, when they catch it at school they git cured of it, when it comes out, by a few doses of judishus kriticism. But he ses he thinks it's a constitootional disease with me, and I better jest let it take its course.

Well, sense my book* has been printed and so many thousand copies of it has been sold all over the country, I've felt a monstrous curiosity to see a little more of the world and the peeple in it, than what a body can see out here in the piny-woods; and as the crap is pretty well laid by now, and things is considerable easy with me, I've made up my mind to make a tower of travel to the big North this summer, jest for greens, as we say in Georgia, when we hain't got no very pertickeler reason for any thing, or hain't got time to tell the real

---

* Major Jones's Courtship, with 21 Engravings. Price 75 cts.

one. I'm gwine to take Mary and little Henry Clay (who's a mazin smart little feller now, I can tell you,) and go to New York, and Filadelfy, and Washington City, and Baltomore, and Boston and all about thar, and spend the summer until pickin time, nockin round in them big cities, mong them peeple what's so monstrous smart and religious and refined, and see if I can't pick up sume idees what'll be worth rememberin. I've got a first-rate overseer to take care of the plantation, and every thing's fixed for the trip. Mary's tickled to deth at the idee of seein New York, and gettin a new bonnet rite from the French milliner ; and the galls is all gwine to send for new frocks to be made in the very newest fashion.

Old Miss Stallins, who you know is one of the economicalist old wimen that ever lived, hain't got much notion of no such doins. She ses its all down-right nonsense to spend so much money jest for nothing but to travel away off among people what we don't know nothin about, and maybe won't never see agin if we was to live to be as old as Methusleum. The fact is the old woman hain't got no notion of them northern people no how. Ever sense that feller Crotchett tried to git round her for one of her daughters, she can't bear the name of the north ; and jest talk to her about water privileges, and it puts her in a passion in a minit. She ses, Lord knows she wouldnt' give a thrippence to see all the bominable Yankees in the world, and as for seein the country, she ses ther's as many fine plantations, and handsum towns, as many big mountains and rivers, and as many cataracks and sulfer springs in Georgia, as she wants to see, 'thout gwine away off on the sea to git shipracked maybe, or blowed up by some everlastin steamboat bustin its biler. Besides, she ses, it's no wonder the southern people is always complainin about hard times, when they go to the north every sumrer and spend all ther money in travelin and byin fineries and northern gigamarees of one kind another what they mought jest as well do without.

Mother's a little more reasonable 'bout it. She ses that bein as I'm a literary caracter I ought to see something of the world, and as it's monstrous troublesome to travel with children, we better go now, when we hain't got but one. She ses it's fashionable to go to the north, and she lon't see why I haint as good a right to be like other folks, as sum people she knows, what goes to the Sarrytogy springs every year, when they can't hardly make out to live at home. All she don't like about it is, takin little Henry so far from home. She ses if he was to git sick at the north then she couldn't be thar to nurse him, and Lord only knows what would come of the child. But she's bundled up a whole heap of things to make yarb tea for the baby when it gits sick, and told Mary all how to do, and Prissy's one of the best nurses in the world; so ther ain't no fear about that. Lord knows, she ses, old misses needn't trouble herself 'bout little massa Harry, for she nussed Miss Mary through all her croops and measels and hoopin-coughs, and all manner of ailments, and she reckons she ought to know how to take care of sick children by this time. I never did see sich a proud nigger before in all my life as she is 'bout gwine to the north. The galls has been makin some new frocks for her, and Mary ses she really does believe the creeter's head is turned; for she can't stand still long enuff to try 'em on. She don't think of nothing else but carryin her little massy Harry 'bout New York to look at the stores, and she's promised every nigger on the plantation to bring 'em sumthing from the north. Ned wants to go too, but I don't think it's hardly worth while to take him along for all the use he'd be to us, and then it would add to the expense.

We're all in a muss now gettin ready for the journey, and sich other fixin and packin you never did see. I do believe old Miss Stallins and mother has packed up 'bout seven trunks full of plunder of one kind and another, and the more we tell 'em that ther ain't no use in takin so much, the more they say we don't know any thing about it. Do you think old Miss Stallins hain't put in a heap of quilts and pillar-cases! and I do believe if we had a trunk big enuff to hold 'em, she'd make us carry a eather-bed or two. She ses people never does know what they want til they find themselves without it, and the best way is always to be on the safe side. She tried her best this morning to git Mary to let her put in 'bout twenty pounds of country soap. She ses she don't care how cheap it is at the north, she knows ther ain't no better in the world than her own make; and she don't see any sense in people gwine and spendin ther money for things what they've got at home. She's a monstrous clever old woman, and I try to humour her all I can in her notions, but I can't stand the soap.

We expect to start day after to-morrow, if nothing don't turn up to prevent, and if you think my letters is worth the postage, I'll give you my impressions of matters and things now and then, whenever I meet any thing in my travels worth noticin.

Hopin you will be alive and able to keep off the muskeeters when I cum back this fall, I must bid you good-by for the present. So no more from
     Your friend til deth,
       Jos. Jones.

LETTER II.

Pineville, Georgia, May 10, 1845.

To Mr. Thompson:—*Dear Sir*—This is a world of ısappintment, shore enuff. All my plans is busted up, and I don't know if any thing ever sot me back much worse before. You know I had evry thing fixed for a journey to the North this summer, with my famly. Well, last nite, bein as we was gwine to start the next mornin, we had a little sort of a sociable party at our nouse, jest by way of makin one job of biddin good by to the nabours. 'Mong the rest of 'em, old Mr. Mountgomery come to see us and wish us good luck on our journey.

Mary and all of 'em was in a monstrous flurryment, and had little Harry all dressed out in his new clothes, to let the nabours see how pretty he looked before he went away. Old Mr. Mountgomery's monstrous fond of children, and always makes a heap of little Harry, cause he's so smart; and the old man tuck him up on his knee and ax'd him whose sun he was, and how old he was, and a heap of other things what the little feller didn't know nothing about.

"Don't you think it'll improve his helth to take him to the North?" ses Mary to him.

"O, yes!" ses he; "no doubt it'll be a great deal of sarvice to the little feller; but he'll be a monstrous site of trouble to you on the road, Mrs. Jones."

"Yes!" ses Mary; "but Prissy's a very careful nurse; and she's so devoted to him that she won't hardly let me touch him."

"O, yes!" ses the old man; "if you could jest take Prissy 'long with you, then you'd do very well. But there's it, you see—"

"What?" ses Mary; "you didn't think I was gwine to the North without a servant, did you, Mr. Mountgomery?"

The old man laughed rite out. "Ha, ha, ha!" ses he; "taint possible you is gwine to take Prissy with you to New York, is it? Why, Majer," ses he to me, "haint you got no better sense than to think of takin sich a valuable nigger as that with you, to have her fall into the hands of them infernal abolitionists?"

"The mischief take the abolitionists," ses I; "I reckon they haint got nothing to do with none of my niggers."

The old man shuck the ashes out of his pipe, and laughed like he would split his sides.

"Why, bless yer soul, Majer," ses he, "you couldn't keep her from 'em a day after you got to New York. No, no!" ses he; "not sich a likely gall as that. They'd have her out of yer hands quicker'n you could say Jack Robinson."

Prissy's eyes looked like sassers, and Mary, and mother, and all of 'em stared like they didn't know what to say.

"Why, Massa Gummery!" ses Prissy, "um wouldn't trouble me if I was long-a' Massa Joe, would dey?"

"To be sure they would, nigger!" ses Mr. Mountgomery; "they'd take you whether you was willin or not, in spite of yer Massa Joe, or anybody else."

"But," ses Mary, "Prissy wouldn't leave us on no account—she knows as well as anybody when she's well treated; and I'm sure she couldn't be better taken care of no whar in the world."

"That don't make no manner of difference," ses the old man. "They wouldn't ax her nothing about it. The fust thing you'd know she'd be gone, and then you mought as well look for a needle in a haystack, as to try to find a nigger in New York."

Then he took a paper out of his pocket and red what

a gentleman had his nigger tuck from him, somewhar in Providence, and carried rite off and put in jail.

"Ki," ses Prissy, lookin like she was half scared out of her senses, "den I aint gwine to no New York, for dem pison ole bobolitionists for cotch me."

"But aint ther no law for nigger stealin, at the north?" ses old Miss Stallins.

"Law!" ses Mr. Mountgomery, "bless you, no! They've sold all ther niggers long ago, and got the money for 'em—so the law don't care whose niggers they steal."

Mary sot and looked rite in the fire for 'bout a minit without sayin a word. I jest saw how it was. It wan't no use for me to think of her gwine with me, 'thout Prissy to take care of the baby; and after what Mr. Mountgomery had sed to her, I mought jest as well try to git her to stick her hed in the fire as go to New York. I never thought of them bominable abolitionists before, and I never was so oudaciously put out with 'em. It was enough to make a man what wasn't principled agin swearin, cus like a trooper. Just to think—every thing reddy to start, and then to have the whole bisness nocked rite in the head by them devils."

"Well," ses Mary, "thar's a eend to my jurney to the north. I couldn't think of gwine a step without Prissy to take care of the child; and spose I was to git sick, too, way off 'mong strangers—what would I do without Prissy?"

"Oh! it wouldn't never do in the world," ses old Miss Stallins.

"But," ses Mr. Mountgomery, you could git plenty of servants at the north when you git thar."

"What!" ses Mary; "trust my child with one of them good-for-nuthin free niggers? No, indeed! I wouldn't have one of 'em about me, not for no considerashun. I never did see one of 'em what had any breedin, and they're all too plagy triflin to take care of themselves, let alone doin any thing else."

"No! but," ses the old man, "they've got plenty of white servants at the north, what you can hire for little or nothing."

"Goodness gracious!" ses old Miss Stallins; "white servants! Well, the Lord knows I wouldn't have none of 'em 'bout me."

"Nor me neither," ses Mary. "It may do well enuff for people what don't know the difference between niggers and white folks; but I could never bear to see a white gall toatin my child about, and waitin on me like a nigger. It would hurt my conscience to keep anybody 'bout me in that condition, who was as white and as good as me."

"That's right, my child," ses old Miss Stallins; "no Christian lady could do no such thing, I don't care who they is."

I know'd the jig was up, and I was like the boy what the calf run over—I didn't have a word to say.

"But," ses Mr. Mountgomery, "the're brung up to it."

"Well," ses Mary, "the more sin to them that brings 'em up to be servants. A servant, to be any account as a servant, is got to have a different kind of a spirit from other people; and anybody that would make a nigger of a white child, because it was pore, hain't got no Christian principle in 'em."

"But," ses Mr. Mountgomery, "you know, Mrs. Jones, when you're in Rome, you must do as Rome does. If the northern people choose to make niggers gentlemen, and their own children servants, you can't help that, you know."

"Yes; but," ses Mary, "niggers is niggers, and white folks is white folks, and I couldn't bear to see neither of 'em out of ther proper places. So, if I've got to have white servants to wait on me, or stay at home, I'll never go out of old Georgia long as I live, that's what I wont."

"Then, Mary," ses I, "is our journey to be busted up, shore enuff?"

"O no, Joseph; you can go, and I'll stay home with mother. Maybe I won't have many more summers to be with her, and I'd feel very bad afterwards, to think I neglected her when she was with us."

The old woman put her arms round Mary's neck, and squeezed her til the tears come into her eyes.

"My sweet, good daughter," ses she; "bless your dear hart, you always was so kind to your pore old mother."

That made Mary cry a little; and little Harry, thinkin' something was the matter, sot up a squall, too, til his mother tuck him and talked to him a bit, and then Prissy come and carried him in tother room.

I didn't know what to do. I always hate terribly to be backed out of any thing what I've sot my mind on; but to go to the north without takin' Mary along, was something I didn't like to think about. But then, after all my 'rangements was made, and I'd shuck hands and bid good-by to 'most everybody in Pineville, it was too 'bominable bad to be disappinted thataway. But after a while I told Mary I'd stay home, too, and go some other time.

"No, no, Joseph," ses she; "I know you want to go, and I want to have you go, cause it'd do you good to see the north and git acquainted with the world. When little Harry gits big enuff so he can take care of himself, then we can take a journey together in spite of the old abolitionists; and then you'll know all about the country, and it'll be a great deal pleasanter for us all."

"That's a fact; Mrs. Jones is right, Majer," ses Mr Mountgomery. "You'd better leave your family at home this time. You wont be gone more'n a month or so, and I reckon Mrs. Jones ain't afraid to trust you that long 'mong the Yanky galls."

Mary blushed terrible.

"But," ses I——

"O! you ain't 'fraid of her runnin off with anybody fore you git back, is you?" ses he. Then the old feller aughed like he would die.

"Ain't you 'shamed, Mr. Mountgomery, to talk that a-way?" ses Mary.

"You needn't be 'fraid of that, brother Joe," ses sister Calline, "for me and Kizzy 'll watch her monstrous close while you're gone."

"Shaw," ses I; "you can't make me jealous."

"Nor me, neither," ses Mary.

Then old Mr. Mountgomery laughed till he knocked the fire out of his pipe all over himself, and that sot the galls and all of 'em to laughin worse than ever.

But I tell you what, Mr. Thompson, (and you're a married man and will blieve what I say,) I didn't feel much like laughin myself. I never did like this Yanky way of married people livin' all over creation without seein one another more'n once in a coon's age; and the idee of 'gwine off and leavin' Mary, for a whole month, tuck all the rinkles out of my face whenever I tried to laugh. But the difficulty was, I couldn't help myself. If I staid home, I couldn't be contented about it, and all the fellers would be rigin me, 'cause I could'nt leave my wife long enough to go to the north. So I made up my mind to go anyhow, and make the best I could of it.

Bimeby old Mr. Mountgomery 'lowed it was time to be gwine home; so he bid us good-by, and promised to come and see me off to-morrow mornin.

After the old man was gone we all sot round the fire and talked the thing over in a family way. Mary looked monstrous serious, but she's got too much good sense to make a fuss 'bout sich things. She ses I must rite to her every day, and I must be very careful and not git shipracked or blowed up in any of the steambotes or rail-rodes, and I must take care and not ketch no colds by exposin myself in the cold weather at the north, whar people, she ses, dies off with the consumption like sheep does with the distemper.

All our trunks has got to be overhauled and my things put by themselves, so I can't start til to-morrow mornin. I'm gwine as far as Augusty in my carriage, and then take the rail-rode to Charlston. If no other botherment don't turn up to pervent, you shall hear from me on my Travels pretty soon. So no more from
  Your frend, til deth,   Jos. Jones.

P. S. Prissy's raised a perfect panick 'mong the niggers on the plantation 'bout the abolitionists. Pore creeter, her hart's almost broke cause she can't go to the north with her misses and little massa Harry; and I do blieve she's as fraid of the abolitionists as she is of the very old Nick himself. You ought to hear some of the niggers' descriptions of 'em. When Prissy told old Ned what Mr. Mountgomery sed—how they carried off all the niggers they could ketch, and put 'em in jail so they couldn't never go back to ther white folks, ses he to her—" Ki, gall, youna no tell dis nigger nuffin bout dem cattle; cus 'em, me hear ole massa tell bout 'em fore you born. Aligator aint no suckemstance to 'em. 'Em got horns like billy-gote, and big red eyes like ball ob fire; and 'em got grate long forkit tail like sea-sarpent, and jes kotch up pore nigger, same like me hook 'em trout. Ugh, chile, dey wusser'n collerymorbus."

LETTER III.

Augusty, Georgia, May 12, 1845.

To Mr. Thompson:—*Dear Sir*—This far I have travelled in the bowels of the land without any diffikilty, as Mr. Shakespeer ses; but whether I'm gwine to git safe to my jurny's eend, or find myself like Jony in the bowels of a whale's belly before I git home agin, is a bisness what opens a fine field for speckelation, as the cotton byers ses.

But that's neither here nor thar. I sot down to tell you 'bout my jurny to this city. Well, this mornin all the famly was up before the crack of day gettin reddy for me to start. Evrything was reddy three or four days ago, but it seemed like the nearer the time come to start, the more ther was to do. Thar was old Miss Stallins in the kitchen raisin a harrycane among the niggers 'bout gettin breckfust for me—the niggers was all crazy 'bout my gwine away—Ned was rairin and pitchin 'bout the lot cause one of the little niggers let the horses git out of the stable--some of the harness was lent—old Simon had tuck the tar-bucket off with him, so ther wasn't no way to grease the carrige—Prissy upsot the tea-kittle, gittin some water for me to shave—Fanny tripped up and spilt all the biskits in the yard—the galls was lookin for the kee of my trunk, what couldn't be found no whar—little Harry was squallin like blazes cause he couldn't have on his new hat and cote and go with me in the carrige—and in the middle of the everlastin rumpus, I like to cut my nose off with the razer!

Bimeby though, things all settled down into a pretty considerable calm. Ned cotcht the horses—the harness was brung home—the wheels was greased—the kee was found rite whar Mary had put it herself—little Harry stopped cryin—my nose stopped bleedin, and breakfust was sot; but after all ther wasn't one could eat a mouthful, spite of all the 'swadin old Miss Stallins could do.

Mary tuck on considerable, pore gall; though she tried to hide it all she could. She didn't have much to say, but she looked monstrous droopy; and whenever I tried to cheer her up by tellin her I wouldn't stay no longer than I could help, her lips would sort o' quiver, and she'd turn round to tend to the baby or something; but when she looked at me agin, her long eyelashes was damp with tears. Ah! Mr. Thompson, me and you know how to preciate the deep pure founting from whar them tears flowed—we married men know how to vally the ever-gushin feelins of a true woman's hart, which, like the waters of the spring what no summer can't dry up and no winter freeze, is coolest when the day is hottest and grows warmer when the world grows cold. I felt monstrous bad myself, but it wouldn't do to let on, for I know'd it would only make her worse.

By this time old Mr. Mountgomery, and cousin Pete, and a heap more nabors, and all the niggers on the plantation, was come to bid me good-by. Old Termination, my driver, was mounted on the box, with his clean clothes on, and a bran new lash to his whip, the proudest nigger you ever did see. He couldn't notice none of the rest of 'em for his shirt collar, but if any of the little niggers come too close to his team, axin him to by 'em something in Augusty, he was monstrous apt to anser 'em with a little tetch of the lash.

When the trunks was tied on, and old Miss Stallins was sure ther wasn't nothin forgot—which she sed she know'd ther would be—I went through the shakin hands with the nabors.

"Good by, Majer," ses old Mr. Mountgomery, "I wish you a plesant jurny and a safe return."

"Thank you," ses I.

"Good by, Joe," ses Pete—"don't you git in no ass with them abolitionists—if you do, old feller, you won't find no frends thar, mind I tell you."

"Don't you fear for me," ses I—"Good by, and take care of yourself."

"Good by, Majer," ses all of 'em, as they shuck my hand.

Then here come all the niggers.

"Good by, Massa Joe," ses all of 'em.

"Good by," ses I, "and be good niggers till I come back."

"Don't let none of dem pesky old bobolitionists kotch you, Massa Joe," ses Prissy.

"Massa Joe, massa Joe, ant Moma say cum da!" ses one of the little niggers.

Pore old Moma was the fust nigger my father ever owned. She's more'n a hundred years old now, and her hed's as white as the cotton she use' to pick for us when she was a gall. She's been monstrous porely this winter, and hain't been able to go out of her little house in the yard, whar she's lived ever sense she was too old to do anything on the plantation. She was 'fraid I was gwine off without bidden her good by, and that's the reason she sent for me. She was settin in the door when I went to her, and she raised her old dim eyes, almost white with age, and looked at me.

"Why, Massa Joe, God bless you; you gwine away widout tellin pore ole Moma good by?—ole Moma what use to nuss you, when you was leetle baby like leetle massa Harry. Moma no able run after Massa Joe now—maybe ole Moma neber see you gin. Pore ole Moma, lib too long—make trouble for white fokes; but Moma's time mose come."

"No, no, Moma," ses I, "you musn't talk that-

"Old Moma was sittin' in the door when Major Jones went to her, and she raised her old dim eyes, almost white with age, and looked at him. 'Why, Massa Joe, God bless you; you gwine away widout tellin' poor old Moma good-by!'"—*Letter* iii. *p.* 34.

away. You know you aint no trouble to us, and you was always a good servant."

The pore old creeter brightened up, and tried to smile.

"Good by, Moma," ses I, as I tuck her pore old hand in mine; "take good care of yourself till I cum home, and let your young misses know whenever you want any thing. Good by, old nigger."

"Bless ye, bless ye, Massa Joe—bless Miss Mary and leetle massa Harry. God bless you all—good by."

The faithful old creeter tried to press my hand, but she was too weak, and when I let go her hand it drapt into her lap, and she follered me with her eyes as far as she could see me through her tears.

Then cum the kissin bisness. I took the worst job fust, and kissed old Miss Stallins and mother. I didn't mind kissin mother, cause it seemed all right and natural; but I always did hate to kiss old wimmin what hain't got no teeth, and I was monstrous glad old Miss Stallins had her handkerchef to her face, for in the hurryment I kissed it, and the old woman was in such a flustration she didn't know her lips from any thing else. I kissed the galls two or three times a piece, rite afore cousin Pete, who smacked his lips, and looked sort o' cross-eyed every time. But when I cum to look for Mary, she was gone in the house. Thar she was, sittin in her rockin chair, leanin her face on her hand, and the tears runnin down her cheeks in a stream. When I got close to her she riz up and put her arms round my neck.——I can't tell you what she sed, nor how many, nor how long, nor how sweet them kisses was. Them's famly affairs, and ain't for nobody to know. After she dried her eyes as well as she could, she went with me to the carrige. Prissy was holdin little Harry reddy for his kiss. I tuck the little feller in my arms and gin him one good lor squeeze, and then got in. Termination popped his whip and away he went, leavin Mary and all of 'em cryin cause I was gone, and the baby kickin and squallin like rath cause he couldn't go too.

Separashuns is monstrous tryin things to peeple what ain't use to 'em, and I couldn't help feelin very sollumcolly all the way to Augusty. The rode is one of the lonesummest in the world, and I never was so put to it to keep my sperits up. Ther was nothin new or interrestin to attract my 'tention, and whenever I thought bout home the worse I felt. Mary's partin injunkshuns was still soundin in my ears, and whenever I shut my eyes I could see her standin on the piazzy lookin after me, with the grate big tears runnin down her cheeks, and sparklin like dimonds in her curls, that was hangin in disorder 'bout her sweet face; and then thar was little Harry puttin out his dear little arms and cryin like his hart would brake, cause he couldn't ride in the carriage with me. It wouldn't do to think of them things, so I tried to sing, and the fust thing I know'd, I was hummin the song what begins:

> Ther's meetins of pleasure and partins of grief,
> But a inconstant loveyer is worse nor a thief;
> A thief he will rob you, and steal all you have,
> But a inconstant loveyer'll take you to the grave.

You mustn't think that song was suggested by any jellous fears on my part; no indeed, not by a jug full: but you know how wimmin will talk sumtimes on sich occasions. They say a heap, jest to see what you'll say.

I got here about noon and stopped at the Globe Hotel, and sent Termination back home with the carrige. Pore feller, he hated to leave me monstrous, and when he shuck hands with me, he couldn't hardly speak, and his eyes looked like two peeled unions

"Then cum the kissin' business. I took the worst job fust, and kissed old Miss Stallins and mother, and then kissed the gals two or three times a-piece, all around."—*Letter* iii. *p.* 35.

swimmin in their own juice. "Good bye, Massa Joe," ses he, "but don't stay away from Miss Mary long, if you spec to see her live when you cum back."

After dinner I tuck a walk down the street to see the town. Augusty's a monstrous pretty city, but it ain't the place it used to was, not by a grate site It seems like it was rottin off at both eends, and ain't growin much in the middle; and the market-houses what a few years ago you couldn't hardly see for the wagons, looks more like pretty considerable large martin-boxes standin in the middle of the grate wide street, than places of bisness. The peeple that laid out the city must been monstrous wide between the eyes, and made very large calculations for bisness; for they've got it stretch'd out over ground enuff to make two or three sich towns, and Broad street, whar the stores is, is wide enuff for the merchants to charge exchange from one side to tother. I see by the papers that they're gwine to dig a big canal, as they call it, and turn the river up stream into the common, so they can go into the mannyfacterin of cotton. That's a sort of bisness I don't know nothin about, and I can't say how it'll turn out, but there's one thing very certain, and that is, if the Augusty people don't do something to start bisness agoin agin, all the houses in the city won't rent for enuff to feed 'em. The fact is, if the people of Georgia don't take to makin homespun and sich truck for themselves, and quit their everlastin fuss 'bout the tariff and free trade, the fust thing they'll know, the best part of their popilation will be gone to the new States, and what'll be left won't be able to raise cotton enuff to pay for what they'll have to buy from the North.

The fust man I met in Broad-street was Mr. Peleg. "Why, hellow, Majer Jones," ses he, "what's brung you to town?"

I told him I was gwine to the North.

"Well!" ses he, "Majer, you must spend a day with us, enny how, and I'll interduce you to some of my friends here. They're all admirers of your's, and would be very glad of a oppertunity to make your acquaintance."

Well, I walked along with Mr. Peleg to his store, and on the way he interduced me to 'bout twenty gentlemen, most all of 'em Pelegs. 'Mong the rest, Mr. Peleg introduced me to Doctor Klag, perfesser of horticulteral science in Augusty. Mr. Peleg told me that the doctor was the greatest man in his line in them parts, for he could make trees *grow twice in two places.* Dr. Klag certainly looks like he might be a genus of some sort, and seems to be very much tuck up with his perfession, for the fust thing he sed to me was something 'bout cedars and arbor-vites, what he sed he'd warrant not to dy. Ther was some mistake about it, which wasn't very clearly explained by Mr. Peleg. The Doctor's got one very curious sort of a oyster-lookin eye, and tother one has a kind of sky-rakin look, so you can't tell what upon yeath he's lookin at. He sed he'd call agin, and Mr. Peleg and me stepped into a watch store whar ther was some more Pelegs, and then, rite next door, we went in whar ther was a lot more of 'em. They was all very glad to see me, and invited me to come up to Mr. Lampblack's that evenin, to hear a lecture on the moon, by some great perfesser, whose name I've forgot. They all seemed like monstrous clever fellers, but I couldn't see how upon yeath they was all named Pelegs, for they didn't look no more alike than any body else. But jest before tea, my old frend Whiskers, what scared Mary so up to Athens, you know, (would you believe it, Mr. Thompson, every bit of his sorrel hair drap't out when he read that Athens letter of mine, and now it's grow'd all out as black as your hat!) come round to see me and told me al' about the Pelegs.

Well, they is the devilishest set of fellers for playin tricks on peeple ever was trumped up any whar, you may depend. Every now and then they're ketchin up some green feller, and *puttin him throo*, as they call it. I'll jest give you a instance. T'other day one of General Kittledrum's lutenants come over from South Carolina to git up a singin skool in Augusty. He brung his commishun from the Guvernor as a recommendation. That was enuff for the Pelegs, who tuck him in hand and soon got up all sorts of a skool for him. He had 'bout a hunderd of 'em down on his list, at twenty-five dollars a quarter, in no time. The feller was almost out of his senses at the idee of makin his fortin so soon, and was willin to do any thing the Pelegs sed was necessary to stablish his repetation as a music-master. In the fust place, they tuck him into a back room and made him put his hands on the globes, and swore him 'bout his faith in certain doctrinal pints which they sed was very important in a singin master. One of 'em red out, in a very solem voice, bout the rain fallin upon the yeath forty days and forty nites; and then another one sed to him, "Lutenant Odin, with your rite hand on the celestial globe and your left hand on the terestial globe, do you swar to that?" Ses he, "I do." Then they swore him bout Samson killin the Fillistines with the jaw-bone of a jackass, and bout Faro and his host gettin swallered up in the Red Sea, and a heap of other things. Then, after puttin him throo the manuel exercise for bout two owers, rite in the brilin sun, they sed he must give 'em a specymen of his vokel powers at the theatre, before all his skollers. Well, they rigged him out on the stage, and had him howlin all manner of meeters and kees, and givin explanashuns, afore a whole theater full of Pelegs, till they got tired of the fun, when the fust thing the feller knowd, a man stepped on the stage, and rested him for hos steelin, rite in the middle of Old Hunderd, on a high kee. The pore feller was skared almost tc deth, and swore he never tuck a horse nor nothin else what didn't belong to him, in all his born days—he tuck out his comishun and show'd the guvernor's hand-ritin. But all he could do or say didn't signify nothin. The constable tuck him to a room whar the Pelegs hold their courts, and thar they put him throo a reglar trial, and made a convicted hos theaf out of him by the strongest kind of testimony. Some of the Pelegs was his frends, and done all they could for him; but it was no use—he was condem'd to be hung according to Carolina law, and was to be sent to jail to wait till the day of execution. The pore feller trembled so he couldn't hardly stand, and the swet started out of his face like he'd been mawlin rails all day. His frends told him his only chance was to escape when they was takin him to jail, and promised that they'd try to git him loose from the constable, and then he must run across the bridge into Carolina as if the very old Harry was after him. Shore enuff, when they got him near the bridge, his frends got him away from the constable, and a straiter coat-tail than he made across that old bridge, was never seed in Georgia. And that's the last that's ever been seed or heard of Lutenant Odin, the singin master.

I spected something wasn't rite when I seed so many of 'em; but they know who to project with. They didn't git me to go to none of their lecters on the moon, mind I tell you.

I'm gwine in the morning to Charleston. It's monstrous late, and the rale-road starts before day-light So no more from
    Your frend til deth,   Jos. Jones.

LETTER IV.

Charleston, S. C., May 15, 1845

To Mr. Thompson:—I arriv here last evenin 'bout three o'clock, rite side up, all safe and sound. Fore daylight yesterday mornin the nigger at the hotel in Augusty nocked me up, and told me the omnibus for the railrode was waitin for me. I wasn't no time gettin reddy, and in a few minits I was ridin over the bridg what Lutenant Odin clared so quick when he got loose from the Pelegs, on my way to the Carolina railrode.

I never was in the land of shivelry before, and .. had a good deal of curiosity to see what kind of a place it was whar the people lived what they say all sneezes every time Mr. Calhoun takes snuff—and whar General Kittledrum's men was born " with arms in ther hands," reddy and termined to take Texas from the Mexicans, whether or no. Well, my opinion is, if Mr Dickens was to see Hamburg he wouldn't find the same fault with it that he did with Boston. The white and red paint in Hamburg wouldn't hurt his eyes much, and when he went to sleep at night he might be monstrous certain that he'd find it thar in the mornin. The fact is, Hamburg is like the Irishman's horse—it is little but it's ould. It was bilt long before the flood, and is got the marks of antickuty in evry old rotten shingle, evry unnailed clapboard, and in evry broken pane of glass.

Don't misunderstand me, Mr. Thompson; I ain't like some travellers into foreign parts, what takes pains to humbug ther readers 'bout evry grate city they visit, jest as if nobody was ever thar before. Not by no means. When

I say Hamburg was bilt before the flood, I don't mean the flood what drownded out all creation cept old father Noey and his cargo of varmints, but I mean the flood of 1840, what overflowed the whole country from Shoolts's Hights to the Sand Hills in Georgia, settin the fences and gin-houses a shassain and dancin hands-all-round with the pig-pens and chicken-coops of a thousand river plantations. The oldest inhabitants of Hamburg is all antydeluvians, and some of 'em is sposed to be amfibious. History don't give any satisfactory account of whar they cum from, but it's generally blieved that the illustrious founder of the city is one of the same Dutch of what tuck Holland. He's a monstrous man in his way, and though he didn't bild a ark—cause he had no warnin beforehand—he bilt a bridg what's stood a thousand thunderstorms and freshets, and all the floods sense the days of Noey couldn't tear it up. It was very early in the mornin when we druv through the city to the depo, and I couldn't form much of a opinion 'bout the bisness of the place. At that time o' day it was monstrous still and looked very much like a barn yard does when ther's hawks about.

Jest before we got to the depo, ses the man what's captain of the omnibus, ses he, "Major, I'll take your fare, if you please." Cum to find out, he meant a half a dollar, for carryin me and my baggage to the railrode. He's a monstrous clever little man, but a terrible politishan—so I paid him, and he soon sot us down on the platform by the cars.

Ther was a considerable bustle and fuss bout the depo, gettin reddy to start. The passengers was gittin ther tickets and ther checks for ther baggage, what some fellers was nockin about like they would tear the hide off evry trunk ther was thar, stowin 'em away in the cars—some people was runnin about biddin good-by with ther frends, and tellin 'em not to forgit a heap of things, and sum was kickin up a rumpus cause they couldn't see ther trunks after they was put in the cars. Bimeoy evry thing was fixed, and here cum old Beelzebub, with his fire, smoke, sutbags and thunderations, to carry us to Charlston. When I saw that everlastin, black, ugly thing cum chug up agin the cars for 'em to tackle it on, fizzin and fryin, and smokin like a tar kill, I thought how if I was a hos or a mule, I'd take my hat off to it. If ther ever was a thing what deserves a vote of thanks from all the pullin generation of animals, I think it's the locomotive ingine. Jest to think, the amount of hos flesh it has saved sense it tuck to carryin the mails. A locomotiv always seems to me to cum nearer a livin animal, than any other machine invented by man, specially sense they've got to hollerin at the cows when they git on the track. It's a monstrous fractious, spiteful, headstrong sort of a creeter, and sumtimes it takes it into its hed to run off the track, but generally speakin it's jest about as governable as any other team, and don't take no more to feed it accordin to its size and strength. I can't help but have a sort of feelin for 'em, and I wouldn't no more think of makin 'em go without givin 'em plenty of wood and water, than I would of makin my horses work without givin 'em plenty of corn and fodder.

Ling! ling! went the bell. "All aboard," ses the captain, and the next minit away we went with the thunderinest rattlin, puffin and snortin I ever did hear. In a few minits Hamburg was out of sight, and the pine trees went dancin along behind us, as if ther roots couldn't hold 'em in the ground when they saw us comin among 'em.

Ther ain't nothin much to interest the traveller on the railrode from Hamburg to Charlston; and if a man can't find no company in his thoughts, he's monstrous apt to be lonesome. Along at the fust ther wasn't many passengers, and most of them was preachers what had been up to Augusty to tend a convention. They was the dryest set of old codgers I ever met with, til the joltin of the cars shuck up ther idees a little, and then they fell to disputin about religion like all rath. After awhile one old feller, what had his hed tied up with a red cotton handkerchef, and didn't belong to the same church with the rest of 'em, mixed in with 'em, and in about five minits they got into one of the hottest kind of argyments 'bout sprinklin and dippin. The old hardshell laid about him like rath, and the louder the racket and the more dust the cars made, the louder the old feller fired away at 'em, and whenever he stopped for breth, two or three of the others was down on him like a Yankee thrashin-machine. They kep up one everlastin string of argyment about forty-five miles long, and to them what sot a little ways off from 'em, and could only hear a few words now and then, it sounded zactly like a reglar cussin match; and sumtimes they'd look at one another like they meant jest what they sed. Bimeby the old hardshell caved in for want of breth, and all the rest of the way he was hockin and hemin, and tryin to git the dust and sinders out of his wind-pipe.

Evry now and then we stopped and tuck in more passengers. 'Bout halfway to Charlston we tuck in two ladys and a little baby. One was a old lady, and she held the little boy, which was a butiful little feller, 'bout the size of my little Harry, in her lap. The other was a handsome young gall, and she was cryin. You know how butiful a pretty woman looks when she's cryin, but you know that's the very time no gentleman ought to stare at 'em. Well, she tried to dry her eyes as fast as she could, but every now and then the tears would bust out agin in grate big draps, and then she'd put her handkerchef to her face. Sumtimes she would look at a ring she had on her finger, and then the tears would come agin. I felt monstrous sorry for her, but I tried not to let her see me lookin at her. Bimeby a sort of skimmilk-lookin feller cum and tuck a seat rite close by her, and looked her rite spang in the face, like he was gwine to eat her up. The pore gall hadn't a very strong stummuck, I spose, and turned away from him. He foller'd her, and she turned back again, and thar he was agin, with his everlastin sheep's eyes, lookin her rite in the face. Thinks I, drat your imperence, I wish tha' gall was my cousin. Just then she looked up to me as much as to say, Sir, did you ever see such insurance? and I looked back to her, as much as to say, No, Miss, I'll be drat if I ever did; and the next minit I gin the feller a sort of a cross-cut look, as much as to say he was a infernal imperent puppy. He looked back that he begged my pardon, he didn't know she was any thing to me; then I looked a kickin at him, if he didn't look out, and he looked tother way a little while, and then tuck himself off into another car. The young lady sot thar a minit or two, then looked the sweetest kind of a thank you, sir, to me, and went and tuck a seat by the side of the old lady. They talked together, and looked over now and then towards me.

Nothing didn't turn up of interest on the way, and bimeby I begun to see signs of town. The closer we got to Charlston, the thicker the plantations and houses begun to git. Bimeby I could see the steeples; and in a few minits more we was rollin along among the little old frame houses, til we got to the depo. And now the fuss commenced. Sich a everlastin rumpus I never seed before. Soon as the gates was open here cum a rang of fellers with whips in their hands, poppin and snappin about 'mong the passengers, axin us to go here and go thar, and whar's our baggage, and if we was gwine to the boat, and more'n twenty thousand other questions before we could answer the fust one. The fust thing I knowd a feller had one of my trunks one way and another one had tother carryin it off in another direction, while two more was pullin the life out of my carpet bag to see which should have it. I shuck the two fellers off my trunks monstrous quick, and was jest gwine to tackle the chaps what had my carpet bag when who should I see but my old frend, Bill Wiley, what used to live up to the old Planters' Hotel, in Madison, you know.

"Why, hellow, Majer," ses he, "is that you?"

"I blieve it is, Mr. Wiley," ses I, "but thar aint no tellin how long I'll last, if I don't git away from these oudacious scamps."

"Well," ses he, "Majer, jest pint out your baggage to Patrick here, and then foller me."

I show'd 'em to Patrick, and then went with Mr. Wiley and got into the omnibus, what tuck me, with a whole lot of other passengers, to the Charlston Hotel. When I got thar, they axd me to put my name down in a big book, and then it tuck me 'bout a ower to git the dust and smoke off my face. As soon as I was done washin here cum three or four niggers with little short-handled brooms, and begun to sweep the very life out of me. I hollered at 'em and ax'd 'em what in the mischief they meant; but they jest thrashed away as hard as they could lick it—first at me and then on their hands—keepin up the devlishest drummin I ever heard; and the more I twisted and turned to try to git out of ther way, the harder they kep at it. Bimeby I sent one of 'em a lick aside of his hed, what put a stop to his fun, and the rest tuck the hint; but one tall yaller feller, what wanted to make a few extra flourishes, got a kick jest as he was leavin, that raised him right off the floor. I never did see the like of 'em in all my born days. I do blieve they'd have a brush at a man if they had to throw him down and hold him. Mr. Wiley said it was all right, and that they was only tryin to git the dust off me. That all mought be, but I don't see no sense in brushin the breth out of a man if he is got a little dust on his clothes.

In the afternoon I tuck a walk over the city to look at the fine bildins and the ships. I tell you what,

Charlston aint no fool of a city. Meeting street, and King street, and Market street, is very fine, and has got sum monstrous handsum bildins in 'em. The best part of the streets is too narrow and crooked, but Meeting street is a butiful width, and from the Charlston Hotel down to the bay, has got sum as pretty views as I ever seed in any picter. After tea I went down to the place they call the Battery. The wind was blowin monstrous still, and the waves from the sea cum rollin in and slashin the nasty salt water all over me. It was a very lonesum place, and smelled like a old shot-gun what hadn't been cleaned out for a long time. They tell me here it's nateral for the sea to smell so, and that people soon gits use to it, so they don't mind it. The place made me feel sort o' sollemcolly, and I started to go to the Hotel. It was sum time before I could find the way, and as I was walkin along in the moonlight, I passed lots of ladies and gentlemen. I heard sum sweet female voices and saw sum butiful faces which made me think of Mary, and by the time I got to the Hotel I was homesick as the mischief. I went to my room and tried to go to sleep; but ther was a company of midshipmen and navy officers in the next room what had jest cum home from a long voyage, and they was drinkin wine and singin "we wont go home til mornin," and makin speeches, and breakin glasses, so I couldn't sleep a bit; and the merrier they was the worse I felt.

This mornin I tuck another walk to look at the soldiers. They had a general musterin of the shivelry here to bury a officer, and I tell you what's a fact, Charlston can parade a pretty respectable showin of the nation's bullworks. There was sum fust rate companys and a good many fine lookin officers among 'em. The Guvernor was thar in his regimentals, but I could'nt see General Kittledrum. Ther was one little officer thar what had so much military sperit in him.

that it put him cumpletely out of shape. He didn't
stick more'n 'bout three feet out of his boots, and he
looked like a jack-knife that was opened so far that it
bent over back. Its a terrible pity that he couldn't
grow a little bigger, or simmer down his sperit a little
more, for the sword is certainly too much for the skab-
bard. They say he's a fust rate officer, only he's a
little out of proportion. The fact is, we may say what
we please, and laugh as much as we've a mind to, 'bout
Carolina shivelry, but ther ain't no mistake about it,
Carolina is a gallant little state, and every sun she's
got's a soldier.

I'd like to stay in Charlston two or three days, but
I hain't got time now. When I cum back from New
York I'll know more about cities, and then I can make
up my mind better about Charlston. I'm gwine to
Wilmington in the steamboat this afternoon. Pervidin
she don't bust her biler, nor git blow'd to ballyhack by
sum bominable harrycane, you will hear from me agin
soon. So no more from
                    Your frend til deth,
                                    Jos. Jones.

P. S. I've jest bought me a hickory stick what I'm
gwine to toat, and it won't be well for these fellers to
come pullin and haulin 'bout my baggage and brushin
all the buttons off my clothes, wharever I stop in futer.
You know I'm a peaceable man, but I can't stand **evry
hing.**

LETTER V.

Washington City, May 18, 1845.

To Mr. Thompson:—*Dear Sir*—I left off my last letter to you only a few minits before the omnibus cum to take me from the Hotel to the steambote. Well, I was a little behind the administration in gettin my trunks packed agin, and cum monstrous nigh gettin left. But Patrick got me down to the wharf jest as the last ring was dyin out of the bell, and in a few minits I was afloat on salt water for the fust time in my life. You must know I fell in a mill-pond once when I was a boy, and was pulled out by old nigger Ned, jest when I had 'bout tuck my last swaller, and I spose it's that what's always made me have sich a mortal dred of water whar I can't tetch bottom ever sense. I felt monstrous jubus 'bout gwine aboard, and if ther was any possible way of gettin round it I wouldn't a run no sich risks you may depend.

It was a butiful afternoon, and the passengers was all as lively as crickets, talkin and laughin and lookin at the city as the steambote went spankin along with her flags a flyin, and her wheels turnin the sea into soapsuds, and leavin a white track in the water behind us. Ther was a heap of ships and steambotes all about—sum standin still, sum gwine out and sum cumin in; and little boats not bigger than a feedin-trough was dodgin all about, with ther white sails a shinin in the sun like sand-hill cranes in a rice-field. The city kep gettin smaller and smaller, til bimeby Fort Moultry, whar you know the Carolina boys licked the British so in the revolution, didn't look no bigger than a fodder-stack. I looked around for the shore, but the sky seemed to cum down to the water on every side, til it looked jest like the crystal of my watch, 'thout a spot of yearth to put one's foot on as far as my eyes could see. I begun to feel monstrous skary, and I don't blieve I ever did draw sich long breths before in all my born days. I do l lieve I thought of all the ship-racks I ever red of in my life, and I would a gin ten per-cent. of all I had in the world to had my life insured. I held on to the side of the boat with both hands, and kep as fur off from the biler as I could. But the ladys and the little children didn't seem to mind it a bit, and after we was out of sight of land about a ower I got a little over my skeer.

Bimeby a nigger feller commenced ringin a bell as hard as he could ring, and hollerin out—"Gentlemen what hain't paid ther passage will please to walk up to the captin's office and settle!" As soon as I could git a chance I paid for my tickets, and pretty soon after that the bell rung agin for supper. We had a fust rate supper, but sumhow it didn't seem natural to be swimmin and rockin about in the sea, and eatin at the same time, and I didn't eat much. Besides, ther was a sort ot sickish feelin cum over me in the supper room, and I went up on the roof agin as quick as I could to smoke a segar, thinkin it mought make me feel better.

By this time it was night, but the moon and stars was shinin above and below—the only difference in the sea and the heavens bein that the stars and moon in the water was dancin and caperin about like they was out of ther senses, while them in the sky was winkin and twinklin in ther old places as quietly and sober as ever. I got a light for my segar and was jest beginnin to smoke when a nigger feller cum up to me, and ses he:

"Massa, no smokin lowed aft the machinery."

"The mischief ther ain't!" ses I, and I went away back to the hind eend of the boat and tuck a seat, and commenced a right good smoke to myself. But I hadn't been thar more'n a minit before here cum the nigger feller agin.

"You musen't smoke aft the machinery," ses he.

"Well," ses I, "I ain't near yer machinery."

"No; but," ses he, "you is aft."

"Aft what?" ses I.

"The place for gentlemen to smoke is forard," ses he.

"Well," ses I, "my buck, I don't understand your gibrish, but if you'll jest show me whar I can smoke 'thout any danger to your machinery, I'll go thar."

With that the bominable fool begun to snicker, til he seed my cane was takin the measure of his hed for a nock down, when he straitened up the pucker of his face and sed—

"Cum this way, sir; this is the forard deck, massa."

I follered him over to the fore eend of the boat, whar sum more gentlemen was smokin. I hadn't tetched a drap of licker in a coon's age, but I was never so put to to walk strait in my life. Sumhow I couldn't make no sort of calkelation for the floor—one minit it was up to my knee, and the next step I couldn't hardly reach it—and my legs kep gittin mixed up and tangled so I didn't know one from tother. All the passengers seemed like they was tite—sum of 'em looked monstrous serious, and one or two was caskadin over the side of the boat into the sea with all ther might. I felt a little sort o' swimmy in the hed myself, and I begun to spicion I was gettin sea-sick, so I tuck a seat by the side of the boat and smoked my segar to settle my stummick.

Well, thar I sot and smoked til all the passengers went down into the bed-room to sleep. It was a butiful night, and the scene was jest the kind to set a man's brains a thinkin. The sea is a roomy place and ther's nothin thar to prevent one's givin free scope to his imagination —it's a mighty thing, the sea is, and if a man don't feel some sublime emotions in its presence, it's because his hed works is on a monstrous small scale. Thar it was, the great, the everlastin ocean, dressed out in its star-bespan-gled night-gown, dancin to the soft music of the sighin winds, and the liquid cadence of its ever-splash.n waves; while down deep in its coral caverns the whales and porpoises was spoutin ther love ditties to ther sweetharts, and the maremaids was puttin ther hair in curl to break the harts of the young sea-hoses. It was monstrous still—the monotonous splashin of the wheels, the gruntin and groanin of the ingine, the rushin of the foam, and the rumblin and squeakin of the timbers of the boat, all keepin time together, made a sort of noisy silence that fell negatively on the ear. I leaned over the side and looked at the fiery foam, as it rolled sparklin away from the bow: but it faded from the face of the sea while I looked at it, and a few yards behind us ther remained no track of our passage. I felt alone on the vast ocean, and a feelin of isolation cum over me, which, fore I got rid of it, made the boat seem no bigger than a teapot, and myself about the size of a young seed-tick. I could preached a sermon on the sublimity of creation, and the insignificance of man and his works, but I had no congregation then, and it's too late now. I don't know what made me think of home—but sumhow I felt like I'd gin a heap to be thar. I thought of the butiful bright eyes that was closed in sleep on my pillar, and the dear little cub that was nestled in my place. Bless ther dear souls—perhaps they was dreamin of me that very minit—perhaps I was never to see 'em in this world again. These thoughts made me feel monstrous bad, and the more I reflected about it, the worse I felt, til I blieve I would gin all I had in the world jest to be sure I wouldn't die before I got back.

Bimeby, I thought, I'd try to go to sleep, so I wen down into the bed-room, and tried it. But it was no go. I got into one of the little boxes, what they call berths, but I couldn't stay born no way I could fix it. In the first place I couldn't git stowed away no how, and in the next place, whenever I shut my eyes, it seemed like the boat was whirlin round and round like a tread-wheel. I got up agin, and went up stairs, and smoked another segar, til I got pretty tired, and then I went in the gentlemen's parlor, and stretched myself on one of the seats. I fell asleep thar sumtime between that and daylight, and never waked up til most breckfust time the next mornin, when they sed we was in Cape Fear, gwine right up to Wilmington.

Cape Fear is a very fine river, and ther's some fine plantations and houses on the banks when you git near to Wilmington. Pretty soon after breckfust we got in sight of the city, and a few minits afterwards we was long side the wharf, and the niggers was cartin our baggage up the hill to the railrode. Wilmington presents 'bout as curious a aspect from the river, as any other town in my knowins. The fust thing you see is everlastin piles of turpentine barrels, piled up on the wharf in evry direction, and on the vessels in the river. That's the front rank. The next is a plattoon of wind mills, enuff to lick all the Don Quicksots in Spain. In them they bile the spirits of turpentine out of the gum. The rare rank—and that's scattered all over the hill—is made up of houses, and old brick walls and chimneys of houses what's been burnt down, with here and thar a few more barrels of turpentine. They've had two or three fires here lately, what's burnt up the best part of the town; but I don't wonder at it, for I would as soon think of puttin out a powder-house as a place what's so perfectly soaked with turpentine. All I wonder at is, that the river don't ketch a fire too.

We waited about a ower in Wilmington, which afforded us a opportunity of lookin about a little. After travellin over it, and lookin at sum very handsum bildins, among which was the new Piscopal Church, a monstrous pretty bildin, we went back to the cars. When we got thar, I ax'd a nigger fellar whar I could git sum segars, and he told me to go into a house what stood rite over a branch, on stilts 'bout twenty feet high, whar he sed Lucy Ann would sell 'em to me. Well I went into the house, and ses I, "Is Lucy Ann here?"

"Dat's my name," sed a little outlandish person with a coat and britches on.

"I want to see Lucy Ann," ses I.

"Dat's me," ses he. "What shall I have the plaisure to sell you to day, ha?"

I looked up at the old feller's whity-brown sort of a face, and ses I, "I don't spose it makes any difference, but they told me Lucy Ann kep this store."

"Well, sare, my name be Lucy Ann; I keep dis store, and sell you sum vary fine orange, banana, soda-water, and so forth."

I bought sum segars and sum oranges and went out, but I couldn't help thinkin ther was sum mistake about it. If Lucy Ann was a woman, her pearance and dress wasn't very flatterin to the North Carolina galls.

Bimeby the bell rung, and the passengers was all aboard agin in the cars. The lokymotive man pulled the wire what sot the steam agwine, and away we went, licky-teklink, rite among the tar and turpentine what was strung all along the road, evry here and thar, for most a hundred miles. Like all the southern rodes this railrode don't run through the most interestin part of the country, so it wouldn't be fair to judge of the old North State by what one sees on the railrode. The country ain't much else but one everlastin turpentine plantation; and all one can see for miles, is millions upon millions of pine trees with the bark half off, and the white turpentine runnin down ther sides, and lookin like so many tall ghosts standin in the dark shade, with ther windin-sheets on. The rode runs through a very level country, and is the straitest in the world—having a single stretch of upwards of seventy miles without a single bend in it. The cars ain't quite so stylish as them on the Georgia Railrode, but the conducters is very obligin, attentive, clever men, and git along with as few accidents as any other conducters in the world, only they don't low no smokin in the cars.

We got to Weldon a little after dark, and thar we

tuck a very good supper. Here we bought tickets agin, and ther was a big fat feller thar what seemed termined to make us all go the Bay route, as he called it, whether we would or no. He banged all the fellers to talk I ever heard in all my born days. He got ahed of evrybody else, passengers and all; and when I told him I'd be very glad to commodate him, only I wanted to go by Washington; he sed, he'd be dad fetched if he didn't have the seat of government moved down on the Bay, jest for the commodation of the public what travels on his line. He's a monstrous good agent, and ought to be well paid for his trouble.

I didn't git much good sleep the night before, in the steambote, and by the time we got to Petersburg, I was pretty well done over, and I never was so glad in my life to go to bed. I remember sumthing 'bout gettin up the next mornin fore daylight, and gettin in a omnibus, and then gettin in sum more cars, and whizzin along through Virginy like a streak of ligthnin. Towns and bridges, and rivers, and mountings went whirlin past us so rapid that I hadn't no time to ax any thing about 'em. Like Cassio when he got sober, "I remember a heap of things, but nothin very pertickelerly," from the time I went to bed in Petersburg, til I found myself in the steambote on the Potomac gwine to Washington.

These railrodes play the mischief with a man's observations. One mought as well try to count the fethers in a pigeon's tail when he's on the wing, as to look at the country he's travellin through in the railrode cars. He gits a kind of flyin panorama of trees and houses, and towns and rivers, and fenses and bridges, all mixed up together—one runnin into tother, and another beginnin before the last one's left off—so he can't make heu tor tail to 'em. And when he does stop a minit he's so pestered with hack-drivers and porters, that he hain't hardly got time to buy his ticket or eat his breckfust, ler alone doin any thing else. I was anxious to have a good look at the Old Dominion, for a good many reasons—I wanted to see the state whar my father and mother was born, and what had given birth to the great Washington. But I had sich a bominable pore chance, I don't blieve I'd know any more about Virginy when I see it agin, than Captain Marryat did about America when he went home to write his everlastin book of lies.

The Potomac is a noble river; and as ther was no waves to set the bote a rollin, I had a fust rate chance to look at the scenery on its banks. I never shall forgit my feelins when the bell rung to let us know we was near Washington's grave, at Mt. Vernon. I felt that it was a grate privilege to be allowed to look at that sacred spot, where the ashes of the father of his country was reposin—to look at the mound of yeath that had taken to itself the noble form in which had centred so much virtue, so much patriotism, so much valor, so much wisdom, so much of evry thing that ennobles human nater. I remembered how on the bosom of the very stream on which I was, a British fleet once floated, and that when they passed the grave of our country's sainted hero, they lowered ther proud banner, in token of respect to the illustrious ded—and when I thought of that, it made me half forgive 'em for destroyin the city that bore his name. Fort Washington stands high up on the bank, and looks down monstrous sassy; and I reckon if the John Bull's was to try that game agin, they'd find the Potomac sumwhat rougher navigashun now than it was then.

In a few minits more we was in sight of Washington city, with the great umbrella top of the Capitol loomin up into the heavens, grand, gloomy, and peculiar. We wasn't long gettin to the wharf, and after a terrible encounter with 'bout five hundred cab-men and porters, I made out to git my baggage into a hack and druv to Gadsby's hotel, whar I got a good supper and soon went to bed.

I dreamed all night of cog-wheels and steam-ingines

—sumtimes my bed was a car, then it was a steambote, and then it was a omnibus, but it was gwine all the time, at the rate of twenty-five miles a ower. My brains hain't got more'n 'bout half settled yet, so you must excuse this monstrous pore letter. I hope to git regelated in a day or two, and then I will tell you sumthing 'bout Washington City and its lyons. No more from Your frend til deth,
Jos. Jones.

LETTER VI.

Washington City, May 19, 1848.

To Mr. Thompson:—*Dear Sir*—It was pretty late before I got up this mornin, and then it was 'bout a ower before I found my way down stairs after I did git up. You hain't no idee what a everlastin heap of rooms and passages and stair-ways ther is to these big hotels, and to a person what aint use to 'em it's 'bout as difficult to navigate through 'em as it is to find one's way out of a Florida hammock.

As soon as I got my breckfast I sot out for the Capitol, what stands on the hill, at the upper eend of the Avenue, as they call it, which is a grate wide street runnin rite through the middle of the city. When I looked up to it—from the street—it seemed like it wasn't more'n twenty yards off, but before I got to it I was pretty tired walkin. The gates was open, and I walked into the yard, and follered round the butiful paved walks til I cum to the steps. The yard, round the bildin, is all laid off in squares and dimonds, jest like Mary's flower-garden, and is all sot out with trees. Rite in frunt of the bildin, on the side towards the city, is a curious kind of a monument, standin in a basin of water, with little babys and angels, all cut out of solid marble, standin all round on the corners of it, pintin up to a old eagle what looks like he'd gone to roost on the top of it. It's a very pretty thing, and the water what it stands in is full of little red fishes, playin all about as lively as tadpoles in a mill pond. I looked at the monument sum time, and red sum of the names on it, but sum I couldn't make out and the rest I've forgot.

After gwine up two or three more pair of stone stairs, I cum to the door of the Capitol. I couldn't see nobody about, so I nocked two or three times, but nobody didn't answer. I waited awhile and then nocked agin with my stick, but nobody never sed a word. Thinks I, they can't be home. But the door was open—so thinks I, I'l go in and see the bildin any how. Well, in I went, anc the fust thing I met was two pair of stairs agin, botl gwine the same way. I tuck one of 'em, and after gwine a little ways I cum to another green door. Thinks I, it wont do to be too bold, or I mought git into a fuss with the kitchen cabinet, and I knowd a whig wouldn't find no frends thar. So I nocked agin, louder and louder, but nobody answered. Well, thinks I, the government can't be to home sure enuff, and I was jest thinkin what a bominable shame it was for them to neglect their bisness so, when here cum a feller, what had whiskers all over his face, with three or four galls, laughin and gigglin at a terrible rate, and in they went, without ever nockin a lick. Well, thinks I, I've got as good a right here as any body else what dont belong to the administration, so in I follered into the rotunda.

I tell you what, Mr. Thompson, this rotunda is a monstrous tall bildin jest of itself. Why you could put the Pineville court-house inside of it, and it wouldn't be in the way a bit. A full grown man dont look no bigger in it than a five year old boy, and I cum very near nockin a pinter dog in the hed for a rat, he looked so little. The sides is all hung round with picters, and over the doors ther is some sculptures representin William Penn swindlin the Ingins out of ther land, and Columbus cumin ashore in his boat, and old Danel Boon killin off the aborignees with a butcher knife, and other subjects more or less flatterin to the national character. The figers is all cramped up like they'd been whittled down to fit ther places, and don't look well to my likin at all. The places would be a great deal better filled with single figers representin our grate generals and statesmen. The picters is very good, and it's worth a trip from Georgia o Washington to see them great national paintins, the

Signers of the Declaration of Indepencence, the Sur
render of Cornwallis, Washington givin up his Com
mission, the Baptism of Pocahontas, and the Pilgrim
Fathers on board ther ship. I could looked at 'em a
whole day, but I had so much to see and so little time
to spare, that I only gin 'em a passin examination.

Bimeby I went up to a chap what was sitin by the
door with a book in his hand, and ax'd him whar the
government was.

"Who?" ses he.

"The government," ses I,—"Polk and Dallas."

"Oh, ses he, the President is at home at his house,
I believe, but I don't know whar Mr. Dallas is."

"Don't the President live here?" ses I.

"No *sir*," ses he. "He lives in the White House
at the other eend of the Avenue. This is the Capitol
whar Congress sets, but it aint in session now."

"Beg your pardon sir," ses I, "I thought the government
all lived at the Capitol."

"Your a stranger here then, it seems," ses he. "My
business is to show strangers over the Capitol. Do you
wish to see it?"

"That's jest what I cum here for," ses I, "and I'd
like very much to see whar Congress makes the laws."

"Very well," ses he, "jest foller me."

Well, he led the way and I follered up stairs and
down, through passages and round pillars and corners,
under arches and over roofs, through the Senate Chamber,
the Hall of the Representatives, and ever so many offices
and committee rooms, til he brung me out on the top of
the dome. I never was so high up in the world before.
Thar was the "city of magnificent distances," literaly
stretched out at my feet, and I looked *down* upon the dignitaries
of the land. I was indeed elevated above Presidents
and Cabinets, and Ministers of State. Houses looked
like martin boxes, men looked no bigger than seed-ticks,
and carriages and horses went crawlin along over the
ground like a couple of ants draggin a dead blue bottle.

The eye ranges over half the nation; Virginy and Maryland comes into the ten miles square, and the Potomac looks like a little branch runnin through a meadow of trees ; while the Tiber don't look no more like " the angry Tiber chafing with its shores" in which Julias Cæsar and Mr. Cassius went a swimmin with ther clothes on, than our duck pond does like the Atlantic Ocean.

Well, after takin a good look from the dome, I follered the man what keeps the Capitol, down agin into the Rotunda, and ax'd him what was to pay for his trouble. " Nothing at all," ses he, and then he told me whar the statues was on the eastern Portico, and pinted out the place whar they kept Mr. Greenough's Washington.

I went out on the portico, and what do you think, Mr. Thompson! the very first thing I seed was a woman without so much as a pettycoat on! Not a real live woman, but one cut out of marble, jest as nateral as life itself. Thar she was, sort of half standin and half squattin by the side of a man dressed off in armour and holdin a round ball in his hand. At first I never was so tuck aback in my life, and I looked all round to see if anybody was lookin at me. I couldn't help but look at it, though it did make me feel sort o' shamed all alone by myself. Every now and then somebody would cum by, and then I would walk off and look tother way. But sumhow I couldn't go away. The more I looked at it the handsumer it got, til bimeby I seemed to forgit every other thought in the contemplation of its beauty. Ther was sumthing so chaste, and cold, and pure about that beautiful figure, that I begun to be in love with it, and I couldn't help but think if I was Columbus and wasn't marble myself, I'd be tempted to give her a hug now and then, if she *was* a squaw. I went down off the portico and took a front view of it—and then I looked at it sideways—and then I went up the steps and looked at it thar agin, and every way it presented a image of beauty to dream of years to come. Bimeby the gall what I sa'' when I was nockin at the door, cum up with that chap with the whiskers and I backed out.

Ther is two other statues standin on the east frunt of the Capitol, one representin the godess of Peace, and the other General Mars, the god of War. They are both very handsome. Mars carrys his hed like a genewine South Carolina militia captain, and Peace looks like she wouldn't hurt anybody for the world; but ther is something tame about 'em—they look somehow like they was cast in a mould.

After lookin at them a while, I went out to the bildin what stands in the yard, and tuck a look at Mr. Greenough's Washington, and to tell you the truth, I never was so disappinted in my life. This statue has some terrible bad faults, and on first view, before one has time to study and understand the design of the artist, creates any thing but a favorable impression. In the fust place the position is out of keepin with the character of Washington; in the second place, the costume is worse than the position, and in the next place, the mouth is not good, and destroys the character and expression of the face. Ther ain't nothing Washington about it, to my notion. The idea of puttin a Roman togy on Gen. Washington, is ridiculous; as if he wasn't jest as much entitled to be a type of his age and generation, as Julius Cæsar or any other Roman hero is of the age when ther was no tailors to make coats. It made me feel bad when I looked up and saw Washington's bare busum. The veneration which Americans feel for the character of Washington is shocked at the exposure of that noble breast, whose every throb was for his country. It seems like a desecration to represent him in any other way than as he was, when he was alive; and though ther is something imposin and grand in the artist's design, the effect is uestroyed by the want of fidelity to the character of the man. I tried my best to overcum my prejudices agin the Washington, because it was a American work, but t was no go, and I went back and tuck another look at

Columbus an.1 his Ingin gall, before I went down to my hotel.

After dinner, I went to see the President, up to the White House as they call it, what stands at the other eend of the Avenue. All along the way the hack-men kep settin at me to ride in one of ther carriages. It looked like only a little ways, and I wanted to see the city as I went along ; but if I stopped for a minit to explain to one of 'em, I was sure to have a dozen of 'em round me at once, all pullin and haulin at me, and cusin one another for every thing you could think of. Washington's so bominably scattered all over creation, that most every body rides, and these fellers think it's a outrage on ther rights to see a gentleman walkin in the street. I cum mighty nigh gettin into three or four fights with 'em fore I got half way to the President's house. It was a monstrous long walk, and I was terrible tired fore I got thar. What makes it so deceivin is, the Capitol at one eend, and the White House at the other eend of the wide street, is so large that one loses all idee of distances and proportions.

When I got to the house, I nocked at the door, and a gentleman opened it and told me to cum in.

" Good evenin, Mr. President," ses I, " I hope yourself and famly is all well," offerin him my hand at the same time.

" Good evenin, sir," ses the gentleman, givin me a real Georgia shake by the hand. " It's not Mr. Polk your spakin too, ses he, but no offence, sir, walk in."

" Why," ses I, " don't the President live here," beginin to think I never would find him.

" To be sure, sir ; this is the Prisident's house, but it's Cabinet day, and his excellency can't be seen by strangers."

" Well, I'm very sorry for that," ses I.

" And so am I," ses the gentleman. " But," ses he, " since you can t see his excellency, you can have the honor of taking a pinch of snuff wid his lagal ripresintative," and with that, he poked his snuff-box at me

4

and I tuck a pinch of his Irish blackguard, that liked to put my neck out of jint a sneezin.

As soon as I got over it a little, ses he: "walk this way, sir, and I'll show you through the public rooms if you would like to see them."

After walkin about awhile we cum into the great East room, which is a real stylish place you may depend, with gold chairs, and marble tables, and the richest kind of carpets, with lookin-glasses clear down to the floor. I knew that was the room whar pore old General Harrison lay before he was buried, so I ax'd the man if he knowd General Harrison.

"To be sure I did," ses he; "I cum here in General Jackson's administrashun, and I've bin here iver since. Ah, sir!" ses he, "General Harrison was a great and good man. He was a true dimocrat, he was. We waked him here two days in this room, sir, and I shall niver, til the day of my deth, forgit that melancholy sight. The gineral was none of yer blarneyin politicians, but a true man, sir. When he cum to the White House I wint to him, and ses I—'Gineral, I'm a dimocrat, and if I'd had a vote I'd voted agin you, and now I'm reddy to give up my place.' 'Don't think of it, Martin,' ses he; 'I'm tould yer attentive and faithful in the discharge of yer duties. I'll need such a man about me, and it's not myself that'll discharge any man for his political opinions.' I kep my place, sir, but the pore ould gintleman, rest his sowl, wasn't spared to keep his. He was kind to ivrybody 'bout him, from the highest to the lowest; I used to walk out wid him whin he was sick; and if you'd seen us togither you couldn't a tould which was the best dimocrat, the Prisident of the United States, or his Irish futman."

"Giv me yer hand, Martin," ses I; "I'm a Georgia whig, and I'm glad to hear you speak well of the man I loved so much."

"Dimocrat or whig," ses he, "the truth's all the same But are ye all the way from Georgia?"

"I am," ses I; "my name is Jones, Joseph Jones of Pineville."

"Majer Joseph Jones?" ses he.

"That's my name when I'm at home," ses I.

"Then giv me yer hand agin, Majer," ses he, "and tell me, how did you lave Mary and the baby—how is little Henry Clay Jones, and the good wife? Faith, I've red yer book, Majer," ses he, "and I'm rite glad to make yer acquaintance. Will you take another pinch of snuff?" ses he.

"No, I thank you, sir," ses I; "I ain't much used to snuffin."

"Well, no matter for that, Majer," ses he; "if it don't agree wid you—I know you used to chew tobacco. But you see I'm a bit of a litterary man myself, and I'm writin a jurnal of my life in the White-house, for these last fifteen years. Now what do you think of the idee, Majer?"

Then he went into a description of his book, and you may depend it's gwine to be one of the most interestin books ever published in this country. You know Martin's bin jest as familiar as a mushstick with the Kitchen Cabinets under Gen. Jackson, Mr. Van Buren, Capt. Tyler, and Mr. Polk—he knows evry politician in the country, and all ther tricks and intrigues; and it'll be monstrous strange if a man of as much natural smartness as Martin, with sich opportunities, couldn't pick up enuff materials in fifteen years to make a interestin book. I told him I thought he had a fortune by the tail, if he'd only hang on to it, and not let anybody git it away from him. He gin me a Irish wink, as much as to say, he wasn't quite so green, and after a little more chat 'bout literature, politics, and matters and things in general, I bid him good by and went back to my hotel. And here I must drap my pen for the present. So no more from

Your friend til deth,

Jos. Jones.

LETTER VII.

Baltimore, May 21, 1848.

To Mr. Thompson:—*Dear Sir*—I left off my las letter whar I went to my hotel. Well, after tea I red the papers a little while, and then went out and tuck a walk by moonlight to see the city. I straggled round all over the place without payin much attention whar I went, lookin at the public bildins and fine-dressed ladies and gentlemen what was in the streets, til the fust thing I know'd I found myself at the gate in frunt of the Capitol. Thar it was agin with its stupendous white walls, and its monstrous high, dark dome, standin in the bright moonlight, loomin up agin the heavens, vast, majestic, and sublime, like the stone mountain in De Kalb county. It didn't seem possible sich a everlastin pile could be bilt with hands; and I could almost imagine it was sum inchanted castle, and that the goblins and fairys was caperin and dancin in the rotunda at that very minit.

I tuck a seat on the stone steps and looked up at it as it stood out agin the blue, star-bespangled sky. Thinks I, this is the hed of the nation, the place whar Uncle Sam does his thinkin; and with that I got to ruminatin 'bout the falibility of national wisdom as well as individual judgment. Public men, thinks I, is like idees: sumtimes they's good, and sumtimes they's monstrous bad—and when they git into the Capitol at Washington, they're jest like thoughts in a man's hed, and make the nation do a monstrous silly thing or a very sensible thing, jest as they happen to be wise or foolish. If ther's any truth in the science of frenology, it must effect the Capitol in the same way it does a man's skull, and I don't doubt that a rite scientific Yankee professor could discover the bumps by feelin the walls of the bildin, and could tell what organ was developed the most. Lately the organ of secretiveness has been pretty strongly developed, and sense we've pocketed Texas, ther ain't no tellin whar we'll stop. Combattiveness, too—which is very prominent, if you notice the projections on the north and south side of the dome—is very active; and I wouldn't be much surprised if we was to lick sum nation like blazes before long. If it wasn't for the excess of veneration which is indicated by the fullness of the dome on the top, we'd been monstrous apt to pitch'd into John Bull before now. Too much veneration is a very bad fault, but maybe it's all the better whar ther's so much combattiveness. I ain't much of a frenologist myself, or I'd go on and give you a full description of Uncle Sam's knowledge-box. I think ther ought to be a scientific committee appinted evry session to make out a complete chart of its bumps, so the people might know what to depend on.

I couldn't leave the Capitol 'thout gwine round and takin one more look at the Ingin gall on the East Portico. Like all butiful wimen, she looked handsumer in the soft, pale moonlight, than she did in the daytime. The outlines and shadows was not so hard; ther was sumthing dreamy and indistinct about her form, and the 'magination was allowed a freer scope in givin the finishin touches to the picter. You know all that is necessary to create in the mind a image of buty, is the mere idee of a woman, with a object for the 'magination to work on. Ther are certain times when a man's 'magination will make a angel out of a bed-post. Well, as I gazed at her, she seemed to becum livin flesh and blood; and, as she looked at Columbus, stoopin over, with her hands raised in a attitude of wunder, I almost fancied I could hear her say—"Christofer! why don't you speak to me?" I tuck a long, long look at her, and then went to the hotel to dream of Mary.

In the mornin, as soon as I got my breckfust, I went to see the Nashunal Institute, whar they told me the government kep all its curiosities. Since as they hadn't the politeness to tell me to cum in when I nocked at the dore of the Capitol yesterday, I tuck it for granted the government was too democratic republican to stand on ceremony; so I didn't nock this time, but jest walked rite in. Well, when I got up stairs, the fust room I got into was the patent-office, whar, the Lord knows, I seed more Yankee contraptions of one kind and another, than ever I thought ther was in the known world. Ther was more'n five hundred thousand models, all piled up in great big glass cages, with ther names writ on 'em, rangin from steam saw-mills down to mouse-traps. Ther was ingines, wind-mills, and water-wheels; steam-botes, ships, bridges, cotton-gins, and thrashin-machines; printin-presses, spinnin-ginnies, weavin-looms, and shingle-splinters—all on a small scale. But it would take a whole letter to give you the names of one half of 'em. I didn't understand much about 'em, and so I went into another room whar they had a ever-lastin lot of shells, and stones, and ores, and fish, and birds, and varmints, and images, and so forth, what was brung home from the North pole, by the explorin expedition. I spose, to sum people, what can find "sermons in stones and good in any thing," these things, what cost the government so much to git 'em, would be very interestin; but I hain't got quite fur enuff in the ologies for that yet—so I went into another apartment, whar they keep the relics of the revolution and other curiosities. This is the most interestin part of the show, and contains a heap of things that must always be objects of the deepest interest to Americans. 'Mong the rest is Gen. Washington's military cote; the same cote that has been gazed on by so many millions of adorin eyes, when it enveloped the form of the great father of his country. It made me have very strange feelins to look upon General Washington's clothes—it caused in my mind the most familiar impression of that great man I had ever felt, and which no paintin or statue could ever give. I was lookin upon what had been a portion of the real, livin Washington ; and I almost felt as if I was in his presence. Close by hung the sword, and below was the camp-chest what he used in the war of the Revolution. What a sight! to behold in one glance the garment that sheltered his sacred person, the provision-chest, cracked and shattered in the great conflict, and the sword with which he won for us the blessings of liberty, which we enjoy. How many thousands, in centuries to come, will look upon the remains of these sacred relics, and bless the memory of the great and good man.

Not far from Washington's cote, in a case by itself, is the cote what General Jackson wore at the battle of New Orleans. I stopped and looked at it with feelins of sincere veneration. Few would suppose the victory of New Orleans was won in sich a coarse cote—but it is like the lion-harted hero who wore it—corse, strong, and honest, without tinsel or false gloss. It looks like the General, and will be preserved as a priceless relic of the brave old patriot, whose days are now drawin to a close. I never voted for General Jackson, cause I thought his politics was wrong; but I always believed him to be a honest man, and a true patriot, and I don't blieve ther's a lokyfoky in the land that's prouder of his fame, or will hear of his deth with more unfeigned sadness.

Ther's a heap of other curiosities in this part of the bildin, that is well worth the attention of the visiter. Among the rest is Gen. Washington's Commisshun, and the original Declaration of Independence, besides treaties in all sorts of outlandish languages, and guns and pistols and swords, all covered with gold and diamonds, that have been made presents to our government from foreign powers. Ther's a heap of Ingin picters, and among 'em some portraits of the Seminole chiefs, what fit us so hard a few years ago. I seed old Alligator settin up thar, as dignified as a turky-cock in a barn-yard, and I couldn't help but think of the time I seed the old feller fall off a log into the St. Johns with all his fancy rigins on, and a jug of rum in his hand. Ther's sum very good likenesses among the Ingin portraits, but they've got sum of the triflinest fellers in the whole nation settin up thar as grand as Mogulls.

After lookin at the other picters, and busts, and statues, (and ther's sum butiful things among 'em,) I went down into the lower story, and thar I saw the grate Sarcofagus what Com. Elliott brung over from Egypt to bury Gen. Jackson in. I don't blame the old General for backin out from any sich arrangement. In the fust place, I don't think it in very good taste for to be in too big a hurry to provide a coffin for a man before he's ded; and in the next place, I've got no better opinion of old second-hand coffins than I have of second-hand boots. I'd a grate deal rather walk in the footsteps of a dozen livin, illustrious predecessors, than to fill the coffin of one ded King Fareo. No, indeed; the old hero is too much of a proud-spirited republican for that —he's not gwine to lay his bones in a place whar sum bominable old heathen King has rotted away before, and I glory in him for it. Such men as Jackson finds a sarcofagus in every true patriot's heart, that will preserve his memory, from generation to generation, to the eend of time.

After gettin out of Uncle Sam's curiosity shop, I went out into his flower garden, what is kep in a long, low house, with a glass roof. It's got about five hundred kinds of cactuses in it, and that's about all. True, ther's a good many little bushes and weeds, with monstrous hard names, and sum few with flowers on 'em, but Mary's flower-garden at home would beat it all holler for buty and variety.

I tuck a walk round by the Post-Office and up to the War Department, and the President's house. The new

Post-Office, the National Institute, and the War Department is most magnificent bildins, of grayish, coarse stone; and if they don't paint 'em like they have the Capitol and the President's house, they'll look ancient enuff to suit the fancy of Mr. Dickens, or anybody else, who never saw a new country before, and who think none of the rest of the world ain't fit to live in, cause it ain't as old and musty as London.

By the time I got down to Gadsby's I was pretty tired; and after eatin a fust rate dinner, I got reddy to go to Baltimore. I paid my bill, which was very little, I thought, for sich comfortable livin, and got my trunks all packed and reddy sum time before the cars started.

Bimeby long cum the omnibus and tuck my trunks; but the depo was so close that I jest fit my way through the hack drivers to the cars, without any serious accidents. It was a very plesant afternoon, and ther was ever so many ladys and gentlemen in the cars, gwine to Baltimore, and among 'em sum of the most outlandish specimens of human nater I ever met with. I thought I'd seed whiskers and bustles before, but I find the further north I git, the bigger they grow. After a while the bell rung and away we went, the houses, Capitol and all waltzin round behind us, til we was out of sight of the city; and the posts of Professor Morse's Telegraph, as they call it, gettin closer and closer together the faster we went.

But now the scene is very different from what it is on the Carolina, or even the Virginy rodes. The woods is in little patches, and the fields is smaller, and the houses and towns is thicker. The country is more uneven, and evry mile changes the scenery, and gives one sumthing new to look at. The track, too, is even as a die, and the cars go like lightnin and as easy as a rockinchair. One minit we was whirlin along between butiful farms, in the next we darted into a cut whar the banks shut out the view, and perhaps the next we was crossin over sum butiful valley on a bridge, with mills, and houses, and people far below us. We passed lots of hoses and cattle, and sum of 'em would twist up ther tails and giv us a race, but we went so fast that nothin couldn't keep up with us but the wire lightnin conductors of the telegraph, which kep us cumpany all the way. It's only 'bout forty miles from Washington to Baltimore, and I hadn't begun to git tired before the monuments and steeples and towers of the city begun to show themselves in the distance, gittin nearer and nearer, til we was rite in among 'em.

When we got to the depo in the edge of the city, they unhitched the lokymotive and hitched on sum hoses that pulled us away down into the center of the city to the railrode office. I could find enuff for twenty pair of eyes to do, lookin at this butiful city. I hadn't no idee it was half so large or half so handsum. But I had no time to give it more'n a glimpse before we was at the stoppin place, and in the middle of another regiment of whips, all pullin and haulin, and axin me to go this way and tother, til I didn't hardly know which eend I stood on.

Bimeby one very civil little man with a piece of painted lether on his hat ses to me, ses he—"Sir, giv me yer checks for yer baggage, and I'll take ye to the Exchange Hotel, a very good house, sir." It was Hobson's choice with me, for I didn't know one house from tother, so I jest handed him over the tins, and he went to look out for my baggage. While I was waitin for him a reinforcement of hackmen got round me, and insisted on takin me to the Exchange. Well, I was like the gall what married the chap to git rid of him, and I got into the fust hack and druv off. I wasn't more'n seated, fore we was at the dore of a grate big stone house, with a dome on the top of it like the Capitol at Washington, what the feller sed was the Exchange Hotel. After I got out I ax'd the driver how much was to pay. "A quarter," ses he. I pulled out my purse and paid him, but if I'd know'd it was no further, I'd seed him to Bullyhack fore I'd got into his hack, that's certain.

Soon as I got in the hotel the man in the office laid a big book out before me and gin me a pen. I know'd what he ment, so I put my name down—Jos. Jones, Pineville, Geo., as plain as a pike-staff. I hadn't more'n finished writin my name before here cum the man with my trunks, and in a minit after I found myself up stairs in No. 27, whar I am now writin to you, and whar I expect to remain for a day or two. I mean to go to bed early to-night, and take a fresh start in the mornin to look at Baltimore. So no more from
Your frend til deth,
Jos. Jones

LETTER VIII.

No. 27, Exchange Hotel,
Baltimore, May 21, 1845.

To Mr. Thompson:—*Dear Sir*—I waked up this mornin bright and early, but I felt so monstrous tired that I didn't git rite out of bed. Well, while I was layin thar, lookin round the room at the fine furniture—at the splendid mahogany burow and wardrobe, the marble-top'd washstand and the cast-iron fire-place, and a heap of other curious fixins—I seed a green cord with a tossel on the eend of it, hangin down by the hed of my bed. Thinks I, that must be to pull the winder blinds, to let the light in, and as it was rayther dark, I tuck hold of it and pulled it easy two or three times, but the thing seemed to be hitched sumwhar, and the blinds didn't move a bit. I wasn't more'n done pullin it, before sumbody nocked at my dore, and as I didn't know who it mought be, I covered up good, and ses I, "Cum in."

A nigger feller opened the dore and stood thar for 'bout a minit, lookin at me like he wanted sumthing, 'thout sayin a word.

"Well, buck," ses I, "what's the matter," beginnin to think he had a monstrous sight of imperence.

"I cum to see what the gemmen wants," ses he.

"Well," ses I, "I don't want nothin."

He looked sort o' sideways at me and put out.

After studyin a bit to try to make out what upon yeath could brung him to my room, I put my hand out and tried the curtains agin; and the fust thing I know'd here cum the same chap back agin.

This time I looked at him pretty sharp, and ses I—"What upon yeath do you mean?"

With that he begun bowin and scrapin and scratchin uis hed, and ses he—"Didn't you ring, sir?"

"Ring what?" ses I.

"Your bell," ses he.

I was beginnin to git pretty considerable riled, and ses I—"I don't carry no bell, but I can jest tell you what it is, my buck: if you go to cumin any of yer free nigger nonsense over me, I'll ring yer cussed neck off quicker'n lightnin."

And with that I started to git out of the bed, but ther was no nigger thar when my feet tetched the floor.

It was too dark to dress, so I tuck another pull or two at the blinds; and while I was pullin and jerkin at 'em, here cums another big nigger, to know what I wanted. By this time I begun to spicion thar was sumthing rong; and shore enuff, cum to find out, I'd been pullin a bell-rope all the time, what kep up a terrible ringin down stairs, though I couldn't hear the least sign of it myself. I'd seed them things hangin round in the rooms at the Charleston Hotel, and at Gadsby's, but I never know'd what they was before. Well, thinks I, live and larn— I'll know a bell-rope when I see it agin.

After findin my way down stairs I went in the barber's room and got shaved, and I do blieve if it hadn't been so early in the mornin, I should went spang to sleep while Billy was takin my beard off. That feller's a real magnetiser; and he goes through the bisness so easy, that you can't hardly tell whether he's usin the brush or the razor; and by the time he's done, your face is so smooth that it takes a pretty good memory to remember whether you ever had any beard or not. After brushin and combin a little, I went out into the readin-room and ooked over the papers til breckfust.

I was settin on the sofa readin in the National Intelligencer, when the fust thing I know'd I thought the whole roof of the bildin was cumin down on top of my hed—whow! row! whow-wow! went sumthing like the very heavens and yeath was cumin together. I couldn't hear myself think, and I was makin for one of the winders as fast as I could, when the everlastin rumpus stopped. I ax'd sumbody what in the name of thunder it was. "O, you needn't be larmed," ses he, "it's nothin but the breckfust gong." I was jest about as wise then as I was before, but I know'd it had sumthing to do with breckfust, and my appetite soon cum back to me agin.

You know I always used to drink coffee, and I'm monstrous fond of it yet; but bein as I didn't feel very well this mornin, when the waiter ax'd me which I'd have, I sed "tea."

"Black or green?" ses he.

I looked at the feller, and ses I—"What?"

"Will you have black or green tea?" ses he.

I didn't know whether he was projectin with me or not, so ses I, "I want a cup of tea, jest plain tea, without no fancy colerin about it."

That settled the bisness, and in a minit he brung me a grate big cup of tea that looked almost as strong as coffee; but it was monstrous good, and I made out a fust rate breckfust.

After breckfust I tuck a walk out to see the city, and shore enuff it is a city! Gracious knows, I thought Charleston, and Richmond, and Washington was big enuff, but Baltimore lays 'em all in the shade. It ain't only a long ways ahed of 'em all in pint of size, but it's a monstrous sight the handsumest. The streets is wide enuff, and then ther ain't no two of them alike, and evry corner you turn gives you a new view, as different from the other as if you was in another city. Monuments and steeples, and minarets and towers, and domes and columns, and piazzas and porticos, and pillars of all orders, sizes, and heights, is constantly changin before you; and the ground rises and falls in butiful hills and hollers, as if it tried to do its share towards givin variety and buty to the view. Baltimore street is the principal street, and you may depend it's got a heap of fine stores on it.

After takin a good stretch on Baltimore street, lookin at the picter-shops and show-winders, I struck out into Calvert street, whar the monument stands what was raised to the brave fellers what licked the British at the Battle of North Pint, in the last war. It's a good deal bigger than the Naval Monument at Washington, and, to my notion, it's a grate deal handsomer. Its proportions is good, and the design is very butiful.

After takin a good look at the monument, I walked along down by sum fine large brick houses with marble porticos to 'em, and winder-glasses so clean you mought see yer face in 'em, lookin back now and then at the woman on top of the monument, when the fust thing I know'd I got a most alfired skeer, that made me jump clear off the side-walk into the street, before I know'd what I was about; "Get out!" ses I, at a cussed grate big fierce-lookin dog upon one of the porticos, that looked like he was gwine to take rite hold of me. "Seize him, Tiger!" ses a chap what was gwine by, laughin, and I raised my stick quicker'n lightnin, but the dog never moved a peg. Cum to find out, it was nothin but a statue of a dog made out of stone or iron, put up thar to watch the dore and keep off housebrakers, I spose. I got over my skare and went along, but I couldn't help thinkin it was monstrous bad taste to have sich a fierce-lookin thing standin rite before a body's dore thataway. If he was lyin down asleep he'd look jest as natural, and wouldn't be apt to frighten any body out of ther senses fore they know'd what it was.

Bimeby I cum to a open place with a butiful little temple standin back in the yard, under the trees, and over the gate was a sign what sed "City Springs." Well, as I felt pretty dry by this time, I thought I'd go in and git sum water. When I got to the house what was standin over the spring on butiful round pillars, and was gwine down the white stone steps, I seed a whole heap of galls down thar playin and dabblin in the water, and sprinklin and splashin one another, and laughin and carryin on like the mischief. I'd heard a grate deal about Baltimore buty, and I thought I'd jest take a peep t 'em while they didn't see me, and when they wasn't suspectin anybody was lookin at 'em. Well, thar they was, five or six of 'em, all 'bout sixteen and seventeen, with ther butiful faces flushed up, and ther dark eyes sparklin with excitement, while ther glossy ringlets, in which the crystal water glittered like dimonds, fell in confusion over ther white necks and shoulders. They was butiful young creters; and as I leaned over the wall, lookin down on 'em as they was wrestlin and jumpin and skippin about as graceful as young fawns, I almost thought they was real water-nymphs, and I was 'fraid to breathe hard for fear they mought hear me and dart into the fountains. Bimeby one of 'em that was scufflin for life to keep two more of 'em from given her a duckin, happened to look up. The next minit thar was a general squeelin and grabbin up of sun-bonnets, and away they went up tother flight of steps. I didn't want 'em to think I'd been watchin 'em, so I went rite down to the spring, like I had jest cum for a drink of water. Ther was three fountains all in a row, and on each side of the fountains was two iron ladles hangin chained to the wall. I tuck up the one on the right, and was holdin it under the spout on that side, when I heard the galls gigglin and laughin up on the steps, whar they was rangin ther dresses. I couldn't help but look round, when I saw one of the prettyest pair of sparklin eyes lookin over the wall at me, that I have seed sense I left home. "The middle fountain's the best, sir," ses one of the sweetest voices in the world. I didn't wait to think, but jest cause she sed so, I jerked the ladel what was already runnin over, towards the middle spout, when kerslosh went the water all over my feet, and the ladel went rattle-teklink agin the wall what it was chained. Sich another squall as they did give I never heard before, and away they all scampered laughin fit to die at me. The fact was the chain wasn't long enuff to reach to the middle fountain no how, even if the water was any better, which I ought to know'd was all gammon. I felt a little sort o' flat, but thinks I, galls, if you only know'd the buties I seed when I was ookin down over your heds, when you was rompin, you'd think we was pretty near even, after all.

From the City Springs I went to the Washington monument, what stands at the hed of Charles street. This is another butiful structure which, while it commemorates the fame of the greatest man what ever lived on the face of the yeath, reflects honor on the patriot ism and liberality of Baltimoreans. At the dore ther was a old gentleman, who ax'd me if I wanted to go up on the monument. I told him I'd like to very well, if ther was no danger. He sed ther wasn't the least in the world; so, after payin him a seven-pence and writin my name in a big book, he gin me a lamp and I started up the steps, what jest kep runnin round and round like a screw-auger. Up, up I went, and kep a gwine til I thought my legs would drap off me. Evry now and then I stopped and tuck a blow, and then pushed on agin, til bimeby I got to the top, whar ther is a dore to go out on the outside.

From that place I could see all over the city, and for miles round the country; and, to tell you the truth, I couldn't hardly blieve my own eyes, when I saw so many houses. The ground seemed to be covered with bricks for miles; and every here and thar some tall steeple or lofty dome shot up from the dark mass of houses below. Streets was runnin in every direction, and carriages and hoses and peeple was all movin about in 'em, like so many ants on a ant-hill. Away off to the south-east I could see the dome of the Exchange Hotel, and a little further was the blue arms of the Patapsco, covered with white sails, gwine in and out of the harbor; while the naked masts of the vessels at the wharves and in the basin, looked like a corn-field jest after fodder-pullin time. I could see "the star-spangled banner" on the walls of old Fort Mackhenry, still wavin "over the land of the free and the home of the brave," as proudly as it did on that glorious night, when

> "The rocket's red glare, and bums bustin in air,
> Gave proof through the night that our flag was still thar."

and I couldn't keep from singin, "O long may it wave!" &c.

By the time I got down from the Monument it was two o'clock, and I begun to have a pretty good appetite agin. I made out to git back to the Exchange, by enquirin the way 'bout twenty times; and pretty soon after I got thar that everlastin gong rung agin, and we all went in to dinner. I never seed sich a handsum table in all my life before. It was long enuff for a fourth of July barbacue, and all dressed out like a weddin-supper. Evry thing looked in order, like a army formed in line of battle. The plattoons of ivory-handled knives, and silver forks, and cut-glass goblets, and wine-glasses, was all ranged in two long columns on each side, with a napkin standin at each place like a file-closer, crimped up as handsum and lookin as white and fresh as a water-lilly. In the middle was the baggage-train, which was made up of a long row of bright covers, with elegant silver casters and tureens, large glass vases full of sallary, and lots of other dishes. I felt jest like I was gwine into battle; and whether Mr. Dorsey, like Lord Nelson, expected every man to do his duty or not, I was termined to do mine. Well, the table was soon surrounded, and then the attack commenced. It was a terrible carnage. The knives and forks rattled like small arms, the corks popped like artillery, and the shampane flew like blood at evry discharge. General Jennings manoovered his troops fust rate—carryin off the killed and wounded as fast as possible, and supplyin ther places with reinforcements of fresh dishes. He had a regular Wellington army, made up of English, French, American, German, Itallian, and all kinds of dishes; but, like Napoleon at Waterloo, he was doomed to come out second best, and in a short time his splendid army was cut to pieces, routed, dispersed, and demolished, horse, foot, and dragoons, or rather roast, boiled, and stewed.

You know I've fit the Ingins in Florida, and can stand my hand as well as the next man in a bush-fight, but I never was in jest sich a engagement before, and I made rather a bad job of it in the beginnin. I hadn't more'n swallered my soup when here cums a nigger pokein a piece of paper at me, which he sed was a bill. Thinks I, they're in a monstrous hurry 'bout the money, so I told him I hadn't time to look it over then. The feller looked and grinned like he didn't mean no offence. and ax'd me what I'd be helped to. Well, I know'd they didn't have no bacon and collards, so I told him to bring me a piece of roast beef. By the time I got fairly gwine on my beef, Mr. Dorsey cum in and tuck a seat at the eend of the table not far from me, and ax'd me how I was pleased with Baltimore. I told him very well, and was passin a word or two with him, when the fust thing I know'd my plate was gone, and when I turned round to look for it, the nigger poked the bill at me agin. I begun to think that was carryin the joke a leetle too fur, and ses I—

"Look here, buck; I told you once I hadn't no time to tend to that now, and I'd like to know what in the devil's name you tuck my plate away for?"

"What'll you be helped to?" ses he, like he didn't understand me.

"I ax'd for sum beef," ses I, "but——" and before I could git it out he was off, and in a minit he brung me another plate of roast beef.

Well, by the time I got it salted to my likin, and while I was taken a drink of water, away it went agin I jest made up my mind I wouldn't stand no such nonsence any longer, so I waited til he brung me a clean plate agin, and ax'd me what I wanted.

"Sum more beef," ses I.

I kep my eyes about me this time, and shore enuff, he moment I turned to nod to sum gentlemen what Mr. Dorsey introduced me to, one of the niggers made a grab at my plate. But I was too quick for him that time.

"Stop!" ses I.

"Beg pardon, sir," ses he; "I thought you wanted another plate."

"I've had enuff plates for three or four men already," ses I; "and now I want sum dinner."

"Very well, sir," ses he; "what'll you have?"

"What's your name?" ses I.

"Hansum, sir," ses he.

Thinks I, you wasn't named for yer good looks then, that's certain; but I never let on.

"Well, Hansum," ses I, "I want you to jest keep a eye on my plate, and not let anybody grab it off til I'm done with it, and then I'll tell you what I want next."

Jest then Mr. Dorsey called him to him and sed sumthing in his ear, and here he cum with Mr. Dorsey's compliments and a bottle of shampane, and filled one of my glasses, and then tuck his stand so he could watch my plate, grinnin all the time like he'd found a mare's nest or sumthing.

The plan worked fust rate, and after that I got a fair showin at the beef. Then I ax'd Hansum what else ther was, and he brung me the bill agin, and told me I'd find it on thar. Shore enuff, it was a bill of things to eat, insted of a bill of expenses. Well, I looked it over, but I couldn't tell the *rari de poulets à la Indienne*, or the *Pigeons en compote*, or the *Anguelles à la Tartare* from any thing else, til I tasted 'em, and then I didn't hardly know the chickens from the eels, they was cooked so curious. Ther was plenty that I did know though, to make out a fust rate dinner, and long before they brung in the custards, and jellies, and pies, my appetite was gone. I was jest gwine to leave the table, when Mr. Dorsey ax'd me if I liked Charlotte Roose. I told him I hadn't the pleasure of her acquaintance. "Well, Majer," ses he, "you better try a little;" and with that he sent me a plate with sumthing on it made out of pound-cake and ice cream 'thout bein froze, which was a little the best thing I ever eat in my life.

Two or three more sich dinners as this would lay me up, so I couldn't git away from the Exchange in a month. No more from

Your frend til deth,
Jos. Jones.

LETTER IX.

No. 27 Exchange Hotel,
Baltimore, May 22, 1845.

To Mr. Thompson :—*Dear Sir*—I've always found that it was the best way to make " good digestion wait on appetite and helth on both," as Mr. McBeth ses, to stir about a little after eatin a harty bate. So after eatin the excellent dinner at the Exchange, what I told you about in my last letter, I tuck another turn round through the city. By this time I begun to git the hang of the place a little better, and wasn't so fraid of gettin lost. I turned up South street as they call it, whar ther's more tailors than would make a dozen common men— even if the old maxim is true, which I never did blieve—and went up Baltimore street agin, whar the fine stores is kep, and whar the galls all go a shoppin and perminadin in the afternoons to show ther new dresses.

Well, sir, I can tell you what's a positiv fact, it would take a French dancin master to git along in Baltimore street without runnin agin sumbody, and even he couldn't shassay his way round through the troops of galls without runnin a fowl of one now and then, or rakin his shins all to pieces on the pine boxes what is piled all along the sidewalk, after you git above Charles street. I done the very best dodgin I could, but every now and then I run spang agin sumbody, and then while I was bowin and scrapin a apology to 'em, ten to one if I didn't knock sum baby over in the gutter what was cumin along with its ma, behind me, or git my cote-tail fast in among the crates and boxes so tite that I run a monstrous risk of losin it bowdaciously. But I wasn't the only one what got hung—two or three galls got ther dresses hitched up, on the nails and hoops, so they blushed as red as fire, and a old gentleman with a broad-brimmed hat, and his stockins over his trowses, tumbled over a wheel-barrow rite into a pile of boxes and tore his clothes dredful. It tuck the old man sum time to gether himself up, and git out of the jam he was in. When he got out he never cussed a word, but he fetched a groan that sounded like it cum from way down below his waistbands, and went on.

I thought, at fust, that the store-keepers must be doin a terrible sight of bisness, to be shure, to be sendin off and receivin 'so much goods, but I knocked on sum of the boxes with my cane, and they sounded as holler as a old empty bee-gum. I spose the city gits a fust rate rent for the pavement, but if the merchants was to keep ther empty boxes in ther sellers, it would be a great deal more convenient for the people to pass along, and I should think it wouldn't hurt ther contents a bit. The fact is a body can't git into the stores to buy nothing, for the piles of boxes round the doors. I wanted a piece of tobacker myself, but I couldn't see no store what I could git into without runnin the risk of breakin my neck or tearin my trowses.

You may suppose I seed a heap of butiful wimmin in Baltimore street. Well, so I did; but, to tell you the truth, I seed some bominable ugly ones too. The fact is, Mr. Thompson, wimmin's wimmin, all over the world; and the old sayin, that "fine feathers makes fine birds," is jest as true here as it is in Georgia. I'm a married man, you know, and can speak my sentiments about the galls 'thout givin offence to nobody; or, at least, 'thout bein spected of selfish motives. Well then, I say Baltimore needn't be ashamed of her wimmin, so far as buty's concerned. "Handsum is as handsum does," is a old and true sayin: and if the Baltimore galls is only as amiable and good as they is butiful, they'll do fust rate, take 'em on a average. But, like every other place, ther's some here that needs a monstrous sight of goodness to make up for ther ugliness.

    I know it used to be a common opinion, that the Baltimore wimmin was the prettyest in the world; and I've heard people what had been here before, advise the young merchants what was gwine to New York to buy goods, that if they didn't want to lose ther harts, they'd better go round this city. But that was a good many years ago, and you know time alters circumstances as well as circumstances alters cases, and this is the way I account for the change. Then the Baltimore galls was most all natives, and come from the same stock, and they was so universally handsum that nobody could help but notice it. But the city is growed a monstrous sight since them days—a great many people from all parts of the world have come into it—and what was the buty of Baltimore, has been mixed up with and distributed about among sich a heap of ugliness, that a great deal of it is spilt altogether; and what does remain pure and unadulterated, aint more'n half so conspicuous now as it used to be. But not withstandin, ther's some monstrous handsum wimmin in Baltimore, some butiful creaters with dark hazel eyes, bright auburn ringlets, Grecian noses, coral lips, and plump, graceful forms, that is enough to melt the ice from round the heart of a old bachellor who had been cold as a lizzard for twenty years; and its my positiv opinion, that a man what couldn't find a gall handsum enuff in this city, would stand a monstrous poor chance of gittin suited short of gwine to Georgia, where the galls, you know, take ther temperments from the warm Southern skies, ther buty from the wild flowers that grow in our fields, and ther voices from the birds that sing in our groves.

    After gwine up as far as Youtaw street, I crossed ove and cum down on tother side of the street, lookin along at one thing and another til I got most down to Charles street. By this time I begun to be monstrous dry, and as I'd heard tell a good deal about the sody water what

"It tuck the breth clean out of me; my tongue felt as if it was full of needles, and I drapped the glass and spurted the rest out of my mouth quicker 'n lightnin', but before I could git breth to speak to the chap, he ax'd me if I wasn't well."—*Letter* ix. *p.* 87.

they have in the big cities, I thought I'd try a little at the fust place whar they sold it. Well, the fust docter's shop I cum to had a Sody water sign up, and in I went to git sum.

Ses I, " I want a drink of yer sody water."

" What kind of syrup will you have?" ses he, puttin his hand on a bottle of molasses.

" I don't want no syrup," ses I, " I want sody water.'

" Ah," ses he, " you want extra sody."

And with that he tuck a glass and put sum white stuff in it, and then held it under the spout til it was full, and handed it to me.

I put it to my hed and pulled away at it, but I never got sich a everlastin dose before in all my life. I got three or four swallers down before I begun to taste the dratted stuff, and you may depend it liked to killed me right ded in my tracks. It tuck the breth clean out of me, and when I cum to myself, my tongue felt like it was full of needles, and my stummick like I'd swallered a pint of frozen soapsuds, and the tears was runnin out of my eyes in a stream.

I drapped the glass and spurted the rest out of my mouth quicker'n lightnin, but before I could git breth to speak to the chap what was standin behind the counter starein at me with all his might, he ax'd me if I wasn't well.

" Well! thunder and lightnin," ses I, " do you want to pisen me to deth and then ax me if I'm well?"

" Pisen!" ses he.

" Yes," ses I, " pisen! I ax'd you for sum sody water, and you gin me a dose bad enough to kill a hoss."

" I gin you nothin but plain sody," ses he.

" Well," ses I, " if that's what you call sody water I'll be dadfetch'd if I'll try any more of it. Why, it' worse nor Ingin turnip juice stew'd down six gallons into a pint, cooled off in a snow-bank and mixed with a harrycane."

Jest then some bilin hot steam come up into my throte, that liked to blow'd my nose rite out by the roots.

Ses he, " Maybe you ain't used to drinkin it without syrup."

" No," ses I, " and what's more, I never will be."

" It's much better with sassypariller, or gooseberry syrup," ses he. " Will you try some with syrup?"

" No, I thank you," ses I, and I paid him a thrip fo the dose I had, and put out.

I wanted some tobacker monstrous bad: so I stepped into a store and ax'd for sum. The man said he didn't sell nothin but staples, but he reckoned I'd find some a little further down, at Smith's. Well, I went along lookin at the signs till I cum to Shaw, Smith & Co. Thinks I this must be the place. So in I went and ax'd a very good lookin man with whiskers, what was standin near the door, if he had any good chewin tobacker.

" No sir," ses he, " we haint got any more of that article on hand than we keep for our own use; but we would like to sell you some carpets to-day."

" Carpets?" ses I; and shore enuff, come to look, ther wasn't another thing but carpets and oil cloths, and mattins and rugs and sich things in the store; and I do blieve ther was enuff of 'em of all sorts and figers to furnish all the houses in Georgia.

After a little explanation he told me the Smith I wanted was J. C. Smith, down opposite to the Museum. He said I'd find lots of tobacker and segars thar, and I'd know the place by a big Ingin standin out before the door. Shore enuff, when I went thar I got some fust rate segars and tobacker, and a box to put it in.

That's the way they do bisness here. They dont keep dry goods and groceries, calicoes, homespun, rum, salt, trace chains and tobacker all together like they do in Pineville, but every kind of goods has a store to itself. If you ever come to Baltimore and want some tobacker or segars, you must go to the stores what's got little painted Ingins or Niggers standin out by the doors;

for you mought jest as well go to a meetin house to borrow a hand-saw, as go to any of the stores here for any thing out of ther line. I spose, like the sody water, it's well enuff to them that's used to it, but it's monstrous aggravokin to them what aint.

As I hadn't been down in the lower part of the city, I thought I'd git into one of the omminybuses and ride over to Fells' Pint, and see how it looked. Well, it's a good long stretch from one eend of Baltimore to the other I can tell you, and after you cross over Jones' falls what runs through to the river and divides the old Town from the new one, you're monstrous apt to think your gettin into another city, if not in another nation. I lik'd to put my jaws out of jint tryin to read sum of the signs. Sum of 'em was painted in Dutch, so I couldn't make out the fust letter, and sum of the people looked so Dutch that you mought almost feel it on 'em with a stick.

I noticed when anybody wanted to git out they jest pulled a leather strap and the omminybus cum to a halt. So when we got down to Fell street, I tuck hold of the strap and gin it a jerk, but the hosses went on fast as ever, so I jest laid my wait on the strap to stop 'em. "Hellow!" ses the driver outside, " do you want to pull me in two?" Cum to find out the strap was hitch'd to the man insted of the hosses, and I liked to draw'd him through the hole whar he tuck his money. He was mad as a hornit, but when he looked in and seed who it was, he had nothin more to say.

I expect some parts of Fells' Pint would suit Mr. Dickens fust rate. It's old as the hills, and crooked as a ram's horn, and a body can hear jest as much bad English thar as he could among the cockneys of London and can find sum fancy caracters, male and female, that would do honor to St. Gileses or any other romantic quarter of the British metropolis.

After lookin about a little while at the sailors that was drinkin toasts and singin songs in the taverns, I went down on one of the wharves whar ther was a ship jest cum from Liverpool. The sailors was singin "All together, oh, heve oh!" and pullin her in to the wharf. Poor fellers, they had been out thirty days, workin hard, in all kinds of weather, and now they was cumin ashore to giv ther money to the sharpers that was lookin out for 'em like sharks for a ded body. I couldn't help but feel sorry for 'em, when I thought how in a few days thay would be without money and without frends, and would gladly go back to the perils of the ocean, to escape the treachery that beset 'em on shore.

I went and tuck a seat on some logs what was layin on the wharf, and smoked a cigar and looked at the vessels sailin about in the harbour. While I was settin thar thinkin of ships and sailors, and one thing and another, a little feller come along with a baskit on his arm, and ax'd me if I wanted to buy some matches. I told him no I didn't want none.

"You better buy some, sir," ses he, "I sell 'em very cheap."

The little feller looked so poor and pittiful that I couldn't help feelin a little sorry for him.

"How much do you ax for 'em?" ses I.

"Eight boxes for a levy," ses he.

They was jest the same kind of boxes that we git two for a thrip in Georgia, and though I didn't want none, I thought I'd buy some of him jest to patronize him.

"Well," ses I, "give me two boxes."

The little feller handed me two boxes and I gin him a sevenpence.

"You may keep the change for profit," ses I.

"Thank you, sir," ses he, and his eyes brightened up as he put the money in his pocket.

"I like to encourage honest enterprize," ses I. "Be honest, and never lie or cheat, and you'll always find friends," ses I.

"With that, the little ragged cuss sot up a big laugh, and put his thumb on his nose and wiggled his fingers at me. 'Do you see anything green,' sez he, 'eh, hoss?'"—*Letter* ix. p. 91.

"Yes sir," ses he, "I never steals nor cheats no body."

"That's right," ses I. That's a good boy."

I went on smokin, and in a few minits, when I thought he was gone, I heard the little feller behind me agin.

"What," ses I.

"My sister died last week," ses he, "and we're very poor, and my mammy's sick, and I can't make money enough to buy medicine for the baby——"

"Well," ses I, "I don't want no more matches, but here's a quarter to add to your profits to-day."

"Thank you, sir," ses he, and he went off agin thankin me, for the quarter.

Poor little feller, thinks I, how much better to give him that quarter of a dollar than to smoke it out in segars. He'll go home to his poor mother, happy, and if he has felt any temptation to be a rogue, the recollection of my kindness will give him courage to be honest. I hadn't got done thinkin about him before here he was, back agin.

"Daddy died last week," ses he, "and sister Betsy got her foot skalded, and we haint had no bred to eat not for a week—ever sense daddy died—and——

"Look here," says I, "you better go before you kill off all your relations: I begin to think you're a little imposter."

"Oh, no sir, daddy *is* ded," ses he, "and mammy and sister lives all alone, and mammy told me to ax you if you would come and see her and give her some money."

I begun to smell a rat, and ses I, "I'll see your mammy to the mischief fust, and if I'd had the same opinion of you that I have now, I'd never gin you the fust red cent."

With that the little ragged cus sot up a big laugh, and put his thum on his nose and wiggled his fingers at me.

"Do you see any thing green," ses he, "eh, hos? What do you think of me now, eh? Would you like to buy another levy's worth of matches? You see," ses he, " I'm one of the b'hoys!—a out and out Fell's Pinter, by J——;" and then he ripped out a oath that nade the hair stand on my hed, and away he went.

I felt like I was completely tuck in, and I never sed another word. But I made up my mind when I gin another quarter away to encourage honesty, it would be to a different sort of candidate; and, throwing the stump of my segar into the water, I left the place and tuck the fust omminybus for the Exchange. I'm done with Baltimore, and shall start to-morrow for the city of Brotherly Love. So no more at present from
Your frend til deth,
JOS. JONES.

LETTER X.

Filladelfy, May 23, 1845.

To Mr. Thompson:—*Dear Sir*—You may be sure I was tired when I got back to the Exchange after my visit to Fell's Pint, last night. I couldn't help but think how I had been tuck in by that bominable little match seller, and I felt rite mad at myself for bein sich a fool.

I had a fust rate appetite for my supper, and by the politeness of Mr. Dorsey—who, tween you and me, is one of the cleverest fellers I've met with sense I left Georgia—I got a invitation to take tea in the lady's supper room. You know when the grand caraven was in Pineville last year, the manager charged a thrip extra for admittin people when they was feedin the annimals. Well, it was worth the money; and if Mr. Dorsey had charged me double price for eatin at the lady's ordinary as they call it, I wouldn't grumbled a bit. Ther was a heap of ladys at the table, rangin from little school galls up to old grandmothers, all dressed out as fine as a fiddle, and lookin as pleasin and happy as the Georgia galls do at a Fourth of July barbycue; and sich a gabblin as they did keep I never heard before. Jest over opposite to me was a bridle party from Virginny, what had jest been gettin married and had come to Baltimore to see ther honey-moon. It was really a interestin party, and it almost tuck my appetite from me to look at 'em, they was so happy and so lovin. They was only married 'bout a week, and of course the world was all moonshine and hummin-birds and roses to them. They felt like ther was no other inhabitants in creation, and that all that was beautiful and bright and good on earth, was made for their enjoyment alone. They had ther bridesmaid and groomsman along, and two or three more young ladys and gentlemen. The galls was all monstrous handsum, but the bride was the handsumest of 'em all. Pore gall, she looked sort o' pale and couldn't eat much supper for lookin at her husband, and he drunk his tea 'thout any sweetenin in it, just cause she looked in his cup with her butiful soft eyes.

They put me in mind of the time when I was married, and of Mary, and by the time supper was over I was as homesick as the mischief. Segars is good for the blues sometimes, and I smoked til my hed whirled round so I couldn't hardly hold my hat on, but it didn't do me not the least bit of good ; so I went to my room and tried to find in the arms of Morfyus a substitute for the arms of her who is a great deal dearer to me than any thing else in this world.

I didn't git much time to sleep for dreamin all night, and when I waked up in the mornin, Hansum sed the second gong was rung, and if I was gwine to Filiadelfy in the cars I better git up rite off. Well, out I got, and dressed and went down to breckfust. After eatin a good breckfust I ax'd for my bill, and Hansum brung down my baggage. Every time I looked at Hansum he was grinnin, but as soon as he seed me lookin at him he straitened up his face and sort o' pretended to scratch his hed. I couldn't think what was the matter with the feller ; and when I looked at him pretty hard he grinned as much as to say, it was the strangest thing in the world to him why I couldn't understand his meanin. Bimeby, when I was puttin my change in my purse, I spected what was the matter. "That's it ; aint it, Hansum," ses I, handin him a quarter. "Yes, sir, thank you, sir," ses he, and he grinned more'n ever, and if you ever seed a ugly nigger he was one.

When I was reddy to start, I went to the door to see if they had put my trunks on the waggon to take them to the cars, and rite in the middle of the hall I met a chap standin with a big painted tin label on his buzzum what had on it, "Boot Black," in big yaller letters. Thar he stood like a sentinel on quarter gard, as stiff as a post, and as I walked by him he kept turnin round, so his sign was all the time in view. When I cum back thar he stood in the same place, with his hands down by is side, and his hed up, lookin me rite in the face. Thinks I, he must be a deaf and dum man what blacks the boots of the establishment, and he want's me to giv him sum change. Well, I didn't know nothin about the deaf and dum language, and as I didn't have no slate and pencil handy, I begun to make signs to him, by pintin at my boots, and then at him, and then doin my hands like I was brushin a boot. He nodded his hed. Then I tuck out my purse and made a motion to him as much as to say, do you want sum money, and he nodded his hed agin, twice. Poor feller, thinks I, he can't dun nobody, and must lose many a debt whar people's always gwine away in a hurry so. So I handed him a half a dollar. When it fell in his hand he opened his eyes and started like he was tuck by surprise. "Thank ye, sir," ses he, scrapin his foot and bowin his hed like a snappin turtle. "Thank ye, sir," ses he.

You may depend that sot me back like the mischief.

"If you ain't dum," ses I, "why didn't you speak before," ses I.

"I had nothin to spake of," ses he.

"Couldn't you sed you was the boot-blacker," ses I.

"I'd tould ye that," ses he, "but I thought you could rade;" ' and where's the use of keepin a dog and doin one's own barkin,'" ses he.

Tuck in agin, thinks I. If I hadn't thought he was a dum man I wouldn't gin him but a sevenpence, nohow.

It was nine o'clock, and I was seated in the cars on my way to Filladelfy. The road runs rite along in the edge of the city, near the wharves, and gives a body a pretty good idee of the heavy bisness part of Baltimore from the basin clear out to Fell's Pint, in Old Town.

After we got out of the city, they took out the horses and hitched in the old steam Belzebub, and away we went, rattle-te-klink, over embankments and through cuts, across fields and over bridges, until we was soon out of site of Baltimore. The mornin was dark and cloudy and the ground was wet; so if we lost any thing by not havin brighter skies and a better view of the scenery, we made up for it by not havin no dust to choke us to deth. This is a butiful railroad, and the cars is as comfortable as a rockin chair with arms to it. You haint got to be bumpin and crowdin up together in the seats like you do on some roads, for every man has a comfortable seat to himself; and another thing that I liked very much was, that the sparks aint always dartin about your face, and lightin down when you aint spectin nothin and burnin your clothes off of you.

I begin to find it a great deal colder here than it was in Georgia when I left home. We had summer in Pineville more'n a month ago, and everybody had gardin vegetables on their tables, and my corn was more'n knee high long before I left. Here ther aint hardly a English pea to be seen, and the cornfield malitia is still on duty to skeer the birds from pullin up the sprouts. But in that line of bisness they can beat us all holler, for I've seed two or three skeercrows standin about in the cornfields here that wouldn't only skeer all the birds in Georgia to deth, but they wouldn't leave a nigger on the plantation in twenty-four hours after they wer put in the field. They looked more like the old boy in regimentals than any thing I can think of.

The road passes through a rather thinly popilated country most of the distance, til it gits to Haver-de-grass, whar it crosses the Susquehanny river. After that it goes through a country that keeps gettin better and better til we git to Wilmington, Delaware, which is a butiful town on the Brandywine river, 'bout thirty miles from Filladelfy. Between Baltimore and the Susque-oanny we crossed over several rivers, on bridges, som of 'em more'n a mile long, but ther aint no changin, only at the Susquehanny, which we crossed in a butiful steamboat to the cars on the other side. From Wilmington all the way to Filladelfy, we wer in site of the broad Delaware on our right, on the banks of which, and as far as we could see on the left, is one of the handsumest agricultural districts in the country—the houses lookin like palaces and the farms like gardens. •

When the cars got to the depo, they was surrounded as usual by a regiment of whips. But the Filladelfy hackmen behaved themselves pretty well for men in ther line of bisness. Ther wasn't more'n twenty of 'em at me at one time, and none of 'em didn't 'tempt to take my baggage from me whether I would let 'em have it or not. Soon as I got so that I knowed which eend I was standin on, I took a hack and druv to the United States Hotel in Chestnut street, rite opposite the old raw head and bloody bones, the United States Bank.

After dinner I tuck a walk up Chestnut street to the old State House, whar the Continental Congress made the Declaration of Independence. The old bildin stands whar it did, and the doorsills is thar, upon which the feet of our revolutionary fathers once rested; but whar are they now? Of all the brave hearts that throbbed in them old halls on the 4th of July, 1776, not one now is warmed by the pulse of life! One by one they have sunk down into ther graves, leavin a grateful pos terity to the enjoyment of the civil and religious blessins for which they pledged ther " lives, ther fortins and thei sacred honors." I felt like I was walkin on consecrated ground, and I couldn't help but think that if some of our members of Congress was to pay a occasional pilgrimage to this Mecky of our political faith, and dwell but for a few hours on the example of the worthy men who once waked the echoes of these halls with ther patriotic eloquence, they would be apt to go back wiser and better politicians than they was when they cum, and that we would have less sound and more sense, less for Buncum and more for the country in ther speeches in our Capitol at Washington.

After lookin about the old hall, I went up stairs into the steeple, whar the bell still hangs what was cast by order of Congress, to proclaim liberty to the world. It is cracked and ruined, and like the walls in which it hangs, the monuments and statues and paintins, and every other relic of them days, it remains a silent memento of the past, and as such it should be preserved as long as the metal of which it is made will stick together.

After takin a good look at it and readin the inscription on it, I went up higher in the steeple, and tuck a look at the city. Well, I thought thar was brick and morter enough under my eyes at one time when I was on the Washington monument in Baltimore; but, sir, Baltimore, large as it is, ain't a primin to Filladelfy. I could see nothin but one eternal mass of houses on every side. On the east, I could see the Delaware, what divided the city from the houses on the Jersey side, but on the north and south, it was impossible to see the eend of 'em. They stretched out for miles, until you couldn't tell one from another, and then the confused mass of chimneys, roofs and steeples, seemed to mingle in the gray obscure of the smoky horizon. The streets run north and south, east and west, at right angles, as strait and level as the rows in a cotton patch. The fact is, I can't compare the city to any thing else but one everlastin big chess board, covered with pieces. The churches with steeples, answerin for castles, the State-house, Exchange and other public bildins, for kings, the Banks for bishops, the Theatres and Hotels for knights, and so on down til you cum to the private houses, which would do to stand for counters. The only difficulty in the comparison is that ther ain't no room to move—the game bein completely blocked or checkmated every whar, except round the edges, and whar ther is now and then a square left for a public walk.

I was standin thar ruminatin and wonderin at the great city that was stretched out at my feet and thinkin to myself what a heap of happiness and misery, wealth and poverty, virtue and vice it contained, and how if I was a Asmodeus what a interestin panorama it would afford me, when the fust thing I know'd I cum in a ace of jumpin spang off the steeple into the tree-tops below. Whang! went something rite close by me, with a noise louder than a fifty-six pounder, that made the old steeple totter and creak as if it was gwine all to pieces. I grabbed hold of the railins and held on to 'em with all my might, til I tuck seven of them allfired licks, every one of which I thought would nock my senses out of me. It jarred my very inards, and made me so deaf I couldn't hear myself think for a ower afterwards. Come to find out it was the town clock strikin in the steeple rite over my head. It was a monstrous lucky thing for me that it wasn't no later, for I do believe if it had been ten or leven o'clock it would been the deth of me.

As soon as I got able to travel I cum down out of that place and went through Independence Square, what's right in the rear of the State House, to Washington Square. This is said to be the handsumest public square in the world—it certainly is the handsumest I ever seed, and I do blieve that on this occasion ther wasn't that spot of earth on the whole globe that could compare with it. I don't mean the square itself, though that is handsum enuff in all conscience, with its butiful gravelled walks, its handsum grass-plats, its shady trees, and ellegant iron fence, that would cost more itself than all the houses in Pineville—but what I mean is the scene what I saw in the square.

If there was one I do blieve ther was fifteen hundred to two thousand children in the square at one time, all rangin from two to seven and eight years old, and all dressed in the most butiful style. Thar they was. little

galls and boys, all playin and movin about in every
direction—some jumpin the rope, some rollin hoops,
nere a party of little galls dancin the polker, and thar
another playin at battledoor or the graces—some runnin
races and some walkin, some of 'em butiful as little
Coopids, and all as merry and sprightly as crickets. It
was a kind of juvenile swoiree, as they call 'em here,
and I never did see any little creaters that seemed to
enjoy themselves so much. I never seed so many
children together before in all my life, and it seemed to
me ther wasn't a sickly one among 'em. Perhaps the
sickly ones couldn't come out when the wether was so
cool. But if they was a fair specemen of the children
of Filladelfy, then I can say there aint a city in the
world that can beat her for handsum, clean, well-dressed,
healthy-lookin children. Ther was lots of nurses among
'em to take care of 'em, and now and then you could see
a pair of little niggers tryin to mix in with 'em; but it
was no go, and the pore little blackys had to sneak
round the corners and look on like pore folks at a frollick, the little children not bein sufficiently edicated yet
to enable them to discover their equals in the sable de-
scendants of Africa.

While I was lookin about in the square who should
I see but the famous Count Barraty, what was out to
Pineville you know about two years ago lecturein on
Greece. Thar he was with the same old shaggy locks
and big moustaches, standin near a groop of servant
galls, with his arms folded, lookin on in the attitude of
Bonaparte at St. Helleny. Poor old feller I couldn't
help but pity him, when I thought what terrible vicissi-
tudes he has passed through sense he was in Georgia.
You know when he left Pineville he told us we would
hear from him in the papers, and in less than a month
we did hear from him shore enuff in the Pickyune, what
gin a account of that terrible encounter he had with a
cowhide in the hands of sum gentleman in New Orleans,
whose lady didn't understand Greek enuff to enable her

to appreciate his foreign manners. The count don't wear so much jewelry now as he use to in Georgia, and his clothes look a little seedy. But he's the same old Count in every other respect. As soon as he seed me he relaxed the austerity of his moustaches and went out of the square.

Bimeby the swoiree was over, and the nurses begun to gether up ther charges and prepare for gwine home. The merry laugh and song soon died away, and troop after troop of little people filed out of the gates in every direction, until the square was entirely deserted.

It was tea time and I went to my hotel. Sense tea I have rit you this letter, informin you of my arrival here. I'm gwine to bed early to-night, and if it don't rain tomorrow I'm gwine to take a early start and see what Filladelfy's made out of before nite. So no more from

Your frend til deth,
Jos. Jones.

LETTER XI.

Filladelfy, May 24, 1845.

To Mr. Thompson :—*Dear Sir*—You know it's the fashion now-a-days for young people at the south, when they git married, to start rite off to the north before the preacher has hardly had time to bless 'em. Well, I never could make out what they done so for—I never could see why they couldn't stay at home til they got rite well acquainted with one another before they went whar they wouldn't see nothing but strangers. One thing I do know though, and that is, they nor nobody else don't come to these big cities to sleep; for if the seven sleepers themselves was to put up in one of these northern hotels, they'd have to take a dose of lodnum to save ther reputations. The omnibusses and carriages, and drays and carts, seems all the time like one everlastin harrycane, roarin and rattlin, and crashin and smashin along over the stones from mornin til night, and from night til mornin; and I don't care if they put you seven stories high, you can hear 'em all the time. and you can't sleep a wink, if you're ever so tired, til you learn to sleep with your ears open, and to dream 'bout bein in sich a infernal racket that you can't hear yourself snore.

I aint very certain whether I waked up at all or not this mornin, but I got up to breckfast, and after sprucin up a little, I went out to see the city. Gwine along up to Sixth street, who should I meet but Mr. More, what you know was out to Pineville winter before last, travellin for his helth. You remember he was almost ded with the consumption, and looked like he was bleeged to carry rocks in his pockets to keep the wind from blowin him away. Well, would you blieve it, he's a sound and well man, and looks this day as if he mought live to be a hundred years old. I never seed such a alteration in any body in my life, and I wouldn't have know'd him from Adam if he hadn't spoke to me fust.

"Why, Major Jones," ses he, "how are you—how d'ye do? I'm so glad to see you. How's Mrs. Jones and the baby, and all of 'em?"

I looked at him right hard while he was shakin my hand, and ses I, "You've got the advantage of me, sir."

"Why, don't you know me, Major—More's my name—don't you remember More, what used to come to your plantation after——?"

"To be sure," ses I. "But is it possible? Why you don't look like the same man. I never should have know'd you agin in the world. What upon yeath has brung you out so?"

"Why, major, when I cum back almost ded last summer, I tuck to drinkin——"

"Taint possible, Mr. More; is you bloated up so?" ses I.

"Oh no," ses he, "I didn't take to drinkin licker. I drunk 'bout fifteen bottles of Schenck's Pulmonic Syrup, and you see what it's done for me."

"Is it possible?" ses I.

"Yes," ses he, "I weigh a hundred and thirty-five pounds now, and I'm indebted to Schenck's Syrup for all but my bones. But no more about that," ses he 'Whar are you gwine, and what can I do for you. Is rer famly along?"

"No," ses I, "I'm jest on a little trip of observation to the north, and am only gwine to stay a day or two to look at your city."

"Well," ses he, "then you'll jest walk with me to the Exchange. When I git through a little bisness I've got thar, we'll take a drive, and I'll show you the wonders of this part of the world."

Well, we went down to the Exchange, a butiful white marble bildin, with columns and porticos, and two monstrous grate big lions layin upon the side of the steps. Its a very handsum bildin, and like all the public bildins in Filladelfy, is as clean and white as a Georgia bred-tray after a hard scrubbin. I looked round the big Change room, at the angels painted on the ceilin, and the other curiosities, til Mr. More got through his bisness, and then we went to the hotel, whar I waited til he could go home and git reddy.

Bimeby here he cum in his carriage, with two splended match greys, and a couple of frends who was gwine with us. After introducin me to Mr. Wiggins and Mr. Hunter, we got in and druv out to Fairmount Water Works on the Skoolkill.

I've seed picters of this place before, but I didn't have no idee it was so handsum, or that it was sich a grate curiosity. I can't take time to describe it to you now, but I can jest give you a idee of it. Well, you must know the river Skoolkill is a grate big river, almost as big as the Savanna or the Chattahooche in Georgia, that runs down by the city til it empties into the Delaware. It used to go sweepin along on its journey to the sea as free as any other river in the nation, til some years ago, when the city authorities tuck it into ther heds that they'd dam it, and set it to work. So they did; and now it don't only furnish the water that the people use, but it is compelled, its own self, to throw that water up into the basins on the hill, so it can run down in the pipes all over the city. Ther is some of the biggest water wheels thar in the world, what make a noise like distant thunder, and remind one of the groans of old Ixion, as ther grate ponderous forms turn gloomily on ther never-resting axis. The house whar the works is, is a dark ugly place, and made me feel bad to be thar, but when I cum out and looked at the butiful basin of water between it and the hill, and seed the statu of a gall standin on a rock jest above, holdin a goose by the legs, with its neck stretched up and squirtin out of its mouth a stream of crystal water, that shot up into the bright sunshine and come down in sparklin dimonds all over her white marble shoulders, and seed the handsum bildins and statues and fountains, and the butiful scenery all around, I thought it was one of the most delightful places I ever seed in my life, and if I'd had time to spare I could spent a whole day looking round it.

After lookin about awhile at the Wire Suspension Bridge and other curiosities, we went to the Girard College, what we've heard so much about for the last fifteen years. You know Mr. Girard was a monstrous rich man, what died in Filladelfy a long time ago, and left a heap of money to bild a college for 'he edication of the pore orfan boys of Pensilvany. The money was left in the hands of directors, who was to see that it was put to the proper purpose. Well, they're bildin a college, sure enuff, but I have my doubts whether it will ever be any benefit to the pore orfans for whom it was intended. It aint done yet, and thousands of pore children have growed up to be men sense it was commenced. When it is done, it will be one of the most aristocratic lookin institutions in this country, and I'm of the notion that if any pore boy ever does go through it, it will be like I did: in at the door and out at the roof, if he don't git kicked out before he gits so high.

They tell me it aint nothin like the bildin Mr. Girard wanted it to be, and all the money has been used up in bildin a palace that wont have nothin to support it after it's bilt. I spose then it'll be seized for its debts and sold to some rich corporation for 'bout half what the ground is worth that it stands on, after which it wil. be come a school whar no pore boy can ever learn his A

B. C's. One thing is certain, it will be the handsumest school house in creation when it is done; but I think if I had the money what one of its white marble pillars cost, I could do more good to the pore orfans of Pensilvany with it than the whole bildin will ever do. Nobody can look at this magnificent pile without bein filled with admiration; but every true frend of the pore orfan would rather see it tumbled to the ground, if the money it has cost could be used to bild log free schools where they're needed, and pay teachers that would edicate the poor children of the country. The greatest wonder to me is, how a man what had sense enuff to make so much money, and filanthropy enuff to give it for such a object, could allow'd himself to be so bamboozled in the management of it. It convinces me of one thing, and that is, if a man really wants to do good in this world with his money, he better be at it when he's on the top of the ground himself.

We went through the bildin from the bottom to the top. It's all solid brick and marble, even to the roof, what is covered with marble shingles on brick rafters. Fire can't git hold of wood enuff to raise a blaze, and the walls is so thick and strong that nothin short of Florida lightnin or a South American yeathquake couldn't knock it down.

While we was standin lookin at its lofty proportions, its white marble walls, and its massive Corinthian columns, two little ragged boys come up to us and ax'd us to give 'em some money. "Please, sir, give me a cent to buy some bred for my mammy," sed one of 'em. He didn't have no matches to sell, and I gin him a thrip, but I couldn't help but think how much more real interest he had in that thrip, than he had in the magnificent edifice that was erectin for him. The old maxim ses, that charity covers a heap of sins, but when the amount of money that is misapplied by the ostentation of the rich, in the name of charity, is deducted from the sum total that is given, ther wouldn't be enuff left to save many souls, I reckon.

The next place we went to, was the Laurel Hill cemetary, a butiful berryin ground what stands on the banks of the Skoolkill, about a mile above the water works. The fust thing we seed after we got in the gate was a butiful group of sculpture in coarse brown stone, representin Walter Scott the great novelist, settin down with his hat in his hand, holdin a interview with "Old Mortality," who is in the act of repairin a old tomb-stone, while his donkey is standin by with his bag of tools on its back. The figures looks like life, and made me feel very solemn, as I recollected the character of that odd old man. It is a great pity that the artist didn't use better materials. Such a work should last as long as the fame of the great author, what will endure til the eend of the granite hills themselves. Mr. More tuck me all through the grounds, and showed me a heap of handsome monuments, and tombs of great statesmen and generals, and rich people, among which was some that cost more than enuff to bild a fine house to live in. It is a butiful place, whar rich people moulder in good society; but whether they rest any better beneath ther costly marble monuments, than the pore people who sleep on the only spot of yeath they ever occupied without payin rent, and who have not even a slab, to perpetuate ther memories, is a circumstance what depends on the character of the lives they led in this world. The monuments of wealth is gratifyin to the pride and grateful to the feelins and affections of the livin, but it is only the wealth of virtuous actions that avails us any thing when we are laid in the grave. A pure unspotted heart in the grave is worth all the costly marble that could be piled upon it.

We looked round and red the inscriptions til we got tired, and then we went to our carriage. It was pretty near dinner time, and the company proposed to go to

Evan's Tavern, at the Falls, and git a dinner of Catfish and Coffy. Well, Mr. More's greys soon brung us to the place, and we had a dinner in no time, and a fust rate dinner it was. I never drunk better Coffy nor eat better Catfish, and we had lots of other good things besides. If you're ever in these parts, you must be sure o take a dinner at the Falls Tavern.

After dinner we went on til we cum to the Wissahicken, and druv along on its banks for about a mile, through some of the prettyest scenery I ever seed in my life. The stream runs along between rocky banks that rise into bold and broken hills on both sides, and are covered with trees that looks as fresh and wild as if they didn't stand in sight of the smoke of one of the largest cities in the world. Every now and then we met parties of boys and galls who was out boat-ridin and gatherin flowers, and once we came across a whole skool of galls who was out on a May frolick, with music and banners, carrying ther armsfull of flowers, and laughin and singin like so many wood nymphs. This is the place whar Fanny Kemble writ sich butiful poetry, and I don't wonder at it, for I do blieve a wheelbarrow would squeak in measured melody if it was rolled along on the bank of this butiful stream without grease. But poor Fanny lives no longer in a world of poetic dreams. She has proved the sad realities of this wicked world, and her eyes, that no longer look upon the lovely Wissahicken, would now see more to make her sad than happy in scenes that was once so delightful to her contemplation.

Turnin away from the Wissahicken, we crossed over to Germantown, the place whar you know the great battle was fit in the revolution. We undertuck to go the whole length of it, but after we got up as far as Chew's House, whar the British made sich a obstinate resistance, I begun to feel sorry for the horses, and told Mr. More we had better turn back. It's a monstrous curious, ancient looking town, with houses all bilt of stone, and looking like the great grand-dadies of all the houses in the world. I would liked to seed tother eend of it, but I'm told it's so long that when people from the Filladelfy eend want to go to tother, they take the steamboats on the Delaware and go round by way of Burlington or Trenton, New Jersey. The inhabitants is most of 'em people who do bisness in Filladelfy and have their residence out thar. Mr. Wiggins pinted out to me the residences of a good many of his acquaintances, and among the rest that of Mr. C. Alexander, the Alexander the Great of the Filladelfy press.

We wasn't long gwine to the city, but it was some time before we got to the United States Hotel. As we druv along through the streets I couldn't help but notice how strait and clean they was, and every now and then we met people what they call Quakers—the stiffest, starchiest, mealy-mouthed lookin people I ever seed. The men had on broad-tailed snuff-colored coats and broad-rimmed hats, and looked as sober and solemn as if butter wouldn't melt in their mouths. The wimmin, most all of 'em, had on drab colored dresses and wore silk bonnets what sot rite down over ther faces like calabashes, so you couldn't hardly see whether they was nandsum or not. But every now and then I got a glimse of a monstrous pretty face from under them bominable wagon-cover lookin bonnets. Ther's a grate many Qua kers in Filladelfy, and they're monstrous good people only they will meddle with what don't consarn 'em, and keep all the time botherin the Southern people 'bout ther niggers. I don't want to say any thing agin the Quaker: —I know that as a class ther aint a more honest, re spectable body of people in the country. But then I really do think that people what claim so much liberty of conscience as to exampt 'em from the discharge of ther duty to ther country, by whose laws they are protected in all the privileges of citizenship, ought at least to allow the people of the South liberty of conscience

to be the judges of ther own domestic institutions. People like them who go for non-resistance under all circumstances, ought to be the last people in the world to make aggressions upon the rights of others. But I musent git on that subject or I'll never git done my letter. It was most tea-time when we got back. I went to the Theatre to see the Opera last night, but I'll tell you all about that in my next. So no more from
                              Your frend til deth,
                                   Jos. Jones.

LETTER XII.

Filladelfy, May 25, 1843.

To Mr. Thompson:—*Dear Sir*—I told you in my last letter that I was gwine to the opery, and that I'd tell you what I thought of 'em. Well, to tell you the truth, I like the opery well enuff, all but the singin. The scenery is very handsum, the actin is good, and the fiddlin is fust rate; but so much singin spiles evry thing. The opery what I went to see at the Chesnut street theatre, was the Bohemian Gall, and the acters was the celebrated Segwin Troop, as they call 'em, and I spose they done it up as well as anybody else could do it; but accordin to my notion, there's monstrous little sense in any such carryins on. If operys didn't cum from Paris, whar all the fashionable bonnets and evry thing else comes from, and it wasn't considered unfashionable not to admire 'em, I don't blieve ther's many peeple in this country what would be willin to pay a half a dollar a night to hear sich a everlastin caterwaulin as they do make.

As soon as I got my tea, I went to the theatre, what ain't a grate ways from my hotel, and after buyin a ticket of a man in a little hole outside of the green dores, I went in and tuck a seat on one of the cushioned benches what they call boxes. Ther was a good many peeple in the theatre and ever so many wimmin, all dressed out as fine as they could be, and sum of 'em lookin monstrous handsum.

Bimeby one of the fiddlers down in the place they call the orkestry, tuck up his fiddle-stick, and rapped on his desk, at which evry musicianer grabbed his instrument. Then the man with the fiddle-stick, after

wavin it up and down three or four times, gin his fiddle
a scrape or two what seemed to set the whole of 'em
agwine; and sich another hurra's nest I never did hear
before. Sumtimes all of 'em stopped but one or two;
then they all struck up agin as hard as they could rip it.
Sumtimes the musick was low and soft as the voice of a
sick kitten, and then it was loud and terrible, as if all
the lions, bulls, jackasses, and hiennys in creashun had
got together, and was tryin to see which could make
the biggest racket. They seemed to have evry thing
in the world that would make a noise, from a base drum
to a jewsharp; and evry feller tried to do his best.
One old feller had a grate big fiddle of about one hundred hoss power, and the way he did rear and pitch
and pull and jerk at it, was really distressin. The old
feller seemed to have the highstericks for fear he
couldn't make as much noise as the rest of 'em, and
he rolled his eyes and twisted his mouth about enuff to
frighten all the ladys out of ther senses. Bimeby they
all blowed out, and at the ring of the bell up went the
curtain.

Then the opery commenced, but for the soul of me I
couldn't hardly make out hed nor tail to it, though I
listened at 'em with all my ears, eyes, mouth, and nose.
The fust thing was a grand singin match by a whole
heap of Bohemian sogers and wimmin, 'bout nobody
could tell what. Then thar was a big fat feller named
Thadeus, what the bill sed was a Polish exile, what
had run away from his country, cum on and sung a song
'bout his troubles, but he put so many dimmy-simmy
quivers in it that nobody couldn't understand what hurt
him. 'Bout this time ther was a gang of Murrelite
lookin peeple, what they called Gipseys, made ther appearance. The hed man among them was a old feller
named Devil's-hooff, what had the whitest teeth I ever
seed in a white man's hed. This old cus sot to robbin
the fat Polander the fust thing, but his wife, who seemed
to wear the trowsers, wouldn't let him; and after a little

sir.gin the Gipseys agreed to take the fat exile into ther gang, and hide him from his pursuers. Then the Gipseys went to whar the Governor of Bohemia and his peeple was, and while they was all singin and carryin on, sumbody cum in and told them that a wild hog or sum other varmint was 'bout to eat up the Governor's baby. Then ther was a rumpus—his excellency and all his sogers run about the stage and looked at one another as much as to say, "Grate Heavens! what's to be done;" til the fat Polander tuck up a gun what was leanin agin the house, and run out and shot the varmint, whatever it was, and brung in the baby safe and sound to its mammy. Then they had another singin match. The Governor was very much obleeged to the fat man for savin his baby, and sung to him if he wouldn't take sumthing to drink. Mr. Thadeus 'lowed he didn't care if he did, and the licker was sot out; but the Governor didn't have no better sense than to propose sum political sentiment what didn't set well on the stummick of the fat Polander, who throwd down his glass and spilled the licker all over the floor. Then ther was a terrible rumpus agin. The Governor made his sogers grab the man what spilled the licker—with that, old Devil's-hooff fell to singin and rearin and shinin, tryin to git his frend out of the hands of the sogers,—but they sung as loud as he did, and tuck him, too, and put him in jail with Mr. Thadeus. But while the Governor and his frends was singin about it, old Devil's-hooff got out of the jail and stole the baby what the fat Polander had saved, and run off with it. They saw him with the baby in his arms, but the sogers was afraid to shoot at him for fear of killin it; and when the old rascal got across the bridge he took out his jack-knife or sumthing else and cut it down, so they couldn't foller him. Then all fell to singin agin as hard as they could, like a barn-yard full of chickens when a hawk has jest carried off one of ther little ones. When they was about out of breth they let the curtain down for 'em to rest.

Well, thinks I, if that's what you call a opery, I'd a monstrous sight rather see a genuine old Georgia corn shuckin frollick, what ther's sum sense in.

Rite close beside me was a feller with three or four alls, what kep all the time lookin round the house at the peeple, with a kind of double-barreled spy-glass, and gabblein and chatterin like a parsel of geese. They was all dressed within a inch of ther lives, and the chap had a red and blue morocco cap on, what sot rite tite down to his hed like a ball-cover. He had a monstrous small hed, and when he had the spy-glasses up to his eyes he looked jest like a double-barreled percussion pistol, and I had half a mind jest to tap him on the hed with my cane to see if he wouldn't go off.

"Now, ladies," ses he, "we've got to wait til that baby grows to be a woman before we see any more of the opery."

"Dear me," ses one of the galls, "I hope they won't keep us waitin so long 'tween the acts as they always do; for I'm so much delighted with the opery."

"And me, too," ses another one. "It's so refreshin to hear sich delightful melody; I shall be very impatient."

"It's exceedingly foin," ses the feller with the percussion cap, lookin roynd the theatre with his spy glasses. "I nevaw heard Segwin in better tune Fwazau is pwefectly delightful. But I must beg the ladies to be patient."

Thinks I, I'll be monstrous apt to be in old Georgia agin before that baby grows to be a gall; but I can set up as long as any of you, and, as I've paid my money, I'm 'termined to see it out.

But I hadn't begun to git sleepy before up went the curtain agin, and the racket commenced. Shore enuff that was the baby grow'd to be a grate big gall, and Mr. Thadeus, as fat as ever, was thar singin love to her. They've both been with the gipseys ever sense, and she's fell in love with the fat Polander. The queen of the gipseys agrees to the match, and the raggymuffins ha: a grand frollick and dance on the occasion. 'Bout this time a Miss Nancy sort of a feller, what's sum relation to the Governor, comes projectin about among the gipseys, falls in love with the Bohemian gall, and wants her to have him. The gipsey queen, who seems to have sum spite agin the pore gall, steals a medal from the booby lover, and puts it on her neck; when the feller, findin he can't git her to have nothin to say to him, has her tuck up for stealin, and carried before the governor. The governor, who's had the blues like the mischief ever sense he lost his baby, is 'bout gwine to punish her, when he finds out by some mark that she is his own daughter. Then he sings to her a heap, and she sings to him, and he takes her home to his palace, and wants her to marry his booby relation. But she's got better sense; besides, she's hard and fast in love with Mr. Thadeus, and won't have nobody else Her father won't consent for her to marry a wanderin gipsey, and thar's the mischief to pay, with singin enuff for a dozen camp-meetins, all mixed up so nobody can't tell hed nor tail to it. 'Bout this time, Mr. Thadeus shows the governor his last tailor's bill, or sumthing else, that proves to his excellency that he was a gentleman once, and he gives his consent to the match. Mr. Thadeus and the Bohemian gall is monstrous happy, and old Devil's-hooff and the governor and all of 'em is takin another sing, when the queen of the gipseys puts up one of her vagabones to shoot Mrs. Thadeus that is to be; but the feller bein a monstrous bad shot misses her and kills the queen, which puts a stop to her singin, though the rest of 'em sing away til the curtain draps.

And that's the eend of the opery of the Bohemian Gall. I hain't got the squeelin and howlin and screechin of them 'bominable gipseys out of my hed yet, and I blieve if I was to live to be a hundred years old I wouldn't go to another opery, unless it was one that didn't have no singin in it. I like a good song as well as anybody, and have got jest as good a ear for musick as the next man, but I hain't got no notion of hearin twenty or thirty men and wimmin all singin together, in a perfect harrycane of noisy discord, so a body can't tell whether they're singin "Hail Columbia" or "Old Hundred." Ther is sich a thing as overdoin any thing; and if you want to spile the best thing in the world, that's the surest way to do it. Well, for peeple what ain't good for much else but music, like the French, Germans, and Italians, a opery full of solos and duetts and quartetts and choruses, as they call 'em, would do very well, if they would only talk a little now and then, so a body could know what they was singin about. But to sing evry thing, so that a character can't say, "Come to supper, your excellency!" without bawlin out—"Co-ho-ho-me to-oo-oo sup-up-up-e-e-er, your-r-r ex-cel-len-cy," with about five hundred dimmy-simmy quivers, so nobody can't tell whether he was called to supper, or whether he was told that his daddy was ded, is all nonsense. Let 'em sing whar ther is any sentiment—any thing to sing about—but when ther is only a word or two that is necessary to the understandin of what comes after or goes before; and whar ther ain't words enuff to make a stave of musick, what's the use of disguisin 'em so that ther ain't neither sense nor musick in 'em.

A body what never seed a opery before would swar they was evry one either drunk or crazy as loons, if they was to see 'em in one of ther grand lung-tearin, ear-bustin blowouts. Fust one begins singin and makin all sorts of motions at another, then the other one sets in and tries to drown the noise of the fust, then two or three more takes sides with the fust one, and then sum more jines in with number two, til bimeby the whole crowd gits at it, each one tryin to out-squall the other, and to make more motions than the rest. That sets the fiddlers a-goin harder and harder—the singers straiten out ther necks and open ther mouths like so many carpet-bags—the fiddlers scrape away as if they was gwine to saw their fiddles in two, wakin up the ghosts of all the cats that ever was made into fiddle-strings, and makin the awfulest faces, as if it was ther own entrels they was sawin on—the clarineters and trumpeters swell and blow like bellowses, til their eyes stick out of ther heds like brass buttons on a lether trunk, and the drummer nocks away as if his salvation depended on nockin in the hed of his drum. By this time the roarin tempest of wind and sound surges and sweeps through the house like a equinoctial harrycane, risin higher and higher and gittin louder and stronger, til it almost blows the roof off the bildin, and you feel like dodgin the fallin rafters. For my part I shall have to go to singin-school a long time, and larn the keys from the pianissimo of the musketer's trumpet, up to the crashin fortissimo of a clap of thunder, before I shall have any taste for a grand opery.

I've always had a great curiosity to see how the free niggers git along in the Northern States. So after breckfust this mornin, I ax'd the man what keeps the books at the hotel whar was the best place to see 'em; for I'd heard gentlemen what had been in Filladelfy say that ther was whole squares in this city whar nobody but niggers lived. The book-keeper told me if I wanted to see free niggers in all ther glory, I must go down Sixth street til I come to 'em.

Well, I started, and sure enuff, I hadn't gone many squares before I begun to smell 'em, and never will I forgit the sight I saw down in Small street, and sum other streets in that neighborhood. Gracious knows, if anybody wants to git ther simpathies excited for the pore nigger, all they have got to do is to go to this part of Filladelfy. I've been on the big rice plantashuns in Georgia, and I've seed large gangs of niggers that had the meanest kind of masters, but I never seed any pore creaters in sich a state of retchedness in all my life. I couldn't help but feel sorry for 'em, and if I was able, I'd been willin to paid the passage of the whole generation of 'em to Georgia, whar they could git good masters that would make the young ones work, and would take care of the old ones.

Thar they was, covered with rags and dirt, livin in houses and cellars, without hardly any furniture; and sum of 'em without dores or winders. Pore, miserable, sickly-lookin creaters! it was enuff to make a abolitionist's hart ake to see 'em crawlin out of the damp straw of the cellars, to sun themselves on the cellar-dores til they got able to start out to beg or steal sumthing to eat, while them that was able was cussin and fightin about what little they had. You couldn't hardly tell the men from the wimmin for ther rags; and many of 'em was diseased and bloated up like frogs, and lay sprawlin about like so many cooters in a mud-hole, with ther red eyes peepin out of ther dark rooms and cellars like lizards in a pile of rotten logs.

This, thinks I, is nigger freedom; this is the condition to which the filanthropists of the North wants to bring the happy black peeple of the South! Well, one of two things is certain:—either the abolitionists is a grand set of hippocritical scoundrels, or they are totally ignorant of the condition of the slaves what they want to git away from ther masters. Materially considered, the niggers of Georgia is as much better off than the niggers of Pensylvany, as the pore peeple of America is better off than the pore peeple of Ireland; and, morally considered, the advantage is equally as great in favor of the slaves of the South over the pore free niggers of the North. For whar social equallity cannot possibly exist, the black peeple are miserable jest in the degree that they approach to equality in wealth and edication with the whites, and are enabled to understand their degraded position. What's the use to talk about equallity when no such thing exists. Ther is as much prejudice agin coler here as anywhar else. A nody sees that in ther churches, and theatres, and courts, and evrywhar else. Nobody here that has any respect for themselves, treats a nigger as ther equal, except a few fannyticks, and they only do it to give the lie to ther own feelins, and to insult the feelins of others. At the South, the relation between the two races is understood by both parties, and a white man ain't at all jealous of the pretensions of his servants; but here, ther is a constant jealous enmity existin between the whites whose occupations brings 'em in contact with 'em, and the niggers, who is all the time aspirin to a social equallity, what they never can attain til ther wool grows strait and ther skins fade white. The races is, naturally, social antagonists, and it is only in the relation of master and servant that they can exist peaceably together. Then, unless the abolitionists can put 'em back into Africa whar they come from, in a better condition than they was when they found 'em, or unless they is willin to take ther turn bein servants, they better let 'em alone.

For my part, I've got as much feelin for the niggers as anybody can have; but sense they are here among us, and I've got to live with 'em, I prefer bein master myself and treatin 'em well, to lettin them be masters and takin the chances of ther treatin me well. But one thing is monstrous certain, if my niggers wasn't better off and happyer on my plantation than these Northern free niggers is, I wouldn't own 'em a single day longer. My niggers has got plenty of hog and hommony to eat, and plenty of good comfortable clothes to wear, and no debts to pay, with no more work than what is good for ther helth; and if that ain't better than freedom, with rags, dirt, starvation, doctor's bills, lawsuits, and the five thousand other glorious privileges and responsibilities of free nigger citizenship, without the hope of ever turnin white and becomin equal with ther superiors, then I ain't no filossofer.

After lookin into sum streets that I wouldn't risk my

life in gwine through, and seein scenes of destitution and misery enuff to make one's very hart sick, I went back to my hotel. I spent the rest of the day lookin about over the city with Mr. More, who wanted me to go to the opery with him agin. But I couldn't stand that, and after tea I paid my bill and got all reddy to leave for New York to-morrow mornin, bright and early. In a few hours more I will be in the great Gotham. No more from   Your frend til deth,

                                              Jos. Jones.

LETTER XIII.

New York, June 2, 1845.

To Mr. Thompson:—*Dear Sir*—I arriv in this city, all safe and sound, yesterday afternoon about three o'clock, but to tell you the truth, if I had cum up minus my coat-tail, or even a leg or arm, after sich a everlastin racket as I have been in ever sense I left Filladelfy, I wouldn't been much surprised. As for collectin my senses and gitin my mind composed so as to know myself or any thing else certain, I don't never expect to do it, as long as I'm in this great whirlpool of livin beins.

A little circumstance happened to me last night, before I had been here only a few hours, that sot me back a little the worst. I never was so oudaciously tuck in in all my born days, and if you had heard me cus about it, you'd thought I was turned a real Hottentot sure enuff. But to begin whar I left off in my last letter.

The porter at the United States Hotel waked me up early in the mornin, and I got to the steamboat jest in time. It was a butiful bright mornin and the storekeepers was openin ther stores, while the servant galls was scrubbin the dore-steps of the houses and washin off the pavements in front of 'em. I looked at 'em as I rode along in the hack, and I couldn't help feelin scrry to see such butiful, rosy-cheeked white galls, down in the dirt and slop in the streets, doin work that is only fit for niggers. They say here that they aint nothing but slewers—but I seed sum that I would tuck for respectable white galls if I had seed 'em in Georgia. Slewers or whatever they is, they is my own color, and a few dollars would make 'em as good as ther mistresses.

in the estimation of them that turns up ther noses at 'em now.

The Delaware is a noble river, and Filladelfy is a city worthy to stand on its banks. From the deck of the steamboat we had a splendid panaramic view of it, as we passed block after block, the streets runnin up from the water's edge, strait as a bee line, and affordin us glimpses of the fine houses and elegant public bildins that makes Filladelfy one of the handsumest cities in the world. But, long as it is, we was soon past it, and in a few minits its numerous steeples and towers and masts faded away in the distance, and we turned our eyes on the butiful country on both sides of the river.

Butiful farm houses and bright-lookin little towns was most all the time in site, till we got to the place what they call Bristol, whar we tuck the cars to New York. The railroad runs along on the bank of a canal part of the way, crosses the river on a splendid bridge, and passes through Trenton, Princeton, Newark, and a heap of other towns in New Jersey, til it gits to Jersey City, what stands on the Hudson river, opposite to the city of New York.

Well, when we got to Jersey City, we all got out and scrambled through the crowd as well as we could to the boat what was thar to take us across the river to New York. When we got up to the gate what encloses the wharf we could see the hackmen and porters peepin at us through the palins, like so many wild varmints in a big cage, ready and eager to devour us and our baggage too. I tuck my cane tight in my hand and kep a sharp eye on 'em, determined to defend myself to the last. As soon as the gates was open we rushed for the boat and they rushed at us. Sich another hellabaloo I never did see before, and I expected every minit to see sumbody git spilled overboard into the river.

I found it wasn't no use to try to keep 'em off without nockin sum of 'em in the hed, and then I would only be like the fox in the spellin book, ready to be worried to deth by a fresh gang. So when they cum round me with "Have a hack, sir?"—"I'm public poorter, sir."—"Shall I take your baggage up, sir?"—"Will you give me your checks, sir?"—"Take you up for two shillins, sir, to any part of the city,"—all of 'em handin ther cards to me at once—I jest backed up agin the side of the boat and tuck evry card they handed to me, without sayin a word, and when they ax'd me for my checks I was deaf and dum, and coudln't understand a word they sed. That sot 'em to pushin and crowdin one another, and hollerin in my ear, and makin signs to me, til they found they couldn't make nothing out of me, and then they started after sum new victim.

Among the passengers ther was a old sun-burnt lookin feller, with green spectacles on, what put me in mind of a Georgia steam doctor, and who seemed to think he know'd more than anybody else 'bout evrything. He was gabbin and talkin to evrybody all the way on the steamboat, and in the cars, and tryin his best to git up a argyment 'bout religion with sumbody. One would supposed he owned half the baggage aboard, to hear him talk about it, and when we got on the ferry boat he was the bissyest man in the crowd, rearin and pitchin among the hackmen and porters like a blind dog in a meat house, and tryin to git into the crowd what was gathered all round the baggage like flies round a fat gourd. Bimeby a honest lookin Irishman cum up to me, and ses he, handin his card, "Shall I take your baggage, sir?" Ther was sumthing like honest independence in the feller's face, and I gin him my checks, and in he went for my trunks. In a minit he cum out safe and sound with one of 'em. "Stand by it, sir," ses he, "til I git the other." I tuck my stand, and it was jest as much as I could do to keep the devils from carryin it off with me on top of it. Ther was sich a everlastin rumpus I couldn't hear myself think. The clerks was callin out the numbers—evrybody was runnin about and ookin after ther baggage, children was cryin, wimmin was callin for ther husbands to look out for ther bandboxes—hackmen and porters was hollerin and shoutin at the people and at one another—whips was stickin in your eyes evry way you turned—and trunks, and carpet bags and boxes was tumblin and rollin in every direction, rakin your shins and mashin your toes in spite of all you could do. In the middle of the fuss thar was old Pepperpod, with his old cotton umbereller in his hand, elbowin his way into the crowd and whoopin and hollerin over evrybody else til he disappeared in the middle of 'em. In about a minit here he cum agin, cusin and cavortin enuff to sink the boat, with a pair of old saddle bags in one hand, sum pieces of whalebone and part of the handle of his umbrelier in the other, his hat gone, and his coat-tail split clear up to the collar. He was mad as a hornit, and swore he would prosecute the company for five thousand dollars damages for salt and battery and manslaughter in the second degree. He cut a terrible figer, but evrybody was too bissy to laugh at him. I thought to myself that his perseverance was porely rewarded that time.

I sot thar and waited til nearly everybody was gone from the boat, and til my Irishman had picked up all the other customers he could git, before he come and tuck my trunk and told me to foller him to his hack. After cumin in a ace of gettin run over three or four times, I got to the hack, what was standin in the middle of 'bout five hundred more hacks and drays, all mixed up with the bowsprits and yards of ships that was stickin out over the edge of the wharves and pokin ther eends almost into the winders of the stores. The hackman ax'd me what hotel I wanted to go to. I told him to take me whar the southern travel stopped. "That's the American," ses he, and after waitin til the way opened so we could git out, we druv to the American Hotel on Broadway, rite opposite to the Park.

It was 'bout three o'clock when I got to the Hotel, and after brushin and scrubbin a little of the dust off, and gittin my dinner, I tuck a turn out into the great Broadway, what I've heard so much about, ever sense I was big enuff to read the newspapers, to see if it was what it's cracked up to be. Well, when I got to the door of the Hotel I thought ther must be a funeral or semething else gwine by, and I waited some time, thinkin they would all git past; but they only seemed to git thicker and faster and more of 'em the longer I waited, til bimeby I begun to discover that they was gwine both ways, and that it was no procession at all, but jest one everlastin stream of peeple passin up and down the street, cumin from all parts of creation, and gwine Lord only knows whar.

I mix'd in with 'em, but I tell you what, I found it monstrous rough travellin. The fact is a chicken-coop mought as well expect to float down the Savannah river in a freshet and not git nocked to pieces by the drift-wood, as for a person what aint used to it to expect to git along in Broadway without gettin jostled from one side to tother at every step, and pushed into the street about three times a minit. A body must watch the currents and eddies, and foller 'em and keep up with 'em, if they don't want to git run over by the crowd or nocked of the sidewalk, to be ground into mince-meat by the everlastin ominybusses. In the fust place, I undertuck to go up Broadway on the left hand side of the pave-ment, but I mought jest as well tried to paddle a canoe up the falls of Tallula. In spite of all the dodgin I could do, sumbody was all the time bumpin up agin me, so that with the bumps I got from the men and givin back for the wimmin, I found I was loosin ground instead of gwine ahed. Then I kep "to the right as the law directs," but here I like to got run over by the crowd of men and wimmin and children and niggers, what was all gwine as fast as if ther houses was afire, or they was runnin for the doctor. And if I happened to stop to look at any thing, the fust thing I knowed I was jammed out among the ominybusses, what was

dashin and whirlin along over the stones like one eternal
train of railroad cars, makin a noise like heaven and
yeath was cumin together. Then ther was the carriages
and hacks and market wagons and milk carts, rippin and
tearin along in every direction—the drivers hollerin and
poppin ther whips—the peeple talkin to one another as
if ther lungs was made out of sole leather—soldiers
marchin with bands of music, beatin ther drums, and
blowin and slidin ther tromboons and trumpets with all
ther might—all together makin noise enuff to drive the
very old Nick himself out of his senses. It was more
than I could stand—my dander begun to git up, and I
rushed out into the fust street I cum to, to try to git out
of the racket before it sot me crazy sure enuff, when
what should I meet but a dratted grate big nigger with a
bell in his hand, ringin it rite in my face as hard as he
could, and hollerin sumthing loud enuff to split the hed
of a lamp post. That was too much, and I made a lick
at the feller with my cane that would lowered his key
if it had hit him, at the same time that I grabbed him
by the collar, and ax'd him what in the name of thunder
he meant by sich imperence. The feller drapped his
bell and shut his catfish mouth, and rollin up the whites
of his eyes, 'thout sayin a word, he broke away from
me as hard as he could tear, and I hastened on to find
some place less like bedlam than Broadway.

By this time it was most dark, and after walkin down
one street til I cum to a grate big gardin with trees in it,
whar it was so still that noises begun to sound natural
to me agin, I sot down on the railins and rested myself
awhile, and then sot out for my hotel. I walked and
walked for some time, but somehow or other I couldn't
find the way. I inquired for the American Hotel two
or three times and got the direction, but the streets
twisted about so that it was out of the question for me
to foller 'em when they told me, and I begun to think
I'd have to take up my lodgins somewhar else for that
night, I was so tired. Bimeby I cum to a street that

was very still and quiet, what they called Chambers street, and while I was standin on the corner, thinkin which way I should go, 'long cum a pore woman with a bundle under her arm, creepin along as if she wasn't hardly able to walk. When she seed me she cum up to me and put her hankerchef to her eyes, and ses she :

"Mister, I'm a pore woman, and my husban's so sick e ain't able to do any work, and me and my pore little children is almost starvin for bred. Won't you be good enuff to give me two shillins?"

I looked at her a bit, and thought of the way the match-boy served me in Baltimore, and ses I—

"Hain't you got no relations nor neighbors that can help you?"

"Oh no, sir; I'm too pore to have relations or neighbors. I was better off once, and then I had plenty of frends."

That's the way of the world, think's I; we always have frends til we need 'em.

"Oh, sir, if you only know'd how hard I have to work, you'd pity me—I know you would."

"What do you do for a livin?" ses I; for she looked too delicate to do much.

"I do fine washin and ironin," ses she; "but I'm sick so much that I can't make enuff to support us;" and then she coffed a real graveyard coff.

"Why don't you git sum of Schenck's Pulmonic Syrup?" ses I.

"O, sir," ses she, "I'm too pore to buy medicin, when my pore little children is dyin for bred."

That touched me—to think sich a delicate young cretur as her should have to struggle so hard, and I tuck ut my purse and gin her a dollar.

"Thar," ses I, "that will help you a little."

"Oh, bless you, sir; you're so kind. Now I'll buy sum medicin for my pore husband. Will you be good enuff to hold this bundle fo me til I step back to that drug-store on the corner? It's so heavy—I'll be back in a minit," ses she.

I felt so sorry for the pore woman that I couldn't refuse her sich a little favor, so I tuck her bundle to hold it for her. She sed she was 'fraid the fine dresses mought git rumpled, and then her customers wouldn't pay her; so I tuck 'em in my arms very careful, and she went to the store after the medicin.

Ther was a good many peeple passin by, and I walked up from the corner a little ways, so they shouldn't see me standin thar with the bundle in my arms. I begun to think it was time for the woman to cum back, and the bundle was beginnin to git pretty heavy, when I thought I felt sumthing movin in it. I stopped rite still, and held my breth to hear if it was any thing, when it begun to squirm about more and more, and I heard a noise jest like a tom-cat in the bundle. I never was so supprised in my life, and I cum in a ace of lettin it drap rite on the pavement. Thinks I, in the name of creation what is it? I walked down to the lamp-post to see what it was, and Mr. Thompson, would you believe me, IT WAS A LIVE BABY! I was so cumpletely tuck aback that I staggered up agin the lamp-post, and held on to it, while it kicked and squalled like a young panter, and the sweat jest poured out of me in a stream. What upon yeath to do I didn't know. Thar I was in a strange city, whar nobody didn't know me, out in the street with a little young baby in my arms. I never was so mad at a female woman before in all my life, and I never felt so much like a dratted fool as I did that minit.

I started for the drug-store with the baby squallin like rath, and the more I tried to hush it the louder it squalled. The man what kep the store sed he hadn't seed no such woman, and I musn't bring no babys in thar.

By this time a everlastin crowd of peeple—men and wimmin—was gathered round, so I couldn't go no whar,

"Says she to Major Jones, 'I'm a poor woman, my husban's sick; won't you hold this bundle for me till I go into the drug store for some medicine?' I did so, got tired of waiting, and walked down to the lamp-post to see what it was. 'It was a live baby,' and the sweat poured out of me, I tell you, in a stream."—*Letter* xiii. *p.* 128.

all gabblin and talkin so I couldn't hardly hear the baby squall.

I told 'em how it was, and told 'em I was a stranger in New York, and ax'd 'em what I should do with the baby. But ther was no gettin any sense out of 'em, and none of 'em wouldn't touch it no more'n if it had been so much pisen.

"That won't do," ses one feller.—"You can't cum that game over this crowd."

"No, indeed," ses another little runty-lookin feller—"we've got enuff to do to take care of our own babys in these diggins."

"Take your baby home to its ma," ses another, "and support it like a onest man."

I tried to git a chance to explain the bisness to 'em, but drat the word could I git in edgeways.

"Take 'em both to the Tooms," ses one, "and make 'em giv a account of themselves."

With that two or three of 'em cum towards me, and I grabbed my cane in one hand, while I held on to the bundle with the other.

"Gentlemen," ses I—the baby squeelin all the time like forty cats in a bag—"Gentlemen, I'm not gwine to be used in no sich way—I'll let you know that I'm not gwine to be tuck to no Tooms. I'm a stranger in your city, and I'm not gwine to support none of your babys. My name is Joseph Jones, of Pineville, Georgia, and anybody what want's to know who I am, can find me at the American——"

"Majer Jones! Majer Jones, of Pineville!" ses a dozen of 'em at the same time.

"Majer Jones," ses a clever-lookin young man, what pushed his way into the crowd when he heard my name. "Majer, don't be disturbed in the least," ses he, "I'll soon have this matter fixed."

With that he spoke to a man with a lether ribbon on his hat, who tuck the baby, bundle and all, and carried it off to the place what they've got made in **New York** a purpose to keep sich pore little orfans in.

By this time my frend, Mr. Jacob Littlehigh, who is a Georgian, livin in New York, had interduced himself to me and 'bout twenty other gentlemen, and I begun to find myself 'bout as much of a object of attraction after the baby was gone, as I was before. I never seed one of 'em before in my life, but they all sed they had red my book, and they didn't know nobody else. So much for bein a author.

They was all monstrous glad to see me, and wanted to know how Mary and the baby was at home; and 'fore they let me off, they made me go down to Bardotte & Shelly's Caffè Tortoni, and eat one of the biggest kind of oyster suppers, and drink sum sherry coblers what would develop the intellect of a barber's block, and expand the heart of a Florida live-oak. They was the cleverest set of fellers I ever seed out of Georgia, and after spendin a pleasant hour with 'em, laughin over the incidents of the evenin, they showed me home to my hotel, whar I soon went to bed to dream of bundles full of babys and oceans of sherry coblers.

You must excuse this long letter, under the circumstances. No more from
Your frend til deth,
Jos. Jones.

P. S.— Don't for the world let Mary know anything about the baby, for she'd want to know what upon yeath I was runnin about the street at night for, holdin bundles for pore wimmin, and I never could explain it to her satisfaction. Ther's one thing monstrous certain —I'll go a hundred yards round the next woman I **meet in the** street with a bundle in her arms.

LETTER XIV.

New York, June 15, 1845.

To Mr. Thompson:—*Dear Sir*—To tell you the plain .ruth, Mr. Thompson, I'm a altered man sense I cum to New York, at least so far as appearance goes, though I blieve my hart is in the same place it used to be. It was sum time before I could giv in to my frend, Littlehigh's argyments, but as I'm always willin to accommodate myself to the wishes of my frends, when it can be done without sacrificin my principles, I consented to have sum new clothes made in the latest fashion. Accordinly the other day he tuck me down to Mr. Lownsberry, in Pine street, and gave the directions to have a fust rate broadcloth suit made for me, jest like his own. Well, in two days afterwards, here cums a bran new suit to my hotel—coat, vest, and trousers. The bootmaker in Fulton street had sent me a pair of new French boots, as he called 'em, and I got a hat from Leary, the great Broadway hat man. I shucked out of my old clothes and got into my new ones, and sich a alteration I don't reckon you ever seed afore. It's a positive fact, I don't blieve Wise or Smart, my coondogs to home, would be able to know me without smellin at me for a while. I don't hardly know myself; and if it hadn't been for my voice which sounded as familiar as a dinner-horn, I would a-had my dowts. Mary wouldn't seed the least resemblance to her husband in me, and I blieve if I had made my appearance in Pineville, my neighbors would been for puttin me in jail for a impostor.

My cote ain't so very outlandish, but my trouses and

jacket is the oddest lookin things in the world. The trouses is "all buttoned down before," like daddy Grimes's old blue cote, and makes me so shamed when I look at 'em that I don't know what to do with myself; and my jacket cums almost down to my knees, and is cut out swaller-tailed in frunt, like General Washington's regimental jacket, what I seed in Washington city. They're all made fust rate though, and fit like they had growd on me. They begin to feel a little better now than when I fust put 'em on, but it will be sum time before I git used to 'em, and before I can pass anybody in the street without feelin like I wanted to turn round to hide my trouses.

You know I told you I had no very grate opinion of operys. Well, that's a fact; but the other evenin when I cum to dinner at my hotel, the clerk handed me a note from Mr. Littlehigh, statin that himself and two or three of his frends would be very glad of Major Jones' company in a private box at the Olympic that evenin, to see the opery of "The Daughter of the Regiment." It wouldn't be perlite to refuse sich a invitation, and I staid home to meet Mr. Littlehigh, accordin to his appintment.

"Well, 'bout six o'clock Mr. Littlehigh called for me, and we went to the Olympic. The house was packed like a barrel of pork, whar ther ain't room enuff left to git another foot or jowl, nor so much as a ear into the barrel, all except my frend's private box, what was pretty close to the stage, and what had nobody in it but three or four gentlemen who belonged to our party. The curtain ris with a everlastin singin and fiddlin, like it did in Filladelfy. Bimeby the daughter of the regiment cum out, and then I thought they would tear the theatre down with ther everlastin rumpus.

"That's our Mary, Majer," ses Mr. Littlehigh, "and now if you want to hear a bird of Paradise, jest buckle back yer ears."

She was a monstrous fine-lookin gall, and the way she could sing was perfectly 'mazin; and then she handled a musket and marched about the stage like a regular sargeant of infantry. How the mischief she ever cum by so many fathers, I couldn't well make out, for the singin, which, as I told you before, spiles evry thing in a opery. But it was very plain to be seen that if the regiment was her daddys, evry feller in the house was in love with her; and I couldn't help but think that the feller with the ribbons on his hat, what kep follerin her about and singin to her how he loved her, loud enuff to be heard all over the house, stood a monstrous pore chance among so many. Whenever she cum on the stage, the peeple all over the house would rap and clap and holler like they was half out of ther senses; and whenever she sung a song by herself, they was certain to make her sing it over agin.

I liked the Daughter of the Regiment myself rather better than I did the Bohemian Gall, but I'd like 'em both a good deal better if ther wasn't so much singin in 'em.

* * * * * * * * *

After the opery was over we went down to the Battery, and after walkin about in the moonlit walks til we got tired, we sot down on the benches and smoked oui segars, while the waves splashed and roared agin the rocks, and the wind played with the tops of the trees behind us. After talkin over matters and things awhile, we started for home.

As we was gwine along up Broadway we saw a smoke comin out of a roof of a house down in one of the cross streets, and turned down to see what it was. When we got opposite to it, we saw a redish sort of a light in the winders on the roof, and the smoke pourin out of evry crack. Mr. Littlehigh run across and rapped at the dore, and in a minit a old man stuck his hed out of the lower winder.

"Your house is a fire," ses Mr. Littlehigh.

The old man grunted out sumthing, but didn't take in his old red night-cap or make any movement like he cared whether his house was afire or not.

"Fire," ses my frend, loud as he could holler, pintin up to the top of the house.

The old man grunted out sumthing in Dutch, and stood as still as a post, starin at us on the other side of the street. Then Mr. Muggins run across and went close up to the old codger, and hollered to him—

"I say, old hoss, your house is on fire—up in the garret."

It was 'bout twelve o'clock, and the street was still as a grave-yard. Mr. Muggins made a good deal of noise, and the old man pulled in his hed and cum back in a minit with a old shot-gun in his hand, and begun to cus in Dutch as hard as he could. Mr. Muggins backed out a little ways, and begun lookin for a brick-bat. Mr. Littlehigh seein that the light was gittin brighter in the winder, stept on the steps and tried the dore. By this time two or three more of the winders was raised, and two or three more red night-caps was stickin out, lookin at us without sayin a word, except the old feller below, who was flourishin his shot-gun and makin a terrible racket.

Just then sum winders was raised on tother side of the street.

"That house is on fire," ses Mr. Muggins.

"Wake 'em up next dore," ses sumbody from tother side. "They can't understand English in that house."

With that we rapped at the next dore, and told the man that cum out what was the matter. The feller sprung into the street and looked up for a second, and then run to the old chap that was cussin with the gun in his hand, and sed sumthing to him. Down drapped the gun, and out of the winder cum the old Dutchman, with nothing on but his shirt and night-cap. As soon as he seed the smoke and light, he sot up a yell that waked the whole neighborhood, and in half a minit they was cumin out of evry winder in the house l:ke cat-squirrels from a corn-crib—climbin down the waterspout, and jumpin out of the winders, men, wimmin, and children—all of 'em half naked and hollerin and yellin like five thousand wild-cats.

By this time the alarm was spread—the peeple cum pourin out of the houses in evry direction, and sich a scene I never seed before in all my life. All we could hear in English was "fire! fire!" and in a few minits here cum the firemen with their ingines, rattlin over the stones, and shoutin and yellin like half the city was in flames. The dores and winders was open, and old trunks and furniture and beds was flyin in evry direction.

And after all what do you think it was? Why nothing but a smoke raised by the family what lived in the garret, to drive out the musketers. Ther was sum ten or a dozen families livin in the house, and all of 'em was frightened almost to deth, and turned out of ther beds into the street, jest because the family in the roof had gone to sleep leavin a pile of old rags afire to drive off the musketers.

The firemen went home cussin the Dutchmen, but we staid awhile with the crowd what was growin bigger and bigger, to see the fun—and I would gin almost any thing if I could jest understood Dutch, so I might know what the pore peeple was sayin to one another when they was gettherin up and disputin about ther plunder. The old chap what had the gun was cumpletely out of his senses. He didn't git the idee that his house was afire for sum time, but when he did git it into his hed, ther was no sich thing as persuadin him out of it. He never tuck time to put on his clothes, but jest grabbed hold of his daughter, a butiful gall, and hollered fire! fire! as loud as he could. The pore gall tried her best to pacify him, but the more she cried and talked to him, the more he tuck on.

Our party got scattered in the crowd, and when we was satisfied that tranquillity was restored in Holland.

Mr. Littlehigh and myself went home, leavin the old Dutchman hollerin fire, and his wife and daughter tryin to git him in the house.

It's beginnin to get pretty warm here now, and ther's a good many Southerners here, and among 'em is sum of my Georgia frends. Tother day, as I was gwine along Broadway, who should I meet but Col. Bill Skimer, of Pineville. You know Col. Bill's one of the cleverest fellers in the world; and as he was 'bout the first old acquaintance I had seed for sum time, I was monstrous glad to meet him. We stopped on the corner of Park place and Broadway, and shuck hands, and was chattin 'bout home, when the fust thing we know'd ther was a crowd of 'bout five hundred peeple gethered round us.

"Look here, Majer," ses he, "I can't stand this. I don't think ther's any danger of ther swallerin me alive, but I don't like to be gaped at like I was a wild animal." So off he started for his hotel, makin a wake among the crowd like a seventy-four in a mill-pond. The fact is, Col. Bill is considered a full-grown Georgian at home, but among us he don't look more'n half so big as he does here, whar the average size of the men is much less than it is in our genial soil, whar men's bodys as well as ther harts git to be as large as ther Maker ever intended 'em to be. The Colonel ain't so sensitive as sum peeple about sich things, and takes a good joke as well as the next man; but when he found they had been puttin him in the Herald, callin him the Georgia giant, and makin him out a heap bigger than he is, he didn't like it a bit.

My old frend, John Hooper, is here, too, from Savannah, and I don't know how many of the Pelegs from Augusta. Col. Shoestring, from the wiregrass settlement, is shinin here in his own peculiar way. The Colonel is one of the oddest specimens of human natur I ever seed in my life, and takes jest as much pride in a ragged cote, a dirty shirt-collar, and a long beard, as the greatest dandy does in his finery. His notions of notoriety, however, doesn't suit this meridean at all. In a small town whar it would be possible for him to be known by most of the inhabitants, perhaps he mought becum distinguished in his line; but here, whar ther is abundance of all kinds of loafers, and whar a person who is a *man* at home is nothing but a *individual*, it is no use to try to git notoriety for sich peculiarities as he indulges in. The Colonel cusses the omminy*buses*, and turns up his nose at the dandies and free niggers from mornin til night, and drinks sassyparilly sody water, and smokes the worst segars he can find. He uses about the Bowery, and goes to Chatham street theatre. He can't bear Niblo's or the Park, and ses that Broadway is worse than a menagery of wild varmints.

I haven't sed any thing to you about the New York ladies, and, as I told you my opinion about the Baltimore galls, I ought to say sumthing of the ladys of this city. Well, so far as dressin is concerned, they beat Baltimore and Filladelfy all holler. But in pint of buty they ain't to compare to the wimmin of the other cities. The fact is, I find the further North I go the more fine clothes and the less handsum faces I see. It would take enuff money to buy a plantation to dress one of these Broadway bells as they call 'em, and after all a man of taste couldn't see much in 'em to fall in love with. They're generally taller than our Southern galls, and with the help of the milliners they is pretty good forms, when they is walkin along before you. But, Mr. Thompson, all ain't flesh and blood that walks, any more'n all ain't gold that shines in Peter Funk's winder; and when you cum to ketch up with 'em an l see ther faces, whatever notions of buty you mought had before is soon gone. And even if you do now and then cum across a handsum face ther's sumthing wrong about 'em, that I can't exactly understand. Sumhow ther ain't enuff difference between the expression of the countenances of the wimmin and the men. The prettiest blue eyes you meet has a kind of a hard, cast-steel expression, so different from the soft, meltin looks o, our modest, blue-eyed Georgia galls. Sumtimes you may see a pair of dark, bright eyes, but ther ain't no depth in 'em. Ther's the same difference between the eves of the Northern wimmin and the eyes of our galls at home, that ther is between a lookin-glass and a deep pool of pure, crystal water. You can look into 'em both, and both reflects your own face ; but the glass is all cold, shallow surface, while you see down deep into the fountain and understand the source from whar its pure waters flow. The Northern ladys' eyes seems like they was only made to look with, while our Southern galls, you know, can speak so eloquently with their's. No doubt livin in sich a grate city, whar they is all the time exposed to the gaze of strangers, has sum effect on the ladys to make 'em less bashful and shrinkin than our Southern galls is, and perhaps ther is other causes of education and habits to make 'em less feminine in the style of ther buty. But certain it is ther is the greatest difference in the world between them and the wimmin of the South, and in my opinion the advantage is all on the side of our Southern galls.

Mr. Hooper and me is gwine to take a trip to Yankeedoodledum in a few days, to see Boston and Lowell I want to see the great Yankee city, and the factory galls what I've heard so much about. I will tell you all about the trip in my next. So no more from
Your frend til deth,
Jos. Jones.

LETTER XV.

New York, June 25, 845.

To Mr. Thompson :—*Dear Sir*—In my last letter I told you I was gwine to Yankeedoodledum. Well, I've been to Boston and Lowell, and seed the live Yankees, Bunkerhill monument and the factry galls, and a heap of other natural curiosities that more'n paid me for the trip.

Hooper, who you know is a Odd Feller as well as a very clever one, wanted to go to the great celebration what was to take place in a few days in Boston, and as I wanted to see that part of the world before I went home, we agreed to go together, and last Monday evenin we tuck passage in the steamboat Narryganset for Boston. We hadn't been gone long from the wharves when the fust thing I know'd the ingine was stopped, the boat commenced slewin round, and the peeple runnin in evry direction. Bimeby the ingine give another lick or two and then stopped agin. Thinks I ther's something out of jint. Thinkin the biler was gwine to bust or the bote was broke, I ax'd a old gentleman what was the matter?"

" We is rite at Hell-gate," ses he.

" The devil we is!—as close as that!" sed a man with mustashys on his mouth.

Hell-gate! thinks I, and I looked out, and shore enuff the water was whirlin round and round, and runnin up stream and crossways and evry other way. Jest then thump went the old bote agin something, and evry woman squalled, and the men stood on ther tip-toes. Thinks I, if we is to go to the bottom, I'd a good deal rather take a swim in some other place. Everybody said don't

be alarmed- -and one man sed it didn't make much dif
ference to him, for he started to go to Boston, any
how. Bimeby the bell rung, the old ingine sot up a
errible puffin and snortin, and in a few minits we was
.eavin the gate of the infernal regions far behind us.
We passed Frog's Neck—whar they're bildin a young
Giberalter to keep the British from coming down to New
York when Mr. Polk drives 'em out of Oregon—before
sundown, and by dark we was in what they call the
Sound. After smokin a segar we went to our berths,
whar we was soon sound asleep.

It was 'bout daylight next mornin when we got to
Stunnington, in Conneticut, whar they say the peeple
live on fish so much that they smell like whale oil and
have scales on their backs. This may be a bug what
they put on me, but one thing I do know—and that is
that they is great whalers, for they whaled the British
out of ther harbor in the last war, a monstrous sight
quicker than they cum in. It was a bominable dark
foggy mornin, and I couldn't see much of Stunnington,
but what I did see made me think it wasn't badly named
—for it is rocks from one eend to tother, and it was long
after we was out of sight of the town fore we could see
any thing but rock-fences and rock-chimneys, and whole
corn-fields of rocks from the size of a goose-egg up to
that of a gin-house. We got a mere squint at Providence, in Rodeisland, when we was crossin the river
in the steambote, and in about a ower more we was in
sight of Boston, which looked at a distance like it
was bilt on stilts in the middle of a everlastin big frog-
pond.

When we got to the depo, the white hackmen cum
rearin and pitchin at us like evry one of 'em had a *capias
ad satisfaction*, as the lawyers say, for us, and to keep
from gittin tramped into the yeath by 'em, we jumped
into the fust hack what had the dore open, and told the
man to drive us to the Purl street Hotel. Well, bein as
t wasn't near dinner-time, we tuck a walk round to see

the city, but we soon found out that wouldn't do. If a man could walk like Mr. Robert Acres wanted to fite his duel, edgeways, he mought possibly manage to git through a square or two of Boston 'thout gittin nocked off the side-walk more'n a dozen times. But for a man of my size to git along in sich little crooked alleys as them Boston streets is, is out of the question. Col. Bill Skimer would be like Mr. Gulliver was in the city of the Lillypushins—the corporation would be bound to accommodate him in the common to keep him from blockin up the streets intirely. Why, they aint much wider than the space between the rows of a pea-patch, and then they are so twistified that it's as much as a common sized body can do to keep both feet in the same street at the same time. And then what makes it worse, is the way the Boston peeple walks. They all go dashin along like they was gwine to die, and hadn't but a few hours left to settle ther bisness. As for givin the walk to a lady, or half of it to a gentleman, they don't think of no sich a thing, and if you don't want to have your breth nocked out of you evry few steps, you mought as well take the middle of the street at once, whar, if you don't keep a monstrous sharp lookout, you is certain to be run over by ther everlastin grate, long, sheep-shear lookin carts. Hooper and me tried to keep together on the side-walk. But it wasn't no use. After bumpin along for 'bout half a square, I found myself in the street and my frend half way into a store dore, whar he was nocked by a feller what was stavin ahead with a armfull of wooden clocks.

We made our way the best way we could in the direction of the Monument, what stands over in Charlestown. The Native Americans had a celebration on the hill, and one of ther orators was makin a speech to a heap of peeple what was crowdin all round the stand, jest like our peeple in Georgia at a Fourth of July Barbycue. As none of ther speeches couldn't make us no better Americans than we is, we left the orator and his flights of eloquence for the flight of steps what tuck us, after puffin and blowin enuff to work a two-hos-power steam ingine, up to the top of the great Yankee Monument, what has been raised on this Sinai of American Freedom. If ther is a man in the nation what don't like the Union and don't feel willin to shed his blood to preserve ., he ought to make a pilgrimage to this consecrated pot. If, standin on this majestic pile and looking down on the ground that received the fust red baptism of Liberty, while he breathes the air that received the expirin breth of so many martyred heroes, and looks upon the sky that witnessed ther heroic valor, he does not feel his bosom glow with patriotic emotion, and imbibe a love of country above all sectional prejudices or interests, then he may be sure he was born on the rong side of the Atlantic.

From the top of the monument, which is about three hundred feet high, we could see half over Massachusetts. Among other things that was pinted out to us in the guide book, was another monument, of which the Boston peeple needn't be so very proud. The ruins of the Ursuline Convent is still standin in sight, to reproach the intolerant spirit of a peeple who have violated the laws and disregarded the principles which ther fathers died to establish in this country.

After cumin down from the monument, we tuck a walk through the navy-yard and the rope-walk, whar they was makin rope's long enuff and strong enuff to pull the Stone Mountain, in De Kalb county, up by the root, and then went back to our hotel.

On the way back, I tuck the opportunity, when we was ridin in the hack, and nobody couldn't run over us, to notice the stores and houses. Exceptin the narrow, crooked streets, Boston looks a good deal like the other Northern cities, though to my taste it aint to compare in no respect to either Baltimore, Filladelfy or New York. In sum parts of the city the streets is wide enuff and very clean, and the houses is very fine, but ther's a aristocratic air about it, a sort of starchy Sundy-go-tomeetin kind of a look about this part of the city, that I don't like a bit better than I do the pinched up, narrow contrived appearance of the rest.

I noticed one thing about the signs in Boston, which accounts for the curious way they pronounce ther words. Ther letters is all littler in the middle than they is at the eends—as for instance, a letter *I* looks like a lady that was dyin of tite lacin. Now, you know the Yankees ses *kyew* for cow, and gives a sort of loud-at-both-eends-and-low-in-the-middle sound to all ther words. Well, it's my opinion that it is the shape of the letters on ther signs that makes 'em do it, or maybe the letters is made by the painters to suit the pronunciation of the peeple. In Filladelfy the most of the signs is painted in grate big block letters, and in New York, in all sorts and kinds. Well, the Filladelfy peeple talk very *square* and plain, and in New York ther aint no peculiarity about their pronunciation—no body can't tell a New Yorker by his accent. So you see what the influence of association is.

After dinner we was gwine to smoke our cigars, but jest as I was biten off the eend of mine, I happened to look up and see a notice what sed, "No smokin 'lowed here."

"Well," ses Hooper, "I spose they consider this room aft the machinery—less go forard."

We went into another room, but the fust thing we seed thar was, in grate big letters, "No smokin 'lowed here." With that we went to the door, thinkin we mought smoke on the steps, but thar was the everlastin "No smokin 'lowed here," stickin up on both sides of the door.

I looked at Hooper and laughed, but he didn't feel like laughin.

"What kind of a place is this; I'd like to know," ses he. "I wonder if they allow peeple to sneeze when they take cold?"

I proposed to git sum matches and go to the common. "Agreed," ses Hooper; "any whar whar we can breathe 'thout violatin the rules."

I ax'd the man in the office, what had been lookin at my cigar all the time, like it was a rattle-snake, for a match.

"I guess you'll find sum in the smokin-room," ses he.

"Smokin-room," ses I, "whar's that?"

"This way, sir," ses he, and he opened a door of a little dirty room that smelled strong enuff of tobacker smoke to nock a man down. Thar was no body in it but a old codger, in a snuff-colored coat, what was smokin one of the worst kind of American segars, and readin "all sorts of paragraphs" in the Boston post. The floor was covered with ashes and old stumps of segars, the walls looked like the inside of a Georgia smoke-house, and the air was strong enuff of smoke to turn a man into well cured bacon in 'bout fifteen minits.

"Majer," ses Hooper, "I can't stand this place—I've had jest as much of Boston as I want. Less go to Lowell this afternoon. Maybe we can smoke a cigar thar, and if you want to see any more of Boston, we can stop when we cum back."

I was jest about as sick of the city of everlastin anty's as he was, and in less than no time we was on the railroad to Lowell.

This is one of the finest roads in the world, leadin through a country that seems like one continual village. The land is poor and covered with rocks, but it's studded all over with butiful country-residences, with churches and mills and factories of one kind and another, til you git to Lowell, which is the handsumest small town I was ever in. We tuck rooms at the Merrymack House, one of the best hotels, and, before tea, tuck a walk over the place. It was a pleasant afternoon, and as we walked along on the bank of the canal what carries the water from the river to the factories, we couldn't help but notice the clean and healthy appearance of the town. The clear cool water went sweepin along, deep and strong, in its rock-banks, over which the green grass and flowers hung to dip themselves in the stream, while a roarin sound, that cum from the direction of the great olocks of five-story factories, reminded us that it was no idle stream, runnin to waste its usefulness on the desert shore, but that it gave its power to aid the industry of man, and to contribute to the wealth of the nation.

We tuck a stroll on the banks of the Merrymack, below the town. From different pints we got a fine view of the place, and found plenty to interest us til tea-time. We was passin up Merrymack street to our hotel when the bells rung, and the fust thing we know'd the whole town was full of galls. They cum swarmin out of the factories like bees out of a hive, and spreadin in every direction, filled the streets so that nothin else was to be seen but platoons of sun-bonnets, with long capes hangin down over the shoulders of the factory galls. Thousands upon thousands of 'em was passin along the streets, all lookin as happy, and cheerful, and neat, and clean, and butiful, as if they was boardin-school misses jest from ther books. It was indeed a interestin sight, and a gratifyin one to a person who has always thought that the opparatives as they call 'em in the Northern factories, was the most miserable kind of peeple in the world.

It was a butiful moonlight night, and after tea we walked out into the street agin. The stores was all lit up and the galls was walkin about in pairs, and half dozens, and dozens, shoppin from store to store, and laughin and talkin about ther purchases, as if it didn't hurt 'em to spend ther earnins no more'n other peeple. Under ther curious lookin cracker-bonnets thar was sum lovely faces and eyes, that looked better by moonlight than any I have seed sense I left Georgia; and poor

Hooper, who you know is a bachellor, bein exposed to sich a constant display of silf-like forms, rosy cheeks, bright eyes, and silver-toned voices, begun to feel montrous weak about the heart long before the ower cum for the galls to retire to ther boardin houses ; and I was monstrous fraid he would need settin up with the balance of the night, his simptoms was so alarmin. By ten o'clock not a cracker-bonnet was to be seen in the streets, though the moonlight was as bright as day, and the stars twinkled and danced in the Heavens above, and a cool breeze played through the branches of the trees and rippled the surface of the canal, while the waters, escapin from ther confinement in many a millrace, sent up a dreamy murmur, that blended harmoniously with the scene, and made it one of the loveliest evenins imaginable. It was a scene and a ower to inspire love—when the world is turned into a Paradice and wimmin into angels—and I couldn't help but feel sorry for the six thousand little nimphs of the spindles, who had no lovers thar to court 'em on sich a night.

It was late before we went to bed. As I'm to the eend of my sheet, I'll stop here, and tell you about my adventures in Lowell, the factories and the factory galls, in my next. So no more at present from

Your frend til deth,
Jos. Jones.

LETTER XVI.

New York, June 26, 1845.

To Mr. Thompson:—*Dear Sir*—I could slep sound as a rock in a shuck-pen, after havin been nockin about all day, and havin my mind constantly on the stretch to take in the wonders I seed in Yankeedoodledum. But in sich a airy room, and sich a soft, cool, clean bed as they gin me at the Merrymack House, I could have gone to sleep with the tooth-ache, and never waked up til Christmas, if it hadn't been for Hooper, who was termined to see the galls gwine to work in the mornin.

I was dreamin about bein in Mahomet's Heaven among the Houries. Ther was more'n ten thousand of 'em, all as butiful as Haydees and Venuses, with cracker-bonnets on, dancin and caperin about under the shadowy arches of the trees, from which hung long festoons of bright flowers, while fountains of crystal water was gushin up in evry direction, and music floated in the air that was perfumed with the breth of roses. Bimeby one of 'em, with butiful eyes and long golden ringlets, what hung down below the cape of her bonnet, cum dancin up to me with a hank of cotton yarn in her hand—

"Cum with me—will you cum with me, my dear?" ses she, smilin so sweet and wavin her hand at me.

"No, I thank you," ses I, blushin to think she would ax me sich a question.

"Say not so, dear," ses she, cumin closer to me. "Say not so, dear—you must be mine;" and with that she begun to undo her hank of cotton.

I soon seed what she was up to, and so I started to quit the place, but the fust thing I knowd she had the yarn round my neck, and the next minit 'bout five hundred of 'em was pullin at me, all singin "Cum with me, my dear," like a pasel of sailors a payin away on a hosser. I pulled and hollered as hard as I could—I told 'em I was a married man—but they never let on they heard me, and jest pulled the harder, each one sayin I 'longed to her.

"Let me go!" ses I, grabbin hold of a tree to hold on by, and kickin at 'em with both feet at a time; "let me loose, you everlastin witches, you. I's got a wife and child to home and can't marry none of you—I tell you I's a married man!"——

Jest then the hank of cotton broke, and away I went, and the galls set up one of the loudest squalls I ever heard.

"What upon yeath's the matter with you, Majer?" ses Hooper, who was laffin like he had the high-stericks. "Why I never seed a body cut sich anticks before in all my life. I jest tuck hold of you and shuck you a little to wake you up, so we mought take a walk before breckfust, and you begun to kick and rare like a wild zebra, cussin and swearin about being a married man, like that had any thing to do with gettin up early in the mornin.

"And was it you that had a hold of my neck," ses I, beginnin to see how it was.

"I jest shuck you a little," ses he.

"Well, if I didn't think——" ses I.

"What was you dreamin, Majer?" ses he.

But I know'd it wouldn't do to tell Hooper what I was dreamin, if I ever wanted to hear the eend of it. So I jest got up and put on my clothes as quick as possible, and went with Hooper to see the galls gwine to work.

The sun was jest up when we went down on to the corporashuns, as they call 'em here, whar the mills is. It was a most lovely mornin. The factorys was all still. The yarls in frunt of the bildins was clean, and

"I soon seed what she was up to, and so I started to go; but the fust thing I know'd she had the yarn round my neck, and the next minit 'bout five hundred of 'em was pullin' at me, all singin' ' Cum with me, my dear.' "—*Letter* xxi. *p.* 148.

the little flower-gardens by the dores was glitterin with due, as the fust bees of the mornin cum to suck the honey from the blossums. Ther wasn't many peeple to be seed in the streets. Now and then we could see sum men gwine to the countin-rooms and offices, or to the factorys, but the cracker-bonnets was in eclipse. The galls was at breckfust at ther boardin-houses, which are neat two, and sumtimes three-story brick houses, what stand in blocks near the factorys, and is owned by the proprietors of the mills.

Bimeby the bells rung. In a minit more the streets leadin to the mills was swarmin with galls. Here they cum in evry direction, laughin and talkin to one another in groops and by pairs, or singly, all lookin as merry and happy as if they was gwine to a frollic, insted of to ther work.

Wimmin look well by moolight, and so they do by early sunlight. The refreshin influence of sleep gives a brightness and animation to the featurs of a healthy young gall, who has been fatigued by the labors of the day, and the mornin ablooshuns, as Mr. Willis calls washin one's face, like the due on the roses, gives freshness to ther cheeks and brilliancy to ther eyes. You may depend thar was sum bright mornin faces in that crowd. I thought of my dream, and I 'termined to take warnin by it. I felt if I was a bachellor it wouldn't be safe to go within the length of a skein of cotton yarn of sum of 'em, and it wouldn't take a very strong or a very hard twisted thread to hold me in the traces.

They poured into the mills by thousands, like bees into a hive, and in a few minits more the noise of the machinery begun to git louder and louder, until each factory sent out a buzzing sound, with which all other sounds soon becum mixed up, until it seemed we was into a city whar men, wimmin and children, water, fire, and light, was all at work, and whar the very air breathed the song of industry.

After breckfust we went to one of the mills, whar we got a little boy to show us the way. The little feller tuck us from one room to another all over the mill, and sich other contraptions I never seed before. The machinery made sich a noise that we couldn't hear ourselves think, let alone sayin any thing to one another, and then we was so cumpletely dumfounded by what we seed, that we couldn't found a word to say even if we could heard one another talk. Thar was the galls tendin the looms and the spindles, mixed all up among the cranks and wheels, and drum-heds and crossbands, and iron fixins, that was all agwine like lightnin, and ther little white hands flyin about like they was a part of the machinery. Bissy as they was, though, they found time now and then to steal a sly glance at us, and then I could see a mischievous smile playin round sum of ther pretty mouths, as much as to say, what green fellers we was that never seed a cotton-mill before. I tried to git the hang of sum of the machinery, but it wasn't no use. Evrything I seed, from the ceilin to the floor, was whirlin, and whizzin, and rattlin, and dashin, as if it would tear evry thing to pieces; but what they was doin or what sot 'em agwine, was more'n I could make out. Buzz-z-z-z, went the spindles and the spools; clank-clank, went the looms, and the white cloth was rollin off in big bolts, but how it was done, was what I couldn't see into.

* * * * * * * *

After gwine through three or four of the mills, which was all pretty much alike, we went into one whar they print calicos. This part of the bisness ain't the nicest work in the world, though it's very interestin. We went into the dryin-room as they call it, but we didn't stay thar but a very short time. If the *other* country is much hotter than this dryin-room, it is not much misrepresented in the accounts we have of it. When I stepped in I felt the hot air, as I breathed it into my lungs, like boilin water, and my hair crisped up like I was in a bake-oven. Hooper, who, you know, takes a good deal of pains with his whiskers, dassent risk 'em in the dryin-room more'n a minit; and when we got out I felt jest like I'd cum out of a steam-bath.

The next place we went to was the whip manufactory, whar we seed a cover braided onto a whipstalk, by machinery, in about two minits. From thar we went to another place, whar they made cotton and woollen cards. That machine banged any thing I ever seed in all my life. I've always thought that a machine that could make any thing as well as it could be made with hands was pretty considerable of a machine. But to see a little iron contraption take a piece of lether and a coil of wire, and cut off the wire and bend it double, punch the holes in the lether, put the wire in the holes, push 'em in and bend 'em, and fasten 'em thar quicker and better than five men could do it, went a little ahed of any thing I ever heard or dreamed of. The man that invented that machine could invent one to eat shad without swallerin the bones, or one that could pick a man's pocket when he was wide awake, without gettin found out. The only wonder is, that he didn't invent sum way to fool Old Deth himself, and live for ever. But the poor man is ded, and, like all men of genius, died very poor.

The next place we went into was a machine carpenter's shop, whar the rough boards cum into one dore in a cart and went out at the other in panel-dores, winder-sashes, pine boxes, &c. Saws and plainers and chissels and awgers was sawin, plainin, chisselin and borin in evry direction by machinery, with men t tend 'em; and for one that wasn't acquainted with the bearins of the place, it was necessary to keep a pretty sharp look-out to prevent havin a shavin tuck off of him sumwhar, or to keep from bein dove-tailed, or havin a awger-hole put rite through him fore he know'd what hurt him. It was most dinner-time, and we didn't stay thar long.

At the Merrymack House we had one of the finest dinners I ever eat in my life. But the dish what tuck my fancy most, was a fine biled Merrymack salmon. What a pity salmons don't grow on pine trees—then we could have 'em in Georgia; but as that can't be, I would advise you, if ever you cum this way in pea-time, to stop at the Merrymack House. Here they git 'em rite out of the water, and if a dish of Merrymack salmon and green peas wouldn't bring a ded man to life, then he may be buried with perfect safety. After the desert we had fruit, and among other things sum of the finest ox-hart cherries. They wer monstrous good, and if the man counted the seeds on my plate, he knows I done 'em justice. Hooper loved 'em too. We sot thar sum time eatin cherries and talkin 'bout the factory galls and the machinery.

"Ain't it a pity," sed Hooper, "that these galls is Yankees. If it wasn't for that," ses he—

"Well, that's a fact," ses I. "But you oughtn't to mind that, Hooper."

"Ah, Majer," ses he, "it wouldn't do. But I did see one gall thar that——"

"Stole your hart," ses I; for I know'd he was very sceptible of the tender passion, and I had hard work to git him out of one room in the Boot Mills.

"No, not 'zactly, Majer; but to tell you the truth, I couldn't keep my eyes of that tall, dark-complexioned gall what was tendin the starchin-machine—the one what was readin in a book. Ther was sumthing so winnin, so amiable, and yet so dignified about that gall, that I shall never forgit her. But she's a Yankee, and maybe a ravin abolitionist."

"Well, Hooper," ses I, to change the subject what

was beginnin to make him serious, "if I was a woodpecker I'd cum to this country evry summer, jest to eat cherries—they're so good."

"Well, if I was a woodpecker I wouldn't do no sich thing!" ses Hooper.

"Why not?" ses I.

"Why, because these everlastin Yankees would be certain to invent sum cussed machine to ketch me."

Ther was sumthing in that, and I had no more to say.

In the evenin we tuck a walk to look at the town. Passin by a book-store, we went in to git sumthing to read. The old gentleman what keeps the store show'd us sum numbers of the "Lowell Offering," what he sed was made up of the writins of the factory galls. Hooper sed he'd bet that gall he seed readin in the mills was one of the writers, and he told the man to let him have all the numbers. Hearin us say we would like to see sum of the writers, Mr. Davis, who is a monstrous clever, obligin man, sed he would be very happy to interduce us to sum of 'em. We tuck him at his word, and in a few minits more he show'd us into a neat little parlor, whar we was soon made acquainted with Miss Harriet F——, the editor of the Offering, and her mother. Miss F—— promised Mr. Davis to take good care of us, and to see that none of the Lowell galls stole our harts, and he went back to his store. We spent a ower in very agreeable chat with Miss F——, who is a true specimen of a New England gall. She has worked in the mills for several years, but now devotes herself to the magazine what she edits, supportin her mother by her own industry. After awhile she proposed to interduce us to sum more of the literary factory galls, and takin my arm, she carried us through several of the mills, and interduced us to the galls who was at ther work.

As we was passin the great machine carpet factory, she ax'd us if we had seed 'em weavin carpets on the power-looms. We told her no—that we went thar in the day, but they wouldn't let us in.

"Oh!" sed she, "they didn't know you was Southerners, or they wouldn't been 'fraid of your stealin ther patent."

I didn't know zactly whether she meant that as a compliment or not.

We went to the office, and ses Miss F——:

"Mr. Peters, here's a couple of Southern frends of mine, what wants to see the carpet-looms."

"Well, but, Miss F——," ses he, "you know its entirely agin the rules for anybody to be admitted to see the machinery."

"Yes; but," ses she, "I don't care for the rules—these gentlemen are all the way from Georgia, and they *must* see the looms."

"But—" ses the old man.

"I don't care," ses she; "I'll be answerable for all the damage."

"Well," ses Mr. Peters, "you can go into that room, (pintin to a dore,) and when you're in the packin-room, I guess you can find the way into the looms without my *lettin you in*."

That was sufficient, and in we went. I ax'd Miss F—— if that man wasn't a Yankee inventor.

"O, no," ses she; "he's only a ordinary genius in these parts."

The carpet-looms is a grate specimen of American ingenuity, bein the only power-looms for weavin carpetin in the world; but my hed was so full of wonders that I had seen durin the day, that I hadn't no room for the carpet-looms. Besides, they is such thunderin grate big, smashin iron things, and go at such a terrible rate, that I expected evry minit to git my branes nocked out by 'em.

After takin a look at 'em for a few minits, we went out, and visited sum more of the literati. Miss F——. interduced me to Miss Lucy L——, the author of "*The Wasted Flowers,*" one of the prettyest little alle gorys in the English language; and which JUDGE CHARLTON, of Georgia, and several other popular poets, has tried ther hands on without bein able to improve it a bit. Miss L—— was in the packin-room of one of the mills, as clerk, checkin off the goods as they were bein put up into bales. She had worked in the mills several years. I never met with a more interestin young lady, though I spose she wouldn't thank me for callin her a *lady*, as she gin me her autograf in a very different spirit. It reads—

" MAJOR JONES:

"SIR—I have the honor to be, yours, very respectfully, a *bonâ-fide* factory girl,

LUCY L——."

We found the place still more attractive as our acquaintance extended, and I begun to fear that Hooper would never be willin to quit Lowell. We tuck tea that evenin with Miss F——, and afterwards called on several of our new acqaintances, who, with a party of ther frends, tuck a walk with us on the banks of the Merrymack. Hooper's symptoms was gettin worse and worse every hour, and I was 'fraid to risk him another moonlight night with the factory galls, for fear he mought meet the fate as a man what he would be 'fraid of as a woodpecker. So we bid 'em all good-by, when we parted with 'em for our hotel.

We was off early in the mornin for Boston, whar we spent a few hours til the cars started for New York. I won't stop to tell you 'bout our trip—what a race we had with another steambote, and how we like to got blowd to Ballyhack gwine round Pint Judy, and how

one man lost his bran-new hat overboard, and th
captain wouldn't stop for it. Sufficient that we arriv
safe in this city, though I ain't rite certain that Hooper
didn't leave his hart in the Boot Mills. No more from
Your frend til deth,
Jos. Jones.

P. S. We're gwine to take a trip to Niagary Fall
and the Lakes next week.

LETTER XVII.

New York, July 15, 1845.

To Mr. Thompson:—I told you in my last that we was gwine to Niagary. Well, the Monday after I rit you my last letter, Hooper and me tuck passage on board the steambote Nickerbocker for Albany, up the Hudson river, what you've heard so much about. It was a butiful afternoon, and ther was peeple enuff aboard to make a fust rate campmeetin—men, wimmin and children, of all ages, sorts and sizes, and a merryer crowd couldn't be well raked together. We wasn't long gittin away from New York, and in a few minits our floatin castle was movin through a fleet of vessels of all kinds, gwine and cumin to the city, in one of the largest and handsumest rivers in the world. Some of the passengers had books, and maps, and spy-glasses in ther hands, and was all the time pintin out the interestin places. I had no time to read about 'em, and while they was porin over ther books and maps, and axin which is this, and that, and whar's so and so, I jest tuck my fill by lookin at every thing that was to be seed.

We had a fust rate view of the Pallisades, as they call 'em, what goes jest a leetle ahead of any pile of rock I ever seed before, extendin for twenty miles on the left bank, and risin in sum places more'n five hundred feet rite perpendickiler out of the water. Now and then ther is a fisherman's house standin on the water's edge, lookin 'bout as big as a bee-gum agin the everlastin stone wall behind it.

After passin the Pallisades, we cum into the Tappan Sea, whar the river is more'n four miles wide and looks as quiet as a duck-pond. Sing Sing prison, what stands on the right at the hed of the Tappan Sea, was made to keep the rascals in New York, what they haint got room for on Blackwell's Island, but one man sed he didn't blieve ther was stone enuff in the Pallisades to bild a house big enuff to hold all that ought to be thar.

In a few minits more we was passin Stony Pint, whar old Mad Antony Wayne waked up the British sogers with the pints of his bayonets, one mornin before breckfust, in 1779, and then we was among the highlands. The sun was most down, and the mountains—sum of 'em more'n one thousand six hundred feet high—stood out in bold relief agin the brown evenin sky, throwin their dark shadows far over the river, that crooked and twisted about in evry direction, as if it had got lost in tryin to find its way through 'em.

It seemed as if old Miss Nature had jest tried her hand at makin hills and hollers, wastin yeath enuff in her fancy work to make two or three states like the State of Delaware; and I couldn't help but think what capers old Boreas must cut in the winter time, when he undertakes to have a strait blow among these everlastin crags and caverns, and precipises. One would think it would take a right smart harrycane to git through 'em without gettin scattered into forty thousand directions. Such monstrous mountings I never seed before. They may talk about pilin Ossa on Pelion, but if a body wanted to astonish the world with a mounting, all they would have to do would be to put Crow's Nest on Butter Hill, or Bull Head on Bare Mount, and if that wouldn't lay all the other hills in the shade, then they mought take my hat.

The passengers was all terribly delighted with the scene, and them that had books and maps couldn't git time to see any thing for answerin the questions of them what didn't have none. Thar was one man from New York, with a crowd of ladys, that know'd all about every place we passed, and, to hear him talk, a body would s'posed he had been born and raised all along the shore like the Indian was. The ladys kep him monstrous busy, you may depend.

"Whar's Antony's Nose, Mr. Johnson?" says one of 'em.

"Oh yes," ses another, "I want to see old Antony's Nose. They say it's one of the greatest curiosities 'n the world—it's so perfectly natural."

"Antony's Nose?" ses Mr. Johnson, puttin his spyglass up to his eye. "Let me see. Ah, thar it is. You can jest see the tip eend of it round that projection."

"Whar! whar?" ses a dozen of 'em at once. "Do tell us."

"In a minit, ladies, we'll have a good view. There now, do you see? Thar it is, rite ahead. That's Antony's Nose."

Well, I looked, and so did everybody else, but it looked as much like a fodder stack as a man's nose to me.

"I can't see no nose," ses a old chap what had his hed tied up with a red hankerchicf to keep from ketchin cold.

"Which eend is the nose on?" ses one of the ladys.

"Oh I see it—I see it," ses a long-legged dandy in check trowses. "I see it jest as plain as the nose on a man's face."

"Whar is it?" ses a dozen that was stretchin ther eyes out of ther heds, but couldn't make it out no better than I could.

"Why," ses Mr. Johnson, "rite thar, a little on the right of the wheel-house. Now, can't you see it, Miss Abbigal, jest beyond that big rock in the edge of the water thar? I can almost see the nostrils."

"To be sure," ses the dandy; "if it was a little later we could hear it snore."

"I can't see no sign of a nose," ses a man what was oglin the mountain with all his might, with a one-eved spectacle tied to a black ribbon.

"Nor me nother," sed all of 'em.

"Well, it's monstrous strange," ses Mr. Johnson—"it's so plain. I can't see nothin else."

"Aint you mistaken, Mr. Johnson?" ses one of the ladys.

"Lord, no," ses he; "I know it so well—I've been on it as often as I've got fingers and toes."

'Bout this time the captain of the boat passed along. The passengers stopped him and ax'd him whar was Antony's Nose?

"'Bout five miles ahead," ses he; "you will see it shortly after we pass the next landin."

Mr. Johnson was tuck with a sudden desire to promenade with one of the ladys, and we didn't see his nose no more on the top deck that night.

Bimeby we cum to Antony's Nose, sure enuff, but it had been *blowed* so that nobody couldn't tell whether it was a Roman nose or a pug—not by the old gentleman himself, but by some oudacious stone quarryers, who had to go and blast it all to pieces, as if ther wasn't enuff rock in the place without ther taking such a liberty with old Antony's countenance. Some men, you know, find as much satisfaction in spilin a wonder, as others does in findin 'em.

It was so dark when we got to West Pint—the place whar Uncle Sam teaches the young ideas how to shoot the enemies of our country—that we didn't see but monstrous little of it. The boat stopped at the landin a few minits, and we had time too look round on the hills that seemed to rise to the skies, fencin us in on every side, cuttin off the river above and below us, so it looked as if we was in a little lake among the hills, insted of bein on a river two hundred miles long.

We had a monstrous good supper, but I lost my share of the strawberries and cream jest 'cause I happened to cail one of the waiters "boy." The kinky-headed cus looked at me sideways, and rolled the whites of his eyes at me like he was gwine to have a fit of nidryfoby, and carried the berries and cream rite past me to the other eend of the table. I called some more of the waiters, but it was no use. The fust one had told the rest, and all ther dignitys was up. They kep lookin at me and whisperin to one another, and makin motions, and I could smell the musk so strong that it like to tuck my appetite from me, hungry as I was. If you should ever cum this way a travellin, you musn't call the nigger waiters, boy, nor uncle, nor buck, nor any frendly, home name; and if your trunk happens to have Georgia on it, you'd better scratch it off, if you want any attention or civility from the waiters. They're all misters here, and the she ones is misses, and it puts the old harry in 'em to call 'em by any thing but ther Northern names. You may call pore white men and wimmin waiters, servants, slewers, or any thing you please, but you must take monstrous good care how you speak to the free niggers.

After supper we tuck a smoke on the top deck. If the scenery of the Hudson is "grand, gloomy and peculiar," in the day-time, it don't lose none of its charms by moonlight. To be sure, the mountings don't look so bold, and we don't see so many prominent objects standin out separate and distinct, excitin our admiration on ther own hook as it were, but ther is enuff to be seed to help the imagination to make improvements even on nater itself. Thar's the broad buzum of the river, reflectin the silver light of the moon, with here and thar a little sloop or scooner, glidin along in silence, with its snow-white sails jest filled by the soft breeze that fans the smoke of your segar away from your nose—the curvin banks, now shootin boldly out into the strong light, disturbin the quiet current of the river, and now retirin into the deep shade, whar the water is sleepin still and dark as a nigger baby in a shuck-pen—the lofty peaks raisin ther bald heds into the sky to bathe 'em in the cold moon-beams—the ravines and gorges windin and twistin about between the hills, or spreadin out into broad valleys, and reachin away for miles into the dim haze, whar the dark Catskills rises ther misty forms agin the vaulted Heavens—all conspirin to make a landscape which—which, as the novel riters ses, is more easy to imagine than describe.

Bimeby our segars went out, the moon went down, the ladys went to ther cabin, and we went to look for our berths. After huntin about for half a ower or more for the rite one, I got into a rong one, whar I hadn't more'n jest got into a doze before a old feller cum along and hustled me out, showin me a ticket for the place. By this time sum feller had got into mine, and when I found him out, and got him awake, and show'd him my ticket, he got out, cussin and growlin like a bare with a sore hed, and went to rout out sumbody else that was in his place. And so the thing went round from berth to berth, and 'tween the rumagin about of the servants, who was tryin to find the rite berths for the gentlemen what had got into the rong numbers, the cussin of them that was waked up on suspicion, and the growlin of them that was huntin about for a bed, in ther bare feet and drawers, I didn't git to sleep for more'n two owers.

One little duck-legged man, what sed he was a editor of a newspaper up in Albany, had all the servants on the bote helpin him to find a bed, and made more rumpus than all the rest put together. He didn't have no ticket himself, so he jest kep gwine round, routin evrybody up to see if they was certain they was in the rite bed. What made it worse, his memory wasn't very good, and he would cum to the same man two or three times. Hooper was layin rite under me, and you know how cross old bachelors is at night when they're in bed. Mr. Squib had waked him up once, and I could hear him cussin about it, and I spected evry minit the fussy little feller would cum back, and then I know'd ther'd be a row. Shore enuff here cum Squib with a gang of niggers behind him, all with candles in ther hands. Fust he looked into my curtains. "Boo!" ses I, and the little man's hed disappeared like a shot. The next minit I heard him wakin up Hooper.

"What number's this you're in, stranger?" ses he.

"Ah, ha! I've got you now," shouted Hooper, springin from his berth like a mad tiger, and grabbin Squib by the neck.

"Murder—murder! take him off!" yelled the little man, as they went down on the floor together.

Then thar was a row shore enuff. Hooper hollered stop thief!—the little man hollered murder!—and the niggers hollered help! The passengers cum scramblin out of ther berths in all kinds of costume—tumblin over the chairs and sofas, and grabbin, sum hold of Hooper, and sum hold of Squib. However, nobody didn't git hurt, and as soon as Hooper got a chance to explain how he was subject to the night-mare, evry thing was quiet agin. But the little man found a place to sleep in the other eend of the bote.

Sleep is like the magnetic telegraph—one travels hundreds of miles in no time when he's asleep—and early in the mornin we was at Albany. I had to give a sevenpence for my boots to a nigger what had rubbed off what little blackin ther was on 'em before, and by the time I got dressed and got my face washed, we was at the wharf.

Here was another gang of boddy-snatchers after us and our baggage. Ther wasn't no choice of evils, so we tuck the fust feller in the way, who whirled us off to the railrode depot in a minit. The distance ain't more'n about five hundred yards, and by the time we got our trunks off the coach, here cum the passengers walkin from the bote, with ther baggage in a wagon belongin to the rode, free of charge. This was take in enuff; but would you blieve it, when I gin the driver a five dollar bill to get it changed, so I could pay him his fair, the rascal went to his coach, jumped on the box, popped his whip, and puttin his thumb on his nose, wiggled his fingers at me as he druv off in a canter. It was no time to rectify sich things—they was callin out for the baggage to put it aboard for the place it was gwine to—Hooper was buyin our tickets—the bell was ringin for evrybody to git in the cars—one chap was just caught tryin to steal a gentleman's trunk rite before his eyes—I looked up agin the wall and seed hand-bills stickin all about, what sed, in big letters, "Look out for Pick-pockets!" and I jest put my hands in my pockets and kep my eyes wide open, til I got my seat in the cars. When we started I drawed a long breth, and thanked my stars that we was out of Albany.

And now I am gwine at the rate of fifteen miles a ower, and Albany is fast fadin from my sight. I will stop here while I go on to Buffalow, leavin you to imagin what happens to me on the way, til you hear from me agin. So no more from

Your frend til deth,
JOS. JONES.

LETTER XVIII.

New York, July 18, 1845.

To Mr. Thompson:—*Dear Sir*—When I left off in my last letter, I was whizzin along in the cars at the rate of 'bout fifteen miles a ower, on my way to Buffalow. You know ther ain't no great deal of romance in a railrode jurney, if you don't happen to no mishaps, sich as runnin off the track and bein tilted heels over hed down a fifty feet embankment, into a quagmire forty foot deep, or pitchin into the train what's gwine tother way, and havin a double seat, back and all, jammed rite through your stummick in the collision, or bustin yer biler and havin your arms and legs sent whirlin in evry direction among the tree-tops in a harrycane of bilin hot steam. Well, as none of these accidents didn't happen to us to make our trip interestin, I shan't truble you with a very long account of my jurney through this part of the great Empire State.

It is a Empire State, shore enuff—a empire of cities and towns, standin so thick that, in the railrode cars, it jest seems to be one everlastin Broadway, with here and thar a Bolin Green or a Union Park by way of variety. I tried to keep a run of the towns, but they stood so thick together and the cars went so fast, that when I ax'd anybody the name of a place, before I could make him understand what I wanted, in the bominable racket, we was in the middle of another town, and by the time I could understand the hard name of that one, we was runnin the children and pigs off the track, and settin the dogs a barkin, and the wimmin a lookin out of the winders in another. Jest as we got out of Amsterdam I ax'd one of the passengers what place it was. He was readin a newspaper, and didn't hear me good at fust.

"What town is this?" ses I.

"Eh?" ses he.

"What place is this?"

"This! oh! this is Tripe Hill, I blieve," ses he.

"What Hill?" ses I.

"It looks like Cawnewaga," ses he.

"Cawne-*which?*" ses I.

"Now we are in Fonda," ses he.

Seein I couldn't git no satisfaction out of him, I give it up. And shore enuff, cum to find out, we had been gwine through three towns while I was tryin to find out the name of the fust one.

This is a go-a-hed country, to be shore. I couldn't help but think, as we went dashing along in the middle of cities and towns, over lakes and rivers, through mountings and valleys, wakin the echoes with the thunderin clang of our iron wheels, and settin all the animal creation a caperin over the fields with the snort of our steam-car—how the old codgers what lived three or four thousand years before the Fourth of July would be tuck a-back if ther ghosts was to cum on a jurney to the United States now—how ther old notions would have to stand out of the way before the march of human knowledge which they would see displayed in evry thing around 'em. What, for instance, would old Mr. Abraham think, to see more'n a thousand peeple, with bag and baggage—more'n all the jack-asses and camels in his kingdom could carry—travelin at the rate of fifteen miles a ower, all of 'em as comfortable and snug as if they was settin in ther own parlors? Or, to cum down to the ater times, what would sich fellers as old Pompy and Socrates, and them, think to see Romes, and Athenses, and Troys, springin up all round 'em, thick as toadstools on a foggy mornin, with more commerce, and havin almost as much inhabitants as the cities of ther own day, what they used to think couldn't be bilt short of two or three of ther long-lived generations?

I used to think that the peeple of the old times had a monstrous sight the advantage of us, livin as they did to be five and six hundred years old; but, when I cum to consider, I don't know as they was much better off than we is. For what's the odds if we don't live so long as Mr. Methusleum, if we can accomplish more in our lifetimes than he did in his? If we can git up a bigger nation in half a century than they did in five times as long—if our boys know more about science and other matters at ten years old, than ther's did at a hundred—if we can travel farther and see more of the world in a week than they could in five years—if we can harness up fire and water, and make 'em pull more cars in a train than Faryo had chariots in his hoste—if we can make the lightnin carry our mails from one eend of the yeath to the other in the twinklin of a eye—if we can print more books in a day than they could rite in a century—if we can do all these things and twenty thousand times more than was never dreamed of in ther filosofy—then what's the use of our livin as long as they did?

I blieve Providence regulates these things jest about as well as Congress could if it had the management of 'em. This world is only a state of preparation for another kind of existence—a sort of human cabbage-patch, whar plants is raised from the seed to be sot out in the gardin of immortality—and the higher the state of cultivation the sooner we cum to the proper degree of human development, and of course the sooner we is reddy for transplantin. But a ralerode car ain't no place to filosofise, so I'll drap the subject and go on with my journey.

We got to Syracuse early in the evenin, and as we wasn't in no grate hurry, we concluded to stop thar all night, and take the train the next day. Ther is salt enuff made in this place, you know, to keep all creation from spilin, and I wanted to see how they biled it. We druv up to the salt-pumps, and seed 'em pumpin the water, and I couldn't help but think, when I seed the everlastin vats of salt water and the piles of salt in evry direction, that Mrs. Lott must been near this place when she looked back at Gomorrow. It's a monstrous nice town, with a heap of butiful private houses and high board fences, all as white as table-salt. We tuck a walk round it by moonlight, and then went to our hotel and went to bed. The next mornin, 'bout 'leven o'clock, we tuck the cars agin, and, passin through one of the butifulest countries in the world, arrived at Rochester, a handsum city 'bout as big as Savannah and Augusty both together, a little after dark. Here we tuck another rest til mornin, when we tuck the cars what set us down in Buffalow before dinner time.

After dinner we tuck a walk through the town, which is a fresh-water sea-port, you know, and a pretty considerable of a place. In the afternoon we went aboard of a little steambote what was gwine down the Niagary River to the Falls. While Hooper and me was smokin our segars on the deck, and the passengers was cumin on board, one of the big lake steamers started off with a rigment of sogers, what had been ordered from Buffalow to sum other place up the lake, makin a mighty grand show with her flags flyin and a band of music playin "Hail Columby."

Our bell rung, and in a few minits we was off. But jest as we got out of the mouth of the creek into the lake, we seed a bote with four sailors in it, and a lady, and a little fat man what was wavin his handkerchief to us like he was in grate distress. Our captain stopped his bote til the sailors rowed alongside and put the lady and the little fat man aboard. He wanted us to give chase to the big bote what was gwine up the lake with the sogers, to put the lady on it, who was the wife of the Curnel, and was left by mistake. Ther bote was tied behind ours, and away we went after the big bote, as hard as we could crack it. But it was no use. The big steamer was leavin us fast, and all the signals we could make wouldn't stop her. The lady sot on the seat and cried like her hart would brake, and the little fat man cussed and stamped about like he would kick our smoke-pipe down if he was only big enuff. The lady, who was a young wife, jest married a few months, was left in his charge by the Curnel to see her to the bote while he tended to his sogers; but the fussy old feller didn't git her thar in time, and the bote was gone with the Curnel, leavin the pore gall to cry her pretty eyes out at the idee of bein parted from her husband until sum other bote could take her to him.

It was a mighty hard case, and made me feel monstrous bad, but ther was no help for it; and after tryin his best to catch the big bote, our captain had to put her and the old man in ther battow agin; and the last I seed of 'em the sailors was pullin in to the shore, what was about five miles off—the old man tryin to console the pore wife, and she wipin her eyes with her handkerchef, and gazin after the bote that was fast gettin smaller and smaller as it bore her husband from her.

As we was runnin back to the outlet of the Niagary River, I noticed that our flag didn't have no stars, and the stripes on it run cross-ways. Think's I that's monstrous curious; and I ax'd the captain what sort of a gigamaree he had got up thar for a flag?

"That?" ses he; "That's Saint George's Cross!"

"Who's Saint George?" ses I; "does he live about these parts?"

"Oh, no!" ses the captain, "that's the English colors."

"The English colors!" ses I. "Why, captain, what upon yeath is you doin with the British flag on your bote?"

"This is a British bote," ses he.

"The thunder it is!" ses I.

And shore enuff, thar we was, abord of a British bote, with a English captain, and the British flag flyin over our heds. Hooper sed it was all right; but I couldn't help but feel sort o' queer with that flag over me, and I thought of the time when the gallant Perry made 'em pull it down on that very lake.

The captain was a monstrous clever little man, and tuck a grate deal of pains to oblige his passengers. And if all the British was like him, I don't think we'd have any more rumpus with 'em.

Ther wasn't many passengers, and as we passed down the river, and all engaged in conversation about the interestin scenery on its banks, and the grate wonder we was gwine to see, we got pretty well acquainted. Among 'em was a tall, thin, pale-lookin Englishman, what wore a grass-linen cote and trouses, with a high-crowned, speckled straw hat. He was runnin about all the time with his gide-book and pencil in his hand, axin evrybody questions, and gabblin and talkin on 'bout evry thing, like he was half out of his senses. He was as nervous as a woman; and when he first seed the colum of spray risin from the catarack—which we saw several miles before we got to Navy Island, where the patriots kicked up such a rumpus, you know, a few years ago—he rubbed his hands together, and begun to talk poetry like a playactor.

We was soon at Chipawa, near the old battle ground, whar we tuck a horse railrode for the Falls The moon was up high and bright as the horses trotteo us along over the rode, and we could hear the thunder of the mighty torrent above the noise of the car. We was all bound for the Clifton House; but wher we got within about a mile of it, a man met us, to tel¹ us that ther was no room thar, and all except a old gentleman and two or three ladys what had rooms engaged, went back to the Pavilion Hotel what stands upon the hill jest above the Falls. And I was rite glad we didn't git in the crowd below, for we found plenty of room at the Pavilion—a good supper, a obligin landlord, and excellent accommodations, in evry respect.

With the roar of Niagary in our ears, it was impossible to go to sleep without first satisfyin our curiosity, by takin a view of the Fall by moonlight; so as soon as supper was over, our party, consistin of Hooper, the Englishman and me, and two other gentlemen from Filadelfy, started to find what we thought ther wouldn't be no danger of missin.

We soon cum to a path what had a gide-board to it and led down in the direction of the falls, and follered it down the almost perpendickeler steep, holdin on to the bushes by the way. We didn't go far before the top of the precipice which we was descendin, shut out the light of the moon so we couldn't see a sign of the path. One straggled off one way and one another, each feelin his way and holdin on to the roots and bushes, and callin to the others to foller, until we found ourselves scattered in evry direction, unable to git to one another, and afraid to go any further down the slippery, miery bank. We could hardly hear each other's voices for the heavy thunder of the flood below.

what seemed to snake the foundation of the hill to which we clung, as it rolled its gray mists up among the dark tree-tops below.

"I say, gentlemen," sed our English frend, "let's commisshun the one nearest to the top of the 'ill to go back to the 'ouse for a gide, and we'll 'old on 'ere where we are, till 'e cums."

"I vote for the gide," ses Mr. Kee, from Filadelfy; "but I couldn't let go this bush for all creation, myself."

Them was jest exactly my sentiments: for I begun to feel monstrous ticklish thar in the dark, so close to sich a terrible place. But I didn't say nothin, waitin to see if sum one wouldn't volunteer. Mr. More was nee deep in the mud, 'bout twenty feet from me, and Hooper was on his hands and nees crawlin up the bank. Hooper was 'termined to see the falls by moonlight, so back he went, and in a few minits cum with a gide, who, after collectin us together and gettin us in the path which led rite the different way from what we was gwine, tuck us down to the second bank, and then led us out to the Table Rock. And thar was the mighty Niagary, pourin its eternal flood in thunder down into the dark abyss, from which cum rollin up grate colums of snow-white mist, supportin a pale rainbow arch, at once presentin the most butiful and the most terrible pair of spectacles I ever had before my eyes.

We stood on the bald Table Rock, what juts out over the bilin flood below, whar the white foam, though we can see it dimly through the mist in the moonlight, gives you no fixed idee of heights or distances, out rather helps the imagination to extend the scene upon a scale suited to its awful sublimity. Not a word was spoke for several minits—each one held his breth in silent awe—afraid to breathe in sich a mighty presence. And the fust words uttered was exclamations to ourselves, that seemed to cum from our mouths 'thout our knowin it, as if the very soul within us was amazed, and was givin utterance to its emotions, while our fisical naters was overwhelmed and paralyzed by the terrific display of the majesty and power of the Being that made the Heavens and the yeath.

I went close on the edge of the rock, whar the water dashed over a few inches from my feet, and looked, fust upon the waves of the wide river, as they cum leapin and shimmerin in the moonlight, like mountains of silver, to the verge of the precipice, whar they suddenly melted into a flood of liquid emerald, frosted over with flakes of snow, as they dashed down into the deep, eternal torment of waters below—then upon the misty cavern that yawned at my feet, whar the waves that my eyes had follered in ther descent, in the foam of ther rath, was howlin, and chafin, and surgin like troubled spirits within ther rocky confines—and then upon the pale bow that spanned the dismal vortex, sheddin a calm halo of ethereal buty over the stupend.ous scene of terrific horrors.

No one was anxious to leave the spot, or to disturb the meditations of the others. After a while we gradually fell into conversation. Our English frend, who we had by this time found out to be a perfect gentleman, and a man of excellent good sense, sed he had travelled the best part of his life, and that he had seed the grate waterfalls of Switzerland and South America, but this was *the* waterfall of the world—it was the grate feature of America. He had never seed any thing capable of producin such sublime emotions, and ses he—"If I was to dy to-night, i would be a grate source of consolation to know that I had lived long enuff in the world to see its greatest wonder."

After spendin a couple of hours on the Table Rock,

we returned to our hotel, and soon after went to our beds, to dream of Niagary, and to awake in the mornin to explore its magnificent wonders. I will tell you how it looks by daylight in my next. So no more from

Your frend til deth,
Jos. Jones.

LETTER XIX.

New York, July 20, 1845.

To Mr. Thompson :—*Dear Sir*—I tuck my leave of you, in my last letter, jest as I was gwine to bed in the Pavilion Hotel. Well, you may depend I dreamed al' sorts of terrible dreams that night. I went to sleep with the roar of the cataract in my ears, and it seemed to me that the bed-posts trembled with the jar. The roarin in my ears kep growin louder and louder, til it seemed to me like heaven and yeath was cumin together, and the fust thing I knowed somehow or other, I was standin on the edge of Table Rock agin, and a mounting of water, that reached to the sky, was cumin rollin rite onto me, to sweep me down into the bilin basin below, what seemed to be 'bout five miles deep, and filled with all the devils in the infernal regions. I tried to run, but for the soul of me I couldn't move a peg—on and over it cum rite on top of me, and down I went—down, down, with my mouth chock full of water, so I couldn't even say my prayers,—but jest as I got to the bottom and was 'bout pitchin hed fust into the mouth of a water devil that was as big as a meetin house, I fotched one all-fired yell—and the next minit I found myself on the floor, with the bed-clothes on top of me.

Hooper sed it was the night-mare, and if I hadn't hollered jest as I did, I'd been a gone Jona, shore enuff. Night-mare or no night-mare, I don't blieve I'd felt much worse if I'd gone over the Falls in downright yearnest.

I was afraid to go sound to sleep agin, and so I jes. tuck a turn round the bed-post with one arm, and slep with one eye open the balance of the night.

ın the mornin before breckfust we tuck another look
t the falls from the Table Rock. This time we had
a better view of the Fall itself, as well as the surroundin
scenery. But notwithstandin it was light, and we could
see for miles around, the objects we looked at was on
sich a different scale of proportion from any thing we
was used to, that ther was no sich thing as formin any
idees 'bout hights and distances, or any thing else.
The more I looked the more I couldn't tell how big a
thing was. Sometimes a rock would look like a mounting, and sometimes it was no bigger than a goose's egg
—sometimes the islands would look big as my plantation,
and then agin they wouldn't look no bigger than so
many tater-hills—and I begun to wonder how they could
hold ther holts, thar rite in the middle of sich a racin
river, 'thout gettin washed up by the roots and swept
over the precipice below.

The magnitude of things at Niagary depends alto-
gether on how a body contrasts 'em. When my eye
tuck in nothing but the mighty river, the everlastin
battlements of rock, and the terriffic cateract, why then
they didn't seem to have no partickeler dimensions;
but when I happened to see the houses on the American
side, or a ferry boat crossin below the Fall, or a company
of men clamberin about among the loose rocks, down
by the water's edge, lookin no bigger than so many ants,
then I was able to comprehend the stupendous wonders
of Niagary, and to feel myself no bigger, standing thar
on that rock, than a seed-tick in Scriven county. Some
peeple ses Niagary is a great place to elevate a body's
idees, but with me it had exactly the contrary effect,
and I do blieve if I was to use about thar long, I'd git
sich an insignificant opinion of myself, that I wouldn't
dare to say my soul was my own. I know some peeple
that it would do a monstrous sight of good to go to
Niagary, if for nothin else but to git a correct measure-
ment of ther own importance in the scale of bein—if

they didn't git ther notions tuck down a peg or two, then I'm terribly mistaken.

The stickin in the mud the night before had laid up our English frend, and when we got back to breckfust he was jest gittin out of bed, but he was too sick to go with us to the Falls. After eatin a good breckfust we went down to the museum kep by Mr. Barnet, whar we seed all sorts of varmints, and Ingin curiosities, and minerals and sich likes, and then bought sum tickets to go down under the Fall to Termination Rock, as they call it.

I didn't have much notion of foolin about quite so familiar with sich terrors as the great water-fall itself; but they all sed ther was no danger, and that evrybody went thar, and nothin would do Hooper but we must go. So we went to the house at the top of the stair-way, whar a old nigger feller tuck us into a room and told us we must strip off all our clothes, and put on sum sailor riggins what he would give us, to go under the falls with.

"But whar shall we leave our money and our watches?" ses Mr. More.

"You needn't be 'tall fear'd, gemmen," ses the old nigger, "jest leave evry thing here, and when you cum back you'll find 'em all safe, and ef you never cums back you know, you won't want 'em."

"We won't!" thinks I, and I begun to feel a little jubous 'bout gwine in any sich a place.

"I say, uncle—beg pardon," ses I. "*Mister*, is thar any danger in gwine to Termination Rock?"

"Not a bit," ses he, as he handed me a red flannel shirt, big enuff for Col. Bill Skinner, and a pair of coarse duck trowses, without no buttons on 'em. "Not a bit, if you don't fall into the casum below, and then thar aint no tellin what would becum of you."

I stopped strippin and sot down on a bench, and begun to consider.

"Stop," ses the nigger to Mr. More, who was p...

a par of trowses on over his boots; "you must take your boots off too—evry thing—and I'll give you a par of shoes for your feet."

Thunder!—thinks I—the feller wants to save all he an, if one of us was to cum up missin.

"Cum, Majer," ses Hooper, as he was pullin his shirt over his hed, "no backin out from old Georgy."

"But," ses I, "is you certain thar aint no danger in this bisness?"

"Not a bit, sir," ses the nigger, "though evrybody is a little skeered at fust—ladies go under evry day, and no accident has never happened yet. I was jest jokin you a little."

In a few minits more we was all dressed in our yaller trowses, red shirts, oil-cloth caps, and cowhide shoes, reddy for the adventure. We follered the lead of t guide to the stair-way, what went round and round we got almost out of breth before we reached the bottom, whar we stepped out into the path what runs along on the side of the almost perpendickeler rock bank, 'bout half-way from the top, gittin narrower and slipryer as we git nearer to the sheet of water. The mist from the river was raw and cold, but I blieve I could shivered in a warm bath jest to look at the place whar we was gwine.

The Table Rock above perjected out far over our heds, and the loose rocks what lay in our narrow path rolled from under our feet down into the foamin basin below. The old nigger led the way—Hooper follered close to him, and the rest of us strung along in Injin file behind. Jest before we got to the edge of the fall we all got a terrible shower-bath from a spring of water what falls in the path from the rock above. And now we enter behind the sheet—the path is hardly wide enuff for our feet, and slippry with runnin water—the white spray cums howlin up from the dark pit on our left, and drives in surgin torrents agin the slimy rocks on our right:—in the darkness we can jest see the black, shelvin rock to which we cling on one side, and the curtain of mad waters that is rushin down within arms-length of us on the other—the deep thunder of the water stops our ears to all other sounds, and the spray is so heavy that we gasp for breth as we shrink close to the tremblin rocks, agin which it drives til it falls in rain upon its slipry side. Now the gide turns back, we have reached Termination Rock, and, filled with a terrible awe that can find no words to express it, we face about, and grope our dangerous way back from a scene of terrific grandure and sublimity, which no pen can describe, and which is worth the riskin of one's life to know!

When we got out from behind the sheet, and had got to a place whar the footin was sure, you may depend I felt monstrous comfortable, and when Mr. More proposed " three cheers for Old Niagary," I jin'd in most hartily, and didn't stop til I had gin it at least half a dozen of 'em. I spose I felt very much like a man does after he's been made a Free Mason or a Odd Feller—the skeer was over, I had found out the mistery, and I felt that whenever I met any one hereafter who had put his foot on Termination Rock, I would be able to participate with him in a sentiment what nobody who had never been thar couldn't understand.

I wonder that among all the ways they have of making money here, out of strangers, they never have hit upon a order of brotherhood, the initiation ceremony of which to take place on Termination Rock. A order founded on sich a rock—a rock what the mighty Niagary itself can't move—certainly would stand, in spite of all the Billy Morgans in the world.

Before gwine up to change our clothes, the gide tuck us down to the water's edge, whar a little rock 'bout the size of Parson Stor's church in Pineville, lies a little ways out in the edge of the water. To git a good view of the Fall from the bottom, we clum up the ladder onto the top of this rock and tuck a seat and looked light up agin the great Horse-Shoe Fall, what looked like as if it cum pourin out of the heavens, it was so grand and high. Some ladys was standin upon the Table Rock lookin at us. They seemed to us about as big as my finger, and I spose we looked 'bout the same size to them. They waved ther little parasols to us, and we tuck off our oil-cloth caps and waved 'em at them.

After takin a good look from the top of the rock we went down and paddled about awhile in the water that runs through the broken rocks between the big rock and the bank, til one of us cum monstrous near gettin washed out into the rapids. After that we went back to the room, whar we found our clothes all right.

We hadn't more'n got out of the place before ther was 'bout a dozen hackmen after us to take us all over Canada if we wanted to go. One red-headed feller, what sed he was a patriot in the rebellion, and was put in prison to keep him from takin the country from the British, was so pressin that four of us chartered him to go to the Burnin Spring and Lundy's Lane.

At the Burnin Spring, whar the water blazes up when you touch it off with a Lucifer match, and burns like a fat light-wood knot, we lit our segars, and Mr. More, who is a little hard to blieve, burnt his finger to be certain it was no take in, and then we druv to the battle-ground whar our brave sogers in the last war giv the British sich a delightful evenin's entertainment. A old chap, what ses he fit in the battle in the British army, has got what he calls a observatory bilt on the spot, and tells peeple all sorts of a cock and bull story 'bout how the thing tuck place, for a quarter of a dollar, and always has got a few musket-balls left, that was picked up on the ground. He told us a dollar's worth of his experience, and we bought sum bullets of him, and then druv back to the ferry to go over on the American side.

On this side of the river ther is a pretty considerable

of a town, and the Yankee character is strikingly illustrated by the way that they have sot the Niagary itself to work for 'em, makin it turn saw-mills, grist-mills and other machinery. I wouldn't be surprised much if they was to set the whole American Fall to drivin cotton-looms and spinnin-ginnies before long.

We went to the old Curiosity Shop, as they call it, whar a feller has got a Niagary Falls in operation by machinery. The thing would do very well out in Pineville, but what upon yeath could possess a man to try to run opposition to sich a wonder, rite in hearin and in sight of the real cateract itself, is what stumps me. Nobody but a jennewine Yankee would ever undertake sich a thing. He don't charge nothin to see his Niagary, but makes a heap of money by selling Yankee made Ingin fixins, sich as moccasins, bead-bags, *card-cases*, and a heap of fancy articles, such as the Ingins themselves never dreamed of makin.

Then we crossed the bridge to Iris Island. After visitin the Biddle Staircase and the Cave of the Winds, and seein the American Fall in all its best views, we went to the Tarrapin Bridge and the Tower, whar ther was lots of ladys and gentlemen venturin about in places whar a cat-squirrel wouldn't be safe. 'Tween climbin rocks and wadin in the water and travelin about, I was beginnin to be pretty tired; and after takin a view from the tower, we tuck a hack for the ferry, and by sun-down was at our hotel agin on the Canady side, whar our clever landlord had a fust rate supper reddy for us.

The next mornin our red-headed coachman tuck us down to Queenston, by way of the Great Whirlpool, which is the next greatest curiosity to the Falls. The river gits very narrow before it enters the whirlpool, whar it runs in and out at right-angles, and whirls round and round, and boils over and over in its grate rock basin, what is sed to be more'n five hundred feet deep.

After takin a good look at the Whirlpool, we passed on to the Devil's Hole, and then to the Little Devil's Hole, and from thar to Queenston Hights, whar we stopped to take a look at Brock's Monument, what sum mean rascal tried to blow up durin the late rebellion. This was a butiful monument, standin in a butiful place, and it makes one sorry to see it busted and ruined as it is. The scoundrel what could be gilty of sich a mean act as the destruction of a monument to a brave man who shed his blood for his country, ain't fit to live among honorable men, and would be a disgrace to a nation of heathens.

We walked from the monument down to Queenston, while our Jehu tuck our baggage to the bote that was to start in half a ower for Montreal. Queenston is a wondrous dull, dirty-lookin little place, what stands rite at the termination of the Highlands, through which the Niagary runs on its way from Lake Ery to Lake Ontario. The effect is strikin, after follerin the river from the Rapids above the Falls to this place, with the roar of its tumultuous waters constantly in one's ears, and the leapin, angry current constantly before one's eyes, to see it suddenly spread out its broad, smooth bosom in the quiet vale, as placid and calm as if its flow had been unobstructed from its source. Ther is indeed a "change cum over the sperit of its dream" at Queenston, and the traveller is monstrous apt to discover that his thoughts is not wholly without sympathy with the stream.

But I have tuck up a whole letter in tryin to hurry over 'bout seven miles. I'll try to travel further in my next. So no more from

Your frend til deth,
Jos. Jones.

P. S.—I spose you know that they hain't got no Fourth of July in Canady, and I was so cumpletely tuck up with tne wonders of Niagary that I forgot all about it. It's the fust time in my life that that day ever missed a harty welcome from me, and I can't account for it in no other way than bein in this benited country.

LETTER XX.

New York, July 22, 1845.

To Mr. Thompson :—*Dear Sir*—Ther wasn't no grate rush of passengers like ther always is on the North River botes, and nobody didn't git nocked overboard in the confusion and hurryment of gettin aboard of the Chief Justice Robinson. At the ring of the bell we was all on board, and a cumfortabler bote or a more obligin captain ain't afloat on river, lake, or sea, than ours was.

Ther ain't nothin very wonderful to be seed gwine down seven miles on the Niagary to Lake Ontario, except it is the Old Fort Niagary, what's been tuck and re-tuck, and capitilated and surrendered so often, 'mong the French, the Ingins, the British, and the Americans, that it ain't very easy to make out who is got the best rite to it now. It's seed lively times in its day, that old place has; but it's monstrous lonesum now, and they say it's been hanted ever sense they put Billy Morgan in it for blowin the Masons. I hain't got much blief in ghost-stories, but they say it's a positiv fact, and that the pore old feller is to be seed every dark night, dodgin about the dark corners, with a taller-candle in his hand and a Free-mason's apron on, lookin like he wanted to tell sumbody sumthing; but evrybody's so 'fraid of him that he can't git no chance to tell his secret. One thing is very certain 'bout Billy Morgan: if he couldn't keep the Mason's secret, he keeps his own monstrous well.

It was a bright sunshiny day, and the water of the lake as if it wanted to show us how well it could behave itself, after its frollick among the rocks of the Niagary, was as still and quiet as a mill-pond. Our splendid steamer, with its British flag flyin—jest as natural as if it was the banner of a sovereign peeple and had a right to wave "over the land of the free and the home of the brave,"—went spankin along, on its way across the lake to Toronto, while the passengers amused themselves accordin to ther likin. Sum old codgers tuck a set-too 'bout politicks; sum of the gentlemen red books and newspapers; sum smoked ther segars, and sum promenaded with the ladys, while the little ones went to playin romps on the deck, keepin ther mothers in a peck of troubles for fear they mought jump overboard, or brake ther necks climbin on the awnin-posts.

We wasn't long gwine to Toronto, whar we only stopped long enuff to git into another bote, and in a few minits we was under way agin in the steambote 'Sovereign" of the "Royal Mail Line," as they called it, on our way down the lake to Kingston.

The names of things begun to sound monstrous queer to my republican ears, and the red and gold crowns what was painted on the cabin dores, and was sticken about in different places on the bote whar the eagle ought to be, looked odd enuff; but I didn't find that they made the bote go any faster, or that my clothes got any tighter for me, because I was on a British *Sovereign* of the *royal line* gwine to *Kingston*.

One don't see very much to interest him on the lake, as what little is to be seed on the shore is so far off that we don't git much good of it. Hooper and I passed the time very agreeable though, smokin our segars and talkin over what we had seed—now and then pickin up a little fun among the passengers. After tea, and when the moon was up, we was a good deal interested in a courtship what was gwine on, between a young cupple from New York. It seemed

that two very rich familys was tryin very hard to make
a match between a Miss-Nancy sort of a son on one
side, and a Liddy-Languish sort of a daughter on the
other; but neither of the young ones seemed to have
sense enuff to know how to go about it. The old
peeple gin 'em all the chance they could, and helped
'em along now and then, but the young feller seemed
to think more of his sorrel-colored whiskers, what
grow'd all over his unmeanin face, than any thing else;
and the gall, though she didn't seem to have no grate
objections to the arrangement, wasn't willin, or didn't
know how to do all the courtin. The old peeple
managed to keep 'em together pretty well all day, only
when the young spark went down now and then to git
a jewlip; and, in the evenin the feller's daddy made
him go and sing to her; but sich singin I never heard
before—half a ower of it was enuff to kill any young
woman in the world. What effect it did have I can't
say, but he kep it up 'bout six owers, 'thout stoppin to
give the pore gall time to draw a long breth between
his bominable songs. Once or twice the ingine blowd
off the steam, when she couldn't hear his croakin, and
it must really been a grate relief to her. At one
o'clock we went to bed and left him singin the "Minit
gun at Sea," to one of the awfulest sam tunes I ever
heard.

At six o'clock the next mornin we waked up at
Kingston, and as we had but a few minits to stop
before we tuck another bote to go down the Saint
Lawrence, we hurried up into the town to see it. We
had got most up to the grate stone Market House,
what's big enuff for five or six sich towns, when the
Stuard cum runnin after us to ask us if we hadn't left
a watch on the bote. Shore enuff it was Hooper's
gold watch the man had in his hand. When Hooper
offered him a dollar for bringin it to him, he wouldn't
take a cent, and away he went.

'Very well," ses Hooper, " that watch is worth jest

one hundred and fifty dollars more to me, than if it had been left on a New York bote."

After takin a look at the market-house, which is more like a castle than a place to sell meat and vegetables, and which I expect was intended as much for one as the other, we started for the garrison, to see the mornin parade of the sogers. When we got to the gates the 71st rigment of Highland Light Infantry was drillin in the square; but as we went to walk in to see 'em, a ugly-lookin customer, what was standin on gard at the gate, brung his bayonet down within 'bout three inches of my nose.

"Take care," ses I, "Mister! what the thunder is you about?"

He sort o' grinned, and didn't say nothin.

Then Hooper walked upon tother side, and he poked his bayonet rite at him.

"Ain't thar no admission?" ses Hooper.

The feller shuck his hed.

"He must be dum," ses Hooper.

"Or maybe he talks Highland, and can't understand American," ses I.

Jest then a chap with a red cap and sum extra buttons on his cote, cum to the gate, and told us that nobody wasn't allowed to cum in thar, and that we musn't talk to the sentinel on the post; and the feller with the bayonet begun to walk up and down agin as stiff as a handspike, and lookin savage as a meat-axe. By this time the ladys from the bote cum up, and 'fore they know'd thar wasn't no admission, they marched rite through the gate, and the gentlemen all follered 'em. The feller with the bayonet looked monstrous sheepish, but even he couldn't charge bayonet on a plattoon of butiful American galls, and was compelled to surrender to charms such as he wasn't used to seein 'n his own country.

In a few minits after we went in, the rigment was

formed in line—the band struck up, an1 away they marched over a bridge to the barracks on the other side of the river. I couldn't help but think, as I heard the cry of ther bag-pipes, and watched the sad countenances and mechanical movement of them pore sogers, what a sorry life ther's must be—away so far from ther homes and relations—givin ther lives to support a power that only tramples 'em under it's feet. But the monarchical institutions that makes slaves of white men, trains 'em to be contented in ther servile conditions, and teaches 'em to glory in the shallow glitter of a crown that is upheld by ther own sweat and blood.

I would liked monstrous well to tuck a better look at Kingston, but we had no time to spare. After takin a short walk through one or two of the best streets, we went aboard of the steambote Canady, and at seven o'clock we was on our way down the Saint Lawrence.

After passin Fort Henry, what looks a good deal like Governor's Island at New York, we was soon among the Thousand Islands, whar the waters of the Saint Lawrence seems to git lost, and runs in evry direction 'thout havin any shores at all. Sum of these islands is monstrous pretty—the fact is ther's a general assortment of 'em, of all shapes and sizes, and a man would have to be terrible hard to please if he couldn't find sum among 'em to suit his fancy. The water bein scattered all about so, hain't got much current, and runs still and deep, so the bote could pass close to ther sides. One minit we would be sailin by one big enuff for a plantation, and then agin we would be twisten about among sum that wasn't bigger than so many 'ater hills. Who ever counted 'em must had a good deal of patience, but I reckon he wasn't far out of the way. If ther's one ther's at least a thousand of 'em, 1 do blieve.

You remember it was among these islands whar Commodore Bill Johnson sot up for himself durin the Canady rebellion. Bill was a monstrous tall customer in his way, and gin the British a heap of trouble, robbin ther hen-roosts and pig-stys, and skeerin the wimmin and children out of ther senses with his Proclamations. They gin him sum terrible hard chases, but they mought as well looked for a needle in a shuck-pen, as to try to find him in sich a place, and so Bill weathered 'em out, and never was cotched. The Captain of the bote pinted out the place whar he burnt the steambote Robert Peel, and robbed all the passengers; but he sed that "Fort Wallace," whar he used to date his Proclamations, was like Billy Morgan —nobody could tell what had cum of it.

After gettin out of the thickest of the Islands, we cum to Brockville, whar the bote stopped for a few minits, and then we passed Prescott's Landin, and the captain pinted out sum old stone ruins what he sed was the place whar the British sogers fit the wind-mill, and tuck the patriots prisoners what they hung at Fort Henry. None of these towns along here on the Canady side ain't no grate shakes, and all of 'em makes a monstrous bad contrast with the smart bisness-lookin towns on the American side, showin plain enuff that our institutions is best calculated to promote the prosperity of the peeple.

It was a very butiful day, and the scenery as we passed from Island to Island, and Lake to Lake, was very butiful. Sumtimes we could almost reach the branches of the cedar-trees from the deck of the bote, then agin we was in the middle of Lake Howe, or sum other lake whar we couldn't hardly see the shores. Most of the passengers was delighted with the interestin objects that presented themselves in rapid succession. Jest before we got into the Rapids I happened to notice that New York chap what was courtin the young lady—the river didn't have no curiosities for him—and thar he sot on the bench by the side of the pore gall, readin Shakspear to her, and actin it as he went along, while she was sleepin with her mouth wide open, and her green vale over her face to keep the flies off. Pore creater, he had sung her almost to deth the night before, and now he was recitin what little life she had left out of her. The bominable fool didn't know she was sleepin til she begun to snore pretty considerable loud, and then he got up and shut up his book, and went and tuck sumthing to drink. Thinks I, if that's the way peeple courts in these parts, they'd stand a monstrous pore chance of gettin a wife among the Georgia galls.

Bimeby we cum to the Long Sow Rapids, as they call 'em, and you may depend it don't take very much steam to go down 'em. It made the har stand on my hed to go whirlin eend for eend as we did down that racin current, whar the water runs so swift that it makes one's hed swim to look at it, and the bote jest takes her hed and goes whar and how she pleases in spite of all the paddle-wheels and rudder can do. Sumtimes, when we cum to a short turn, we would cum in a ace of runnin rite spang on the rock-shore, and the bote would slew over to one side like it was gwine to spill us all out, and the fust thing we would know while we was all holdin our breth to keep from gettin drownded, we would find ourselves gwine like a streak of lightnin, starn fust, down the next stretch. It was monstrous fine ridin, and the little boys and galls danced and clapped ther hands with joy, but the grown peeple wore monstrous long faces sumtimes, and opened ther eyes tight; while the captain and the man at the wheel had ther hands full to keep the bote off the rocks. The captain sed it wouldn't been so bad if the wind hadn't blowd so hard down the river.

After gettin through the Rapids, we had a little

slower and safer travellin through Lake Saint Francis to Cooto du Lack, whar we arriv a little after dark. Here we was to take stages, sixteen miles, to the Cascades. But they wasn't sich stages as we have in Georgy, not by a long shot. They was sumthing between a New York Omnibus and a Noa's Ark, and would carry 'bout as many passengers as either of 'em. Before the bote got to the landin the bell rung for the number of coaches it would take to carry us, and by the time we got on shore thar they all was, reddy to start. I don't know how many of us, men, wimmin, and children they stowed inside and on the top of each one of 'em, but six coaches, carried 'bout a hundred of us, bag and baggage, without the least difficulty.

Hooper, and me, and five or six more, tuck seats on top, behind the drivers, so we could smoke our segars Pop went the whips, and in the next minit we was rollin along over a plank rode, at the rate of six miles a ower, as smooth as if we was in a ralerode car, and a monstrous sight comfortabler. It was the delightfulest travelin I ever had in my life. The plank rode was as level and as clean as a barn floor, and the little Canadian hosses trotted off with us, 'thout ever stoppin or movin ther heds or tails out of the same position, durin the whole drive, only when we stopped twice to water. The scenery was butiful. On our right was the broad Saint Lawrence, shinin like a sheet of silver in the moonlight, while evry now and then we could look down onto the roofs of the little vine-covered cabins what was dotted all along on both sides of the road, with ther little narrow fields lea lin back to the woods and hills on the left, or the river on the right. Now and then we would cum to a house bigger than the rest, what had shade-trees and a big wooden cross out before the dore, whar the priests lived. But evrybody was gone to bed, and the little cottages themselves seemed to be sleepin in the calm moonlight.

Three owers—what didn't seem longer than one ower in a Georgia stage, whar the horses is wadin nee-deep in the sand, and one don't hear the wheels more'n once or twice in a mile, when they happen to run over a pine root—brung us to the Cascades. After shuckin out the passengers and baggage, and gettin all the children and band-boxes gethered up, they tuck us down a steep hill to the steambote, whar we went to bed.

In the mornin, when we waked up, we found ourselves in the butiful Lake Saint Louis, on our way to La Chin. We got up in time to see sum of the butiful islands—among 'em Nun's Island, what stands high out of the water, and is covered with houses and little plantations. On the highest part of the Nun's Island is a monstrous big cross, what we could see a long ways off, remindin us that we was in a Catholic country. By seven o'clock we was at La Chin, whar we tuck sum more stages over a good rode, eight miles, to Montreal.

This is another butiful country. The rode runs all the way through one continual string of cottages, what stands close by the rode, with little plantations 'bout as big as a good-sized Georgia turnip-patch, runnin down to the river on one side, and back to the Green Mounting of Montreal on the other. It was early in the mornin, and the people was jest gwine to 'ther work; and it was odd enuff to see the men with ther blue frocks, and ther red caps stickin on one side of ther heds, geerin up ther teams, and the pretty little barefooted French galls, with ther short petticotes, gwine to milk the cows. From the top of the stage we could look rite down into the chamber winders, and evry now and then I could see a pair of bright eyes peepin out through the mornin-glorys and trumpet-flowers at us. The whole eight miles was a panorama of buty, and glad as I was to see Montreal, I would liked it very well if the rode had been a little longer.

But the wheels of our coach was soon rollin over the wooden pavements of the city, and in a few minits more we found ourselves all safe and sound at the Exchange Hotel, with good appetites for our breckfusts So no more from

Your frend til deth,
Jos. Jones

LETTER XXI.

New York, July 24, 18 5.

To Mr. Thompson:—*Dear Sir*—After brushin up ι little and gettin a fust rate breckfust, we tuck a stroll through the town to see the curiosities. I could spend a week very well in this city, lookin about among the churches and nunneries and soger's quarters and other public places, but as I didn't have no time to spare, I had jest to give evry thing a passin glance, 'thout stoppin long enuff to know much about it. Under sich circumstances you musn't expect me to give you much of a description of Montryal.

If I was travelin like Mr. Dickens or Captain Marryatt, or any of them English travellers, jest to make a book for a peeple who is so blinded with prejudice that they can't see any thing but faults, it wouldn't make no difference whether I know'd much about the things I described or not; all I'd have to do would jest be to go ahed and find all the fault I could with evrybody, and with evry thing I heard of or seed sot down in the gide-books; and the further I cum from the truth, so I went on the black side of it, the better I would please. But I ain't a writin for no sich peeple, and I'm not gwine to find fault with what I don't know nothin about, jest for the sake of ault-findin.

The fust place we went to was the grate French Cathedral in Notre Dame street, a regular Noah's Ark of a meetin-house you may depend, what holds twenty thousand peeple 'thout crowdin 'em, and takes two hundred and eighty-five steps to go to the top cf its towers. Ther was a grate many picters and sum wax figers in it, but ther names was all so outlandish that I couldn't make 'em out. After lookin about in the church for awhile, we went to the Grey Nunnery. Here we seed lots of nuns and sisters of charity takin care of little chiidren what had no fathers and mothers, and of sich peeple what had no money and no frends to do for 'em. Then we went to the Hotel Dieu, what Maria Monk gives sich a terrible bad account of in her book; then to the Bishop's Chapel, which is one of the finest churches on the Continent; and then to the Parlyment House, whar the Canady peeple make sich laws as ther masters over the water don't care about troublin themselves with. The bildin ain't no grate shakes, compared to what sum of our state capitols is, but it's rigged off in mighty fine style inside, with red velvet and gold-leaf, to keep the peeple in mind of what monstrous fine peeple ther Royal masters is. The gentleman what show'd is in, pinted out the portraits of sum of the kings an queens and other grate characters what was hangin out, and ax'd us if we would like to take a seat on the throne whar the representative of British majesty sot on grate occasions. Rather than to make him feel bad, when he was so perlite and obligin to us, I tuck a seat for a minit, and I couldn't help but think how I would like to give the castin vote on a proposition to annex Canady to the United States. Sich a measure of human emancipation would be worth all the laws ever made in that house.

From the Parlyment House we went to the barracks whar the sogers was. Ther was a everlastin lot of 'em—in fact they was all over the city, and ther red cotes and shinin bayonets was to be seen at evry corner, in evry street and evry ally. They may be sed to be the *strikin* feater of Canady—and one can't help but wonder what upon yeath England can want of territory what takes sich a terrible lot of money and sogers to keep it. What a difference, too, ther is in the sogers' ~de in Canady and in our country. While our sogers

is arm,ed and fed to *protect* the peeple, their's is put
thar to *subject* the peeple who supports 'em. It's enuff
to make a man's blood bile, to see them swarms of
grate lazy hulks sunin themselves about on the pavements, and loungin round ther quarters, waitin like
blood-hounds jest to be sot loose on the pore peeple,
to tear 'em to pieces for the bone that they git from the
table of ther masters. And the pore devils ain't very
well kept nuther, for I seed lots of 'em without the
sign of a pair of trouses to ther legs any more'n a
Seminole Ingin, and with nothin but a sort of red-plad
huntin shirt on, that jest cum down to ther nees.

In the afternoon we tuck a drive round the mounting
to see the guvernor's house, and at five o'clock in
the evenin tuck passage in the steambote Queen for
Quebeck. The scenery on the Saint Lawrence was
very butiful, and we sot up til twelve o'clock to see
Saint Peter's Lake. About seven o'clock the next
mornin we arriv at Quebeck, and druv to Payne's
Hotel in the Place de Armes.

The fust place I wanted to go to was the famous
Gibralter of America, the fortress of Quebeck; but
Mr. Payne sed we'd have to wait til he could git a
permit for us to visit the Citadel; so we tuck a calash
and went out to the Plains of Abraham, whar the grate
battle was fit what lost France her Northern possesshuns
in America. I don't remember to what Saint the gate
we went out at belonged, but that doesn't matter—a
Frenchman tuck us to the Plains, whar we had a quiet
view of that place whar so much gallantry was displayed, and so much blood spilled on the 14th of Sep-
tember, 1759. It's a butiful place to fight a battle, and
I can't see what ever possessed the brave Montcalm
with his undisciplined troops, to give Wolf and his
British regulars battle thar, when he mought have
defended himself so much better in his works, even
poor and weak as they was then. It was a hard piece
of bisness, that contest, in which France lost her Gene-

ral and her cause; and though the English may try til dooms-day to make the French Canadians forgit the injustice they have suffered, by givin ther Catholic churches all sorts of priviliges, and by bildin monu ments, like they have in the Palace Gardin' with Wolf's name on one side and Montcalm's on the other, tryin to make the honors of that day *easy* between 'em,—they never can make loyal, contented subjects out of 'em as long as Cape Diamond stands whar it does. While they're in the reach of British bayonets they don't make any fuss, but rebellion is stickin out of 'em all over, and the fust right good chance they git they'll give ther conquerors plenty to do to keep 'em under. If anybody wants any proof of ther bad feelins agin the British, jest let 'em look at Wolf's Monument what stands on the spot whar he fell. The words "HERE DIED WOLF VICTORIOUS," that was cut deep in the solid marble, is pecked and battered so, rite in sight of the sentry on the walls of the citadel, that if it wasn't for the gide-book nobody could tell what was on it. Every countryman that crosses over the Plains with a basket of eggs for the market, gives it a pelt with a stone, til the whole side of the monument is almost nocked off.

After dinner we got a permit to go in the citadel, but they sent a sargeant with us, who watched us all the time like he was 'fraid we was gwine to tetch off the powder-magazine or spike ther cannons. We musn't go here, and strangers wasn't 'lowd to go thar; and if we went to go up on sum of ther batteries, as they called 'em, voices would cum from evry loop-hole and look-out, to tell us we musn't go thar. They seemed to be dreadful 'fraid we'd find out sumthing. It's a monstrous stanchious place, and commands one of the finest views in the world. One looks down upon the noble Saint Lawrence at his feet, and over the minerets and towers of the churches, and the roofs of the old and curious-lookin stone houses of the upper town, and on the other side, at the ruins of more'n a thousand houses in the Saint Rock District, beyond which the butiful Saint Charles winds its way to mingle its waters with the waters of the Saint Lawrence in the grate basin below, after which they flow away together til they find the sea. All together, Quebeck is a curious and interestin place. It looks like it belonged to another Continent and to another age of the world; and when one looks upon its power and its buty, and remembers that it stands on the boundry of civilization, close to the edge of the wild, unexplored wilderness that extends northward to the regions of everlastin freeze-to-deth, he is apt to exclaim with the poet—" Time's noblest empire is the last."

Sum of the officers—who we found to be monstrous clever fellers, though sum of 'em was dredful green— invited us to see a grand review on the Esplanade. It was a very considerable of a show, and convinced me that the British sogers is under fust rate discipline; but I couldn't help but think how terribly they would git ther fethers siled in a Ingin campain in the hammocks of Florida. We spent the evenin in walkin about through the streets lookin at the public bildins and odd-lookin houses.

* * * * * * * *

The next day was Sunday, and we went to the French Cathedral, what was so full that it was sum time before we could git through the crowd of men and wimmin that was settin on the steps and away out in the street, stringin beads and talkin Lattin to themselves. Bimeby a man cum and tuck us into a fust rate seat, whar we could see and hear all that was gwine on. Ther was any number of priests dressed out in red, white, and black pettycotes, and lots of organ-musick, singin and preachin; but the only word I understood the whole time was "Kebeck, Kebeck," which run all through the sermon.

* * * * * * * * * *

About five o'clock we tuck passage in the Queen

agin for Montryal, whar we arriv the next mornin about breckfust time. As no bote didn't leave til evenin, we tuck another round through Montryal, and spent the time very agreeably til five in the evenin, when we started in the Prince Albert for La Prairy, on our way home.

The steambote Prince Albert ain't no compliment to the Queen's husband; and if his highness's popilarity in Canady is to be estimated by the quality of the bote they have named after him, one would suppose that he didn't stand very high among the loyal Canadians. It ain't much bigger than a New York ferry-bote, and its accommodations is but little better. Ther was a good many passengers, most of 'em Irish emmygrants what had cum to Canady, and was now cumin over into the States. Pore peeple, they was all huddled up together, bag and baggage, on the forecastle, and wasn't 'lowed to take the air on the deck no more'n if they'd been so many cattle. My hart aked for one pore family. The man was dyin with the ship-fever, while his wife and children and young sister, a butiful girl about sixteen, was weepin over him. He lay on the deck on a coarse, dirty mattrass, his pore wife supportin him while the tears poured down her pale cheeks, and his dyin hed was rocked to its last sleep on her heavin bosom. His sister was neelin by his side and bathin his parched lips with water mingled with her tears, and the two oldest children, little girls, was clingin round him, cryin as if ther harts would brake. The youngest child, a fat little boy 'bout two years old, with cheeks as red as the apple he had in his hand, looked at his dyin father and then at his mother, as if he spected sumthing was the matter; but the pore little feller was a stranger to the bitter sorrow that was agonizin the harts of that mournin group.

The emmygrants made as much room round the dyin man as they could, to give him air, and sum of 'em tried to console the family. The sister tuck the cross what she wore round her neck, and put it to her brotner's lips—he kissed it and tried to speak, and then closed his eyes. In a minit after I seed him gaspin for breth, and a loud scream from the wimmin told that he was ded.

The people laid him strait in the bed, whar he remained til the bote arriv at La Parairy.

"It was hard," sed one of the emmygrants as they was leavin the bote, "that pore Dennis should die widout ever puttin his fut in Amirica."

"Ah!" ses another, "he's gone to a better place, rest his soul!"

At La Parairy we tuck the cars for St. John's, leavin the pore wife to berry her ded husband in a strange land; but I couldn't go til I had gin her a dollar to help her in her ower of distress. The look she gin me was more than a recompense for all the good actions I ever done in my life.

The steambote Saranack tuck us through Lake Champlain, whar we seed sum of the finest scenery and interestin places, among the rest the ruins of old Fort Ticonderogy what Ethen Allen tuck from the British by sich high authority in the Revolutionary war. Durin the day we stopped to git sum wood at a place called Burlington, in Vermont, and Hooper and me went ashore to look at the place. But we hadn't got more'n ten steps from the bote when we seed a thunderin grate big sign stickin up over the rode, with "No Smokin allowd here!" "Cus the place," ses Hooper, who had a segar in his mouth, "Majer, let's shake the dust from our feet and go back to the bote; I can't trust myself in the hands of no peeple what would stick up sich a sign as that at a steambote landin,"—and back we went.

* * * * * * * * *

After gwine aboard, the fust thing that tuck my attention was a chap what was rootin round among the baggage after sumthing. I didn't like his looks much, so I jest kep my eye on him to see what the feller was after. Bimeby I seed him grab hold of my trunk. Thinks I that's makin rayther too free, and ses I—" What upon yeath is you up to, Mister, with my trunk?"

"Is that your trunk?" ses he.

"Well," ses I, "I reckon it ain't nobody elses."

"Very well," ses he; "I jest wanted to know what was in it, that's all."

"The mischief you do!" ses I; "I'd like to know what bisness you've got with what's in my trunk."

"I spose ther ain't nothin contraband in it," ses he.

"What the thunder's that?" ses I.

"Why, nothin smuggled."

Smugglin means stealin, down in Georgia, and when he sed that my dander was up in a minit. I looked at the feller what was beginnin to grin all over his face, and ses I—

"Do you mean to insiniwate the likes of that to me, you infernal, imperent cus?"

"Cum, cum, Mister," ses he, "it ain't no use to git into no passion. The law's the law, and ther ain't no use tryin to git round it."

"I'll tell you what," ses I, "I don't know nothin about your law out in these parts; but I know one thing, and that is, if you jest insiniwate to me that I'm a thief, or that I've got any thing what don't belong to me in my trunk, I'll histe you overboard off this bote 'fore you can have time to say yer prayers."

And I was jest gettin reddy to pitch into the oudacious cus, when Hooper cum up and tuck hold of me—

"Shaw, Majer," ses he, "don't git riled—it's the custom——"

"Cus ther customs," ses I; "I know it's a Yankee custom to meddle with evrybody's bisness but ther own. But I'll larn 'em better than to interfere with my consarns."

"It's the custom-house officer, I mean," ses Hooper, "what wants to see all right with the baggage, to keep peeple from cheatin the government. It's only the tariff bisness what you whigs voted for at the last elec tion. It's protection, Majer; and I'm sure you're too good a whig to make a rumpus about it."

By this time I begun to see into the bisness, and of course I hadn't nothin more to say. But you may depend I was hot for a few minits; and what made it worse, the custom-house officer, as he called himself, kep all the time laughin at me like he would bust his sides.

We shuck hands, however, and made evry thing strait. He didn't open my trunk when I told him that it didn't have nothin in it but my clothes, and sum curiosities what I'd picked up in my travels; but you may depend, whenever he cum across a Dutchman or any outlandish foreigner with a big trunk, he made 'em show up. And, shore enuff, he cum across one feller what had a trunk full of English broadcloths and silks, what he was tryin to smuggle into the States. The officer tuck 'em all from him, and how they settled it I don't know; but the feller was quite as much out of humour with the officer as I was.

After runnin Lake Champlain out to the little eend of nothin, til ther wasn't water enuff to float a bread-tray, and we had to dodge the boat along among the hay-cocks that the peeple was makin in the marsh-meadow what we was gwine through, we cum to a place called White Hall, about four o'clock in the evenin. Here we tuck a canal-bote for Mechanicsville.

In the fore part of the evenin, while we was all on deck, evry thing went on pretty well, except 'bout evry five minits we would cum to a bridge, when we would all have to drap down flat on the deck; and bein as it was covered with men, wimmin, and children, as thick as we could stand, the dodgin was rather awkward bisness, and brung us sumtimes in rather close contact with strange passengers.

One old feller what was a little hard of hearin, and was bissy talkin politicks with his back turned the rong way, didn't hear the word "Bridge!" and the fust thing he knowd, kerslosh he went heels over hed, rite into the water. It was monstrous well for him that it wasn't no deeper, or he'd never had another vote in this world—for he couldn't swim a lick, and the hoses was so pore and hard in the mouth that it tuck 'em 'bout ten minits to take in sail, so as to stop the bote. The captain got him out though, and the old chap went below for the balance of the night.

* * * * * * * * * *

They packed us into hammocks, as they called 'em, to sleep—but I'd been monstrous glad to exchanged mine for the worst hammock in Florida. It was nothin more than a layer of canvass, then a passenger, then a layer of dirty sheet, then another layer of canvass, and then another layer of passenger and another sheet, and so on to the top. Ther was no sich thing as turnin over 'thout nockin yer nees into the ribs of the man above you, and when you was once packed in, ther was no gettin out til mornin. I never cum so near suffocatin in my life, and never was so anxious to see the break of day before. The wimmin and children was all packed into one eend of the bote, with nothin but a blanket between us and them; and sich other musick I never heard before—it was worse than a concert of cats all night.

'Bout sunrise we got to the place whar we tuck the cars for Troy. Here we tuck a steamer to Albany, and from Albany we wasn't long cumin to New York in the Knickerbocker.

So here I am, and by the time you hear from me agin I will be home in old Georgia. No more at present from

Your frend til deth,
Jos. Jones.

LETTER XXII.

Pineville, August 6, 1845.

To Mr. Thompson:—*Dear Sir*—Once more I take my pen to tell you that I arriv here safe and sound last Friday night. Nothin didn't happen in the jurney from New York to Pineville out of the usual course of travellin incidents, and to tell the truth, after I sot my face for home, nothin of a common nater—nothin short of a terrible railrode collision or the bustin of a steambote biler could tuck my mind off from thinkin of the joys that was waitin me at home. * * * *

Pore Mary couldn't hardly contain herself for joy, at seein me once more; and old Miss Stallins had to have a fit of the highstericks, jest to show how glad she was. The galls all tuck on monstrous, and 'tween bringin the old woman to, and kissin the baby and Mary, and shakin hands with the niggers and nabors, and tellin evrybody 'bout my travels, I hain't had time to do nothin else ever sense I cum home. * * *

Nothin of importance hain't tuck place on the plantation sense I left, only the deth of pore old Moma. She died 'bout three weeks ago, leavin her dyin blessin for me. Pore old creter, she was very sorry she couldn't see me before she died. Well, she's out of her troubles now, and I have the satisfaction to know that she never was treated bad, and never suffered for any thing while she lived; and as sumthing bad always has to happen when a body's away from home, I spose I ought to be satisfied that it's no worse than it is. I'm certain that no one on the plantation was better prepared or more willin to go than good old Moma, and no one could been so well spared by us all. * * * *

The crap looks fust rate, and the stock is all in good order, and evry thing looks like good attention had been paid to it by the overseer, who ses he hain't got no complaints to make agin none of the niggers except old Saul, what sot the woods afire in one of his possum-hunts, and burnt 'bout twenty panels of fence. Old Saul always was the most bominable possum-hunter and fish-trapper I ever seed in my life; but he's too old to quarrel with him now, and besides, he's a monstrous good old feller. Sum of the little niggers has been cuttin up sum antics, and had to have a little buckin to keep 'em from spilin 'fore I cum home. But on the whole things has gone on much better than I expected, and I've made a proclamation of a general pardon for all offences, and gin 'em all the presents what I bought for 'em in New York.

If you could see Prissy with her New York riggins on, you would think she was the proudest nigger in Georgia. She don't want to do nothin now but go to church and take the baby out a visitin the nabors. Little Henry Clay's grow'd a heap and can begin to talk rite smart, and with his new-fashioned Knickerbocker cote on, and his red velvet cap with a gold tossel on it, what I brung from New York for him, he is the cuninest-lookin little feller you ever did see.

The galls is all tickeled to deth with ther new-fashioned brestpins, and Mary likes her dresses fust rate, only she ses they are too expensive, and won't do to wear until next winter. Pore gall, she ses she never did think she loved me so much til I was away from her, and she ses she wouldn't let me go agin not for all the world. Would you blieve it, Mr. Thompson, she fell away more'n ten pounds while I was gone, jest grievin about me. Her mother ses she never did see anybody take on so, specially when she red in the papers 'bout any railrode accidents or steambote explosions.

Well, it's all over now, and I don't think we will ever be separated agin. Give me home after all. I've travelled more'n four thousand miles—I've seed sum fourteen states, and more'n five hundred cities and towns—I've seed the northern peeple, in ther cities, in ther towns and in the country, and though I've got a good deal better opinion of 'em sense I've been among 'em a little, than I had afore, still I say, give me old Georgia yet. We hain't got so many cities, nor sich fine ones—we hain't got so much public improvements nd all them sort o' things—but we've got a plenty of vry thing that is necessary to make us independent and happy. We've got as fine a soil, a finer climate, as smart men, and handsumer wimmin than any other country in the world, and nothin can hinder us from bein one of the greatest states in the Union, if we go to work as we ought to, and develop our own resources.

I blieve a jurney to the North is calculated to do a southern man a grate deal of good, if he goes thar in the rite sperit and for the rite purpose. He will see thar a grate deal to be proud of as a American, and much to be ashamed of as a white man. He will find all sorts of peeple thar—sum that is examples of patriotism, intelligence, and enterprise, and sum that ain't no manner of account on the face of the yeath, only to kick up a eternal rumpus and keep the world in a everlastin stew about ther new-fangled fooleries; and though, as a peeple the Northerners is very different from us in a grate many things, the majority of 'em is actuated by the same impulses, and is strivin on for wealth and power like all the rest of the world. Ther's a good deal of ignorance and prejudice at the North, to be shore, specially about matters what don't consarn ther own interests; but it is to be hoped that whar ther is so much patriotism and intelligence, they will sum day larn to mind ther own bisness, and leave other peeple's consarns to be regulated by ther own consciences and ther own judgments. Hopin that we may both live to see that day, I sign myself

Your frend til deth,   Jos. Jones.

THE END.

CATALOGUE OF BOOKS

PUBLISHED BY

T. B. PETERSON AND BROTHERS,

PHILADELPHIA, PA.,

And for sale by all Booksellers.

☞ Any of the books named in this Catalogue, will be sent by mail, to any one, to any place, at once, post-paid, on remitting the price of the ones wanted to T. B. PETERSON & BROTHERS, Philadelphia, Pa.

CHEAPEST BOOK HOUSE IN THE WORLD

Is at the Publishing and Bookselling Establishment of

T. B. PETERSON & BROTHERS,

No. 306 Chestnut Street, Philadelphia, Pa.

T. B. PETERSON & BROTHERS, Philadelphia, are the American publishers of the popular and fast-selling books written by MRS. EMMA D. E. N. SOUTHWORTH, MRS. ANN S. STEPHENS, MRS. CAROLINE LEE HENTZ, MISS ELIZA A. DUPUY, MRS. C. A. WARFIELD, MRS. HENRY WOOD, Q. K. P. DOESTICKS, EMERSON BENNETT, T. S. ARTHUR, GEORGE LIPPARD, HANS BREITMANN (CHARLES G. LELAND), JAMES A. MAITLAND, CHARLES DICKENS, SIR WALTER SCOTT, CHARLES LEVER, WILKIE COLLINS, MRS. C. J. NEWBY, JUSTUS LIEBIG, W. H. MAXWELL, ALEXANDER DUMAS, GEORGE W. M. REYNOLDS, SAMUEL WARREN, HENRY COCKTON, FREDRIKA BREMER, T. ADOLPHUS TROLLOPE, MADAME GEORGE SAND, EUGENE SUE, MISS PARDOE, FRANK FAIRLEGH, W. H. AINSWORTH, FRANK FORRESTER (HENRY W. HERBERT), MISS ELLEN PICKERING, CAPTAIN MARRYATT, MRS. GRAY, G. P. R. JAMES, HENRY MORFORD, GUSTAVE AIMARD, and hundreds of other authors; as well as of DOW'S PATENT SERMONS, HUMOROUS AMERICAN BOOKS, and MISS LESLIE'S, MISS WIDDIFIELD'S, THE YOUNG WIFE'S, MRS. GOODFELLOW'S, MRS. HALE'S, PETERSONS', THE NATIONAL, FRANCATELLI'S, THE FAMILY SAVE-ALL, QUEEN OF THE KITCHEN, and all the best and popular Cook Books published.

T. B. PETERSON & BROTHERS take pleasure in calling the attention of the entire Reading Community, as well as of all their Customers, and every Bookseller, News Agent, and Book Buyer, as well as of the entire Book Trade everywhere, to the fact that they are now publishing a large number of cloth and paper-covered Books, in very attractive style, including a series of 25 cent, 50 cent, 75 cent, $1.00, $1.50, $1.75, and $2.00 Books, in new style covers and bindings, making them large books for the money, and bringing them before the Reading Public by liberal advertising. They are new books, and are cheap editions of the most popular and most saleable books published, are written by the best American and English authors, and are presented in a very attractive style, printed from legible type, on good paper, and are especially adapted to suit all who love to read good books, as well as for all General Reading, and they will be found for sale by all Booksellers, and at Hotel Stands, Railroad Stations and in the Cars. They are in fact the most popular series of works of fiction ever published, retailing at 25 cents, 50 cents, 75 cents, $1.00, $1.50, $1.75, and $2.00 each, as they comprise the writings of the best and most popular authors in the world, all of which will be sold by us to the trade at very low prices, and also at retail to everybody. Send for a Catalogue of these books at once.

☞ Enclose a draft for five, ten, twenty, fifty, or one hundred dollars, or more, to us in a letter, and write for what books you wish, and on receipt of the money, or a satisfactory reference, the books will be packed and sent to you at once, in any way you may direct, with circulars and show-bills of the books to post up.

☞ All Books named in Petersons' Catalogue will be found for sale by all Booksellers, or copies of any one book, or more, or all of them, will be sent to any one, at once, to any place, per mail, post-paid, or free of freight, on remitting the retail price of the books wanted to T. B. PETERSON & BROTHERS, Philadelphia.

☞ WANTED.—A Bookseller, News Agent, or Canvasser, in every city, town or village on this Continent, to engage in the sale of Petersons' New and Popular Fast Selling Books, on which large sales, and large profits can be made.

☞ Booksellers, Librarians, News Agents, Canvassers, Pedlers, and all other persons, who may want any of Petersons' Popular and Fast Selling Books, will please address their orders and letters, at once, to meet with immediate attention, to

T. B. PETERSON & BROTHERS, PUBLISHERS,
306 CHESTNUT STREET, PHILADELPHIA, PA.

T. B. PETERSON AND BROTHERS' NEW BOOKS.

Booksellers, News Agents, and all others in want of good and fast-selling books will please send in their orders at once.

ÉMILE ZOLA'S NEW AND GREAT WORKS.

L'Assommoir. By *Emile Zola*. The Greatest Novel ever printed. Price 75 cents in paper cover, or $1.00 in morocco cloth, black and gold.

The Markets of Paris; or, *Le Ventre de Paris*. By *Emile Zola*. Price 75 cents in paper cover, or $1.25 in morocco cloth, black and gold.

The Conquest of Plassans; or, *La Conquete de Plassans*. By *Emile Zola*. Price 75 cents in paper cover, or $1.25 in cloth, black and gold.

The Rougon-Macquart Family; or, *La Fortune Des Rougon*. By *Emile Zola*. Price 75 cents in paper cover, or $1.25 in cloth, black and gold.

The Abbé's Temptation; or, *La Faute De L'Abbe Mouret*. By *Emile Zola*. Price 75 cents in paper cover, or $1.25 in cloth, black and gold.

Hélène, a Love Episode; or, *Une Page D'Amour*. By *Emile Zola*. Price 75 cents in paper cover, or $1.25 in morocco cloth, black and gold.

HENRY GREVILLE'S GREAT NOVELS.

Dosia. A *Russian Story*. By *Henry Gréville*, author of "Markof."
Philomène's Marriages. With Author's Preface. By *Henry Gréville*.
Pretty Little Countess Zina. By *Henry Gréville*, author of "Dosia."
Marrying Off a Daughter. A Love Story. By *Henry Gréville*.

Above are in paper cover, price 75 cents each, or in cloth, at $1.25 each.

Savéli's Expiation. A Powerful Novel. By Henry Gréville.
Dournof. A Russian Story. By Henry Gréville, author of "Dosia."
Bonne-Marie. A Tale of Normandy and Paris. By Henry Gréville.
A Friend; or, "L'Ami." By Henry Gréville, author of "Dosia."
Sonia. A Love Story. By Henry Gréville, author of "Dosia."
Gabrielle; or, The House of Maurèze. By Henry Gréville.

Above are in paper cover, price 50 cents each, or in cloth, at $1.00 each.

Markof, the Russian Violinist. A Russian Story. By Henry Gréville. One large volume, 12mo., cloth, price $1.50, or paper cover, 75 cents.

MRS. BURNETT'S LOVE STORIES.

Kathleen. A Love Story. By Mrs. Frances Hodgson Burnett.
A Quiet Life. By Mrs. Frances Hodgson Burnett, author of "Theo."
Miss Crespigny. A Charming Love Story. By author of "Kathleen."
Theo. A Love Story. By author of "Kathleen," "Miss Crespigny," etc.
Pretty Polly Pemberton. By author of "Kathleen," "Theo," etc.

Above are in paper cover, price 50 cents each, or in cloth, at $1.00 each.

Jarl's Daughter and Other Tales. By Mrs. Burnett. Price 25 cents.
Lindsay's Luck. By Mrs. Frances Hodgson Burnett. Price 25 cents.

☞ Above Books will be sent, postage paid, on receipt of Retail Price, by T. B. Peterson & Brothers, Philadelphia, Pa. (A)

T. B. PETERSON AND BROTHERS' NEW BOOKS.

BY AUTHOR OF "A HEART TWICE WON."

A Heart Twice Won; or, Second Love. *A Love Story.* By Mrs. Elizabeth Van Loon. Morocco cloth, black and gold. Price $1.50.
Under the Willows; or, The Three Countesses. *By Mrs. Elizabeth Van Loon*, author of "A Heart Twice Won." Cloth, and gold. Price $1.50.
The Shadow of Hampton Mead. *A Charming Story.* By Mrs. Elizabeth Van Loon, author of "A Heart Twice Won." Cloth. Price $1.50.

NEW AND GOOD BOOKS BY BEST AUTHORS.

The Earl of Mayfield. *Sixth Edition Now Ready.* Complete in one large duodecimo volume, morocco cloth, black and gold, price $1.50.
The Last Athenian. By Victor Rydberg. Translated from the Swedish. Large 12mo. volume, near 600 pages, cloth, black and gold, price $1.75.
The Count de Camors. *The Man of the Second Empire.* By Octave Feuillet. Price 75 cents in paper cover, or $1.25 in morocco cloth.
Major Jones's Courtship. *Author's New, Rewritten, and Enlarged Edition.* By Major Joseph Jones. 21 Illustrations. Price 75 cents.
Rancy Cottem's Courtship. By author of "Major Jones's Courtship." *Author's Edition.* 8 Illustrations. Price 50 cents.
Angèle's Fortune. By André Theuriet. Paper cover, 75 cents, cloth $1.25.
St. Maur; or, An Earl's Wooing. Paper cover, 75 cents, cloth $1.25.

NEW BOOKS BY THE VERY BEST AUTHORS.

The following books are all printed on tinted paper, and are each issued in uniform style, in square 12mo. form. Price Fifty Cents each in Paper Cover, or $1.00 each in Morocco Cloth, Black and Gold.

The Little Countess. By Octave Feuillet, author of "Count De Camors."
The Amours of Phillippe; or, Phillippe's Love Affairs, by Octave Feuillet.
Sybil Brotherton. A Novel. By Mrs. Emma D. E. N. Southworth.
The Red Hill Tragedy. By Mrs. Emma D. E. N. Southworth.
Fanchon the Cricket; or, La Petite Fadette. By George Sand.
Carmen. By Prosper Merimee. *Book the Opera was dramatized from.*
Miss Margery's Roses. A Charming Love Story. By Robert C. Meyers.
The Days of Madame Pompadour. By Gabrielle De St. Andre.
Father Tom and the Pope; or, A Night at the Vatican. Illustrated.
Madeleine. A Charming Love Story. Jules Sandeau's Prize Novel.
Madame Pompadour's Garter. A Romance of the Reign of Louis XV.
A Woman's Mistake; or, Jacques de Trévannes. A Charming Love Story.
The Story of Elizabeth. By Miss Thackeray, daughter of W. M. Thackeray.
The Matchmaker. By Beatrice Reynolds. A Charming Love Story.
Two Ways to Matrimony; or, Is it Love? or, False Pride.
That Girl of Mine. By the author of "That Lover of Mine."
Bessie's Six Lovers. A Charming Love Story. By Henry Peterson.
That Lover of Mine. By the author of "That Girl of Mine."

Above are in paper cover, price 50 cents each, or in cloth, at $1.00 each.

☞ Above Books will be sent, postage paid, on Receipt of Retail Price, by T. B. Peterson & Brothers, Philadelphia, Pa. (13)

T. B. PETERSON AND BROTHERS' PUBLICATIONS.

☞ Orders solicited from Booksellers, Librarians, News Agents, and all others in want of good and fast-selling books. ☜

MRS. EMMA D. E. N. SOUTHWORTH'S WORKS.

Complete in forty-three large duodecimo volumes, bound in morocco cloth, gilt back, price $1.75 each; or $75.25 a set, each set is put up in a neat box.

The Phantom Wedding; or, The Fall of the House of Flint,............$1 75
Self-Raised; From the Depths..$1 75
Ishmael; or, In the Depths,.... 1 75
The Mother-in-Law,............... 1 75
The Fatal Secret,................. 1 75
How He Won Her,................ 1 75
Fair Play,........................... 1 75
The Spectre Lover,................ 1 75
Victor's Triumph,................. 1 75
A Beautiful Fiend,................ 1 75
The Artist's Love,................. 1 75
A Noble Lord,..................... 1 75
Lost Heir of Linlithgow,......... 1 75
Tried for her Life,................ 1 75
Cruel as the Grave,............... 1 75
The Maiden Widow,............... 1 75
The Family Doom,................ 1 75
The Bride's Fate,.................. 1 75
The Changed Brides,.............. 1 75
Fallen Pride,....................... 1 75
The Widow's Son,................. 1 75
The Bride of Llewellyn,.......... 1 75
The Fatal Marriage,............... 1 75
The Deserted Wife,................ 1 75
The Fortune Seeker,............... 1 75
The Bridal Eve,.................... 1 75
The Lost Heiress,.................. 1 75
The Two Sisters,................... 1 75
Lady of the Isle,................... 1 75
Prince of Darkness,............... 1 75
The Three Beauties,............... 1 75
Vivia; or the Secret of Power, 1 75
Love's Labor Won,................ 1 75
The Gipsy's Prophecy,............ 1 75
Retribution,........................ 1 75
The Christmas Guest,............. 1 75
Haunted Homestead,.............. 1 75
Wife's Victory,..................... 1 75
Allworth Abbey,................... 1 75
India; Pearl of Pearl River,.. 1 75
Curse of Clifton,.................. 1 75
Discarded Daughter,.............. 1 75
The Mystery of Dark Hollow,.. 1 75
The Missing Bride; or, Miriam, the Avenger,...................................... 1 75
Above are each in cloth, or each one is in paper cover, at $1.50 each.

MRS. CAROLINE LEE HENTZ'S WORKS.

Green and Gold Edition. Complete in twelve volumes, in green morocco cloth, price $1.75 each; or $21.00 a set, each set is put up in a neat box.

Ernest Linwood,........................$1 75
The Planter's Northern Bride,.. 1 75
Courtship and Marriage,......... 1 75
Rena; or, the Snow Bird,....... 1 75
Marcus Warland,................... 1 75
Linda; or, the Young Pilot of the Belle Creole,............................... 1 75
Robert Graham; the Sequel to "Linda; or Pilot of Belle Creole,"... 1 75
Love after Marriage,................$1 75
Eoline; or Magnolia Vale,...... 1 75
The Lost Daughter,................ 1 75
The Banished Son,................ 1 75
Helen and Arthur,................. 1 75
Above are each in cloth, or each one is in paper cover, at $1.50 each.

☞ Above Books will be sent, postage paid, on receipt of Retail Price by T. B. Peterson & Brothers, Philadelphia, Pa. (1)

T. B. PETERSON & BROTHERS' PUBLICATIONS.

MRS. ANN S. STEPHENS' WORKS.

Complete in twenty-three large duodecimo volumes, bound in morocco cloth, gilt back, price $1.75 each; or $40.25 a set, each set is put up in a neat box.

Norston's Rest,...............$1 75		The Soldiers' Orphans,...........$1 75
Bertha's Engagement,............ 1 75		A Noble Woman,................ 1 75
Bellehood and Bondage,......... 1 75		Silent Struggles,................ 1 75
The Old Countess,................ 1 75		The Rejected Wife,............. 1 75
Lord Hope's Choice,............... 1 75		The Wife's Secret,............... 1 75
The Reigning Belle,............... 1 75		Mary Derwent,.................. 1 75
Palaces and Prisons,............. 1 75		Fashion and Famine,............ 1 75
Married in Haste,................ 1 75		The Curse of Gold,.............. 1 75
Wives and Widows,............... 1 75		Mabel's Mistake, ... 1 75
Ruby Gray's Strategy,............ 1 75		The Old Homestead,............ 1 75
Doubly False,.... 1 75	The Heiress,.... 1 75	The Gold Brick,... 1 75

Above are each in cloth, or each one is in paper cover, at $1.50 each.

MRS. C. A. WARFIELD'S WORKS.

Complete in nine large duodecimo volumes, bound in morocco cloth, gilt back, price $1.75 each; or $15.75 a set, each set is put up in a neat box.

The Cardinal's Daughter,......$1 75 | Miriam's Memoirs,..............$1 75
Ferne Fleming,.................... 1 75 | Monfort Hall,..................... 1 75
The Household of Bouverie,.... 1 75 | Sea and Shore................... 1 75
A Double Wedding,............... 1 75 | Hester Howard's Temptation,... 1 75
Lady Ernestine; or, The Absent Lord of Rocheforte,..................... 1 75

BEST COOK BOOKS PUBLISHED.

Every housekeeper should possess at least one of the following Cook Books, as they would save the price of it in a week's cooking.

The Queen of the Kitchen. Containing 1007 Old Maryland
  Family Receipts for Cooking,.......................................Cloth, $1 75
Miss Leslie's New Cookery Book,....................................Cloth, 1 75
Mrs. Hale's New Cook Book,..Cloth, 1 75
Petersons' New Cook Book,..Cloth, 1 75
Widdifield's New Cook Book,..Cloth, 1 75
Mrs. Goodfellow's Cookery as it Should Be,....................Cloth, 1 75
The National Cook Book. By a Practical Housewife,........Cloth, 1 75
The Young Wife's Cook Book,.......................................Cloth, 1 75
Miss Leslie's New Receipts for Cooking,........................Cloth, 1 75
Mrs. Hale's Receipts for the Million,..............................Cloth, 1 75
The Family Save-All. By author of "National Cook Book," Cloth, 1 75
Francatelli's Modern Cook. With the most approved methods of
  French, English, German, and Italian Cookery. With Sixty-two
  Illustrations. One volume of 600 pages, bound in morocco cloth, 5 00

☞ Above Books will be sent, postage paid, on receipt of Retail Price, by T. B. Peterson & Brothers, Philadelphia, Pa.

T. B. PETERSON & BROTHERS' PUBLICATIONS. 3

MISS ELIZA A. DUPUY'S WORKS.

Complete in fourteen large duodecimo volumes, bound in morocco cloth, gilt back, price $1.75 each; or $24.50 a set, each set is put up in a neat box.

A New Way to Win a Fortune	$1 75	Why Did He Marry Her?.......	$1 75
The Discarded Wife,...............	1 75	Who Shall be Victor?............	1 75
The Clandestine Marriage,......	1 75	The Mysterious Guest,..........	1 75
The Hidden Sin,.....................	1 75	Was He Guilty?...................	1 75
The Dethroned Heiress,.........	1 75	The Cancelled Will,..............	1 75
The Gipsy's Warning,.............	1 75	The Planter's Daughter,.........	1 75
All For Love,........................	1 75	Michael Rudolph,.................	1 75

Above are each in cloth, or each one is in paper cover, at $1.50 each.

DOESTICKS' WORKS.

Complete in four large duodecimo volumes, bound in cloth, gilt back, price $1.75 each; or $7.00 a set, each set is put up in a neat box.

Doesticks' Letters,.................$1 75	The Elephant Club,................$1 75
Plu-Ri-Bus-Tah,.................... 1 75	Witches of New York,........... 1 75

Above are each in cloth, or each one is in paper cover, at $1.50 each.

JAMES A. MAITLAND'S WORKS.

Complete in seven large duodecimo volumes, bound in cloth, gilt back, price $1.75 each; or $12.25 a set, each set is put up in a neat box.

The Watchman,.....................$1 75	Diary of an Old Doctor,........$1 75
The Wanderer,..................... 1 75	Sartaroe,............................. 1 75
The Lawyer's Story,............. 1 75	The Three Cousins,............... 1 75
The Old Patroon; or the Great Van Broek Property,...................... 1 75

Above are each in cloth, or each one is in paper cover, at $1.50 each.

T. ADOLPHUS TROLLOPE'S WORKS.

Complete in seven large duodecimo volumes, bound in cloth, gilt back, price $1.75 each; or $12.25 a set, each set is put up in a neat box.

The Sealed Packet,...............$1 75	Dream Numbers,..................$1 75
Garstang Grange,.................. 1 75	Beppo, the Conscript,............ 1 75
Leonora Casaloni,... 1 75	Gemma,......... 1 75	Marietta,............... 1 75

Above are each in cloth, or each one is in paper cover, at $1.50 each.

FREDRIKA BREMER'S WORKS.

Complete in six large duodecimo volumes, bound in cloth, gilt back, price $1.75 each; or $10.50 a set, each set is put up in a neat box.

Father and Daughter,............$1 75	The Neighbors,.....................$1 75
The Four Sisters,................... 1 75	The Home,........................... 1 75

Above are each in cloth, or each one is in paper cover, at $1.50 each.

Life in the Old World. In two volumes, cloth, price,.................. 3 50

☞ Above Books will be sent postage paid, on receipt of Retail Price, by T. B. Peterson & Brothers, Philadelphia, Pa.

4 T. B. PETERSON & BROTHERS' PUBLICATIONS.

WILKIE COLLINS' BEST WORKS.

Basil; or, The Crossed Path..$1 50 | The Dead Secret. 12mo........$1 50
Above are each in one large duodecimo volume, bound in cloth.
The Dead Secret, 8vo............... 75 | The Queen's Revenge,............... 75
Basil; or, the Crossed Path,....... 75 | Miss or Mrs?......................... 50
Hide and Seek,...................... 75 | Mad Monkton,........................ 50
After Dark,.......................... 75 | Sights a-Foot,....................... 50
The Stolen Mask,......... 25 | The Yellow Mask,... 25 | Sister Rose,... 25
The above books are each issued in paper cover, in octavo form.

FRANK FORRESTER'S SPORTING BOOK.

Frank Forrester's Sporting Scenes and Characters. By Henry William Herbert. With Illustrations by Darley. Two vols., cloth,...$4 00

EMERSON BENNETT'S WORKS.

Complete in seven large duodecimo volumes, bound in cloth, gilt back, price $1.75 each; or $12.25 a set, each set is put up in a neat box.
The Border Rover,...............$1 75 | Bride of the Wilderness,........$1 75
Clara Moreland,................... 1 75 | Ellen Norbury,..................... 1 75
The Orphan's Trials,............. 1 75 | Kate Clarendon,................... 1 75
Viola; or Adventures in the Far South-West,............................... 1 75
Above are each in cloth, or each one is in paper cover, at $1.50 each.
The Heiress of Bellefonte,...... 75 | The Pioneer's Daughter,......... 75

GREEN'S WORKS ON GAMBLING.

Complete in four large duodecimo volumes, bound in cloth, gilt back, price $1.75 each; or $7.00 a set, each set is put up in a neat box.
Gambling Exposed,...............$1 75 | Reformed Gambler,..............$1 75
The Gambler's Life,............... 1 75 | Secret Band of Brothers,........ 1 75
Above are each in cloth, or each one is in paper cover, at $1.50 each.

DOW'S PATENT SERMONS.

Complete in four large duodecimo volumes, bound in cloth, gilt back, price $1.50 each; or $6.00 a set, each set is put up in a neat box.
Dow's Patent Sermons, 1st Series, cloth,......................$1 50
Dow's Patent Sermons, 2d Series, cloth,...................... 1 50
Dow's Patent Sermons, 3d Series, cloth, ...$1 50
Dow's Patent Sermons, 4th Series, cloth,...................... 1 50
Above are each in cloth, or each one is in paper cover, at $1.00 each.

MISS BRADDON'S WORKS.

Aurora Floyd,....................... 75 | The Lawyer's Secret,............. 25
Aurora Floyd, cloth............... 1 00 | For Better, For Worse,........... 75

☞ Above books will be sent, postage paid, on receipt of Retail Price by T. B. Peterson & Brothers, Philadelphia, Pa.

6 T. B. PETERSON & BROTHERS' PUBLICATIONS.

CHARLES LEVER'S BEST WORKS.

Charles O'Malley,	75	Arthur O'Leary,	75
Harry Lorrequer,	75	Con Cregan,	75
Jack Hinton,	75	Davenport Dunn,	75
Tom Burke of Ours,	75	Horace Templeton,	75
Knight of Gwynne,	75	Kate O'Donoghue,	75

Above are in paper cover, or a fine edition is in cloth at $2.00 each.

A Rent in a Cloud, ... 50 | St. Patrick's Eve, ... 50

Ten Thousand a Year, in one volume, paper cover, $1.50; or in cloth, 2 00
The Diary of a Medical Student, by author "Ten Thousand a Year," 75

MRS. HENRY WOOD'S BEST BOOKS.

The Master of Greylands,	$1 50	The Shadow of Ashlydyat,	$1 50
Within the Maze,	1 50	Squire Trevlyn's Heir,	1 50
Dene Hollow,	1 50	Oswald Cray,	1 50
Bessy Rane,	1 50	Mildred Arkell,	1 50
George Canterbury's Will,	1 50	The Red Court Farm,	1 50
Verner's Pride,	1 50	Elster's Folly,	1 50
The Channings,	1 50	Saint Martin's Eve,	1 50
Roland Yorke. A Sequel to "The Channings,".			1 50
Lord Oakburn's Daughters; or, The Earl's Heirs,			1 50
The Castle's Heir; or, Lady Adelaide's Oath,			1 50

The above are each in paper cover, or in cloth, price $1.75 each.

Edina; or, Missing Since Midnight, cloth, $1, paper cover,			75
The Mystery,	75	A Life's Secret,	50
Parkwater. Told in Twilight,	75	The Haunted Tower,	50
The Lost Bank Note,	50	The Runaway Match,	25
The Lost Will,	50	Martyn Ware's Temptation,	25
Orville College,	50	The Dean of Denham,	25
Five Thousand a Year,	25	Foggy Night at Offord,	25
The Diamond Bracelet,	25	William Allair,	25
Clara Lake's Dream,	25	A Light and a Dark Christmas,	25
The Nobleman's Wife,	25	The Smuggler's Ghost,	25
Frances Hildyard,	25	Rupert Hall,	25
Cyrilla Maude's First Love,	25	My Husband's First Love,	25
My Cousin Caroline's Wedding	25	Marrying Beneath Your Station	25

EUGENE SUE'S GREAT WORKS.

The Wandering Jew,	$1 50	First Love,	50
The Mysteries of Paris,	1 50	Woman's Love,	50
Martin, the Foundling,	1 50	Female Bluebeard,	50
Above are in cloth at $2.00 each.		Man-of-War's-Man,	50

Life and Adventures of Raoul de Surville. A Tale of the Empire,... 25

☞ Above Books will be sent, postage paid, on receipt of Retail Price by T. B. Peterson & Brothers, Philadelphia, Pa.

T. B. PETERSON & BROTHERS' PUBLICATIONS. 7

MRS. HENRY WOOD'S BEST BOOKS, IN CLOTH.

The following are cloth editions of Mrs. Henry Wood's best books, and they are each issued in large octavo volumes, bound in cloth, price $1.75 each.

Within the Maze. By Mrs. Henry Wood, author of "East Lynne," $1 75
The Master of Greylands. By Mrs. Henry Wood,........................ 1 75
Dene Hollow. By Mrs. Henry Wood, author of "Within the Maze," 1 75
Bessy Rane. By Mrs. Henry Wood, author of "The Channings,".... 1 75
George Canterbury's Will. By Mrs. Wood, author "Oswald Cray," 1 75
The Channings. By Mrs. Henry Wood, author of "Dene Hollow,".... 1 75
Roland Yorke. A Sequel to "The Channings." By Mrs. Wood,...... 1 75
Shadow of Ashlydyatt. By Mrs. Wood, author of "Bessy Rane,".... 1 75
Lord Oakburn's Daughters; or The Earl's Heirs. By Mrs. Wood,... 1 75
Verner's Pride. By Mrs. Henry Wood, author of "The Channings," 1 75
The Castle's Heir; or Lady Adelaide's Oath. By Mrs. Henry Wood, 1 75
Oswald Cray. By Mrs. Henry Wood, author of "Roland Yorke,".... 1 75
Squire Trevlyn's Heir; or Trevlyn Hold. By Mrs. Henry Wood,..... 1 75
The Red Court Farm. By Mrs. Wood, author of "Verner's Pride," 1 75
Elster's Folly. By Mrs. Henry Wood, author of "Castle's Heir,"... 1 75
St. Martin's Eve. By Mrs. Henry Wood, author of "Dene Hollow," 1 75
Mildred Arkell. By Mrs. Henry Wood, author of "East Lynne,"......1 75

WORKS BY THE VERY BEST AUTHORS.

The following books are each issued in one large duodecimo volume, bound in cloth, at $1.75 each, or each one is in paper cover, at $1.50 each.

The Initials. A Love Story. By Baroness Tautphœus,................$1 75
Married Beneath Him. By author of "Lost Sir Massingberd,"...... 1 75
Margaret Maitland. By Mrs. Oliphant, author of "Zaidee,"........... 1 75
Family Pride. By author of "Pique," "Family Secrets," etc.......... 1 75
Self-Sacrifice. By author of "Margaret Maitland," etc................ 1 75
The Woman in Black. A Companion to the "Woman in White,"... 1 75
The Autobiography of Edward Wortley Montagu, ... 1 75
The Forsaken Daughter. A Companion to "Linda,".................... 1 75
Love and Liberty. A Revolutionary Story. By Alexander Dumas, 1 75
The Morrisons. By Mrs. Margaret Hosmer,................................. 1 75
The Rich Husband. By author of "George Geith,"....................... 1 75
Woodburn Grange. A Novel. By William Howitt,....................... 1 75
The Lost Beauty. By a Noted Lady of the Spanish Court,............ 1 75
My Hero. By Mrs. Forrester. A Charming Love Story,............... 1 75
The Quaker Soldier. A Revolutionary Romance. By Judge Jones,.... 1 75
Memoirs of Vidocq, the French Detective. His Life and Adventures, 1 75
The Belle of Washington. With her Portrait. By Mrs. N. P. Lasselle, 1 75
High Life in Washington. A Life Picture. By Mrs. N. P. Lasselle, 1 75

Above books are each in cloth, or each one is in paper cover, at $1.50 each

☞ Above Books will be sent, postage paid, on Receipt of Retail Price by T. B. Peterson & Brothers, Philadelphia, Pa.

8 T. B. PETERSON & BROTHERS' PUBLICATIONS.

WORKS BY THE VERY BEST AUTHORS.

The following books are each issued in one large duodecimo volume, bound in cloth, at $1.75 each, or each one is in paper cover at $1.50 each.

The Count of Monte-Cristo. By Alexander Dumas. Illustrated,...$1 75
The Countess of Monte-Cristo. Paper cover, price $1.00; or cloth,.. 1 75
Camille; or, the Fate of a Coquette. By Alexander Dumas,.......... 1 75
Love and Money. By J. B. Jones, author of the "Rival Belles,"... 1 75
The Brother's Secret; or, the Count De Mara. By William Godwin, 1 75
The Lost Love. By Mrs. Oliphant, author of "Margaret Maitland," 1 75
The Roman Traitor. By Henry William Herbert. A Roman Story, 1 75
The Bohemians of London. By Edward M. Whitty,................ 1 75
Wild Sports and Adventures in Africa. By Major W. C. Harris, 1 75
Courtship and Matrimony. By Robert Morris. With a Portrait,... 1 75
The Jealous Husband. By Annette Marie Maillard,................ 1 75
The Life, Writings, and Lectures of the late "Fanny Fern,"........ 1 75
The Life and Lectures of Lola Montez, with her portrait,............ 1 75
Wild Southern Scenes. By author of "Wild Western Scenes,"...... 1 75
Currer Lyle; or, the Autobiography of an Actress. By Louise Reeder. 1 75
The Cabin and Parlor. By J. Thornton Randolph. Illustrated,..... 1 75
The Little Beauty. A Love Story. By Mrs. Grey,................... 1 75
Lizzie Glenn; or, the Trials of a Seamstress. By T. S. Arthur,..... 1 75
Lady Maud; or, the Wonder of Kingswood Chase. By Pierce Egan, 1 75
Wilfred Montressor; or, High Life in New York. Illustrated,....... 1 75
The Old Stone Mansion. By C. J. Peterson, author "Kate Aylesford," 1 75
Kate Aylesford. By Chas. J. Peterson, author "Old Stone Mansion,". 1 75
Lorrimer Littlegood, by author "Harry Coverdale's Courtship,"..... 1 75
The Earl's Secret. A Love Story. By Miss Pardoe,................ 1 75
The Adopted Heir. By Miss Pardoe, author of "The Earl's Secret," 1 75
Coal, Coal Oil, and all other Minerals in the Earth. By Eli Bowen, 1 75
Secession, Coercion, and Civil War. By J. B. Jones,............... 1 75

Above books are each in cloth, or each one is in paper cover, at $1.50 each.

The Dead Secret. By Wilkie Collins, author of "The Crossed Path," 1 50
The Crossed Path; or Basil. By Wilkie Collins,................... 1 50
Indiana. A Love Story. By George Sand, author of "Consuelo," 1 50
Jealousy; or, Teverino. By George Sand, author of "Consuelo," etc. 1 50
Six Nights with the Washingtonians, Illustrated. By T. S. Arthur, 3 50
Comstock's Elocution and Model Speaker. Intended for the use of
  Schools, Colleges, and for private Study, for the Promotion of
  Health, Cure of Stammering, and Defective Articulation. By
  Andrew Comstock and Philip Lawrence. With 236 Illustrations.. 2 00
The Lawrence Speaker. A Selection of Literary Gems in Poetry and
  Prose, designed for the use of Colleges, Schools, Seminaries, Literary
  Societies. By Philip Lawrence, Professor of Elocution. 600 pages.. 2 00

☞ Above Books will be sent, postage paid, on receipt of Retail Price by T. B. Peterson & Brothers, Philadelphia, Pa.

T. B. PETERSON & BROTHERS' PUBLICATIONS. 9

ALEXANDER DUMAS' WORKS, BOUND IN CLOTH.

The following are cloth editions of Dumas' and Reynolds' works, and they are each issued in large octavo volumes, bound in cloth, price $1.75 each.

The Three Guardsmen ; or, The Three Mousquetaires. By A. Dumas,$1 75
Twenty Years After; or the "*Second Series of Three Guardsmen*,"... 1 75
Bragelonne; Son of Athos; or "*Third Series of Three Guardsmen*," 1 75
The Iron Mask; or the "*Fourth Series of The Three Guardsmen*,".... 1 75
Louise La Valliere; or the "*Fifth Series and End of the Three Guardsmen Series*," 1 75
The Memoirs of a Physician. By Alexander Dumas. Illustrated,... 1 75
Queen's Necklace; or "*Second Series of Memoirs of a Physician*," 1 75
Six Years Later; or the "*Third Series of Memoirs of a Physician*," 1 75
Countess of Charny; or "*Fourth Series of Memoirs of a Physician*," 1 75
Andree De Taverney; or "*Fifth Series of Memoirs of a Physician*," 1 75
The Chevalier; or the "*Sixth Series and End of the Memoirs of a Physician Series*,"... 1 75
The Adventures of a Marquis. By Alexander Dumas,. 1 75
The Count of Monte-Cristo. By Alexander Dumas,...................... 1 75
Edmond Dantes. A Sequel to the "Count of Monte-Cristo,"........... 1 75
The Forty-Five Guardsmen. By Alexander Dumas. Illustrated,... 1 75
Diana of Meridor, or Lady of Monsoreau. By Alexander Dumas,... 1 75
The Iron Hand. By Alex. Dumas, author "Count of Monte-Cristo," 1 75
Camille; or the Fate of a Coquette. (La Dame aux Camelias,)...... 1 75
The Conscript. A novel of the Days of Napoleon the First,........... 1 75
Love and Liberty. A novel of the French Revolution of 1792-1793, 1 75

GEORGE W. M. REYNOLDS' WORKS, IN CLOTH.

The Mysteries of the Court of London. By George W. M. Reynolds, 1 75
Rose Foster; or the "*Second Series of Mysteries of Court of London*," 1 75
Caroline of Brunswick; or the "*Third Series of the Court of London*," 1 75
Venetia Trelawney; or "*End of the Mysteries of the Court of London*," 1 75
Lord Saxondale; or the Court of Queen Victoria. By Reynolds,...... 1 75
Count Christoval. Sequel to "Lord Saxondale." By Reynolds,........ 1 75
Rosa Lambert; or Memoirs of an Unfortunate Woman. By Reynolds, 1 75
Mary Price; or the Adventures of a Servant Maid. By Reynolds,... 1 75
Eustace Quentin. Sequel to "Mary Price." By G. W. M. Reynolds, 1 75
Joseph Wilmot; or the Memoirs of a Man Servant. By Reynolds,... 1 75
The Banker's Daughter. Sequel to "Joseph Wilmot." By Reynolds, 1 75
Kenneth. A Romance of the Highlands. By G. W. M. Reynolds, 1 75
Rye-House Plot; or the Conspirator's Daughter. By Reynolds,...... 1 75
Necromancer; or the Times of Henry the Eighth. By Reynolds,...... 1 75
The Mysteries of the Court of the Stuarts. By G. W. M. Reynolds, 1 75
Wallace; the Hero of Scotland. By G. W. M. Reynolds,.............. 1 75
The Gipsy Chief. By George W. M. Reynolds,........................... 1 75
Robert Bruce; the Hero King of Scotland. By G. W. M. Reynolds, 1 75

☞ Above Books will be sent, postage paid, on receipt of Retail Price, by T. B. Peterson & Brothers, Philadelphia, Pa.

10 T. B. PETERSON & BROTHERS' PUBLICATIONS.

WORKS BY THE VERY BEST AUTHORS.

The following books are each issued in one large octavo volume, bound in cloth, at $2.00 each, or each one is done up in paper cover, at $1.50 each.

The Wandering Jew. By Eugene Sue. Full of Illustrations,.........$2 00
Mysteries of Paris; and its Sequel, Gerolstein. By Eugene Sue,.... 2 00
Martin, the Foundling. By Eugene Sue. Full of Illustrations,..... 2 00
Ten Thousand a Year. By Samuel Warren. With Illustrations,.... 2 00
Washington and His Generals. By George Lippard,................. 2 00
The Quaker City; or, the Monks of Monk Hall. By George Lippard, 2 00
Blanche of Brandywine. By George Lippard,...................... 2 00
Paul Ardenheim; the Monk of Wissahickon. By George Lippard,. 2 00
The Mysteries of Florence. By Geo. Lippard, author "Quaker City," 2 00
The Pictorial Tower of London. By W. Harrison Ainsworth,......... 2 50
Above books are each in cloth, or each one is in paper cover, at $1.50 each.

The following are each issued in one large octavo volume, bound in cloth, price $2.00 each, or a cheap edition is issued in paper cover, at 75 cents each.

Charles O'Malley, the Irish Dragoon. By Charles Lever,......Cloth, $2 00
Harry Lorrequer. With his Confessions. By Charles Lever,...Cloth, 2 00
Jack Hinton, the Guardsman. By Charles Lever,..............Cloth, 2 00
Davenport Dunn. A Man of Our Day. By Charles Lever,...Cloth, 2 00
Tom Burke of Ours. By Charles Lever,........................Cloth, 2 00
The Knight of Gwynne. By Charles Lever,....................Cloth, 2 00
Arthur O'Leary. By Charles Lever,...........................Cloth, 2 00
Con Cregan. By Charles Lever,...............................Cloth, 2 00
Horace Templeton. By Charles Lever,.........................Cloth, 2 00
Kate O'Donoghue. By Charles Lever,..........................Cloth, 2 00
Valentine Vox, the Ventriloquist. By Harry Cockton.........Cloth, 2 00
Above are each in cloth, or each one is in paper cover, at 75 cents each.

HUMOROUS ILLUSTRATED WORKS.

Each one is full of Illustrations, by Felix O. C. Darley, and bound in Cloth.

Major Jones' Courtship and Travels. With 21 Illustrations,.........$1 75
Major Jones' Scenes in Georgia. With 16 Illustrations,............. 1 75
Simon Suggs' Adventures and Travels. With 17 Illustrations,...... 1 75
Swamp Doctor's Adventures in the South-West. 14 Illustrations,... 1 50
Col. Thorpe's Scenes in Arkansaw. With 16 Illustrations,.......... 1 50
The Big Bear's Adventures and Travels. With 18 Illustrations,...... 1 75
High Life in New York, by Jonathan Slick. With Illustrations,.... 1 75
Judge Haliburton's Yankee Stories. Illustrated,.................. 1 75
Harry Coverdale's Courtship and Marriage. Illustrated,........... 1 75
Piney Wood's Tavern; or, Sam Slick in Texas. Illustrated,......... 1 75
Sam Slick, the Clockmaker. By Judge Haliburton. Illustrated,... 1 75
Humors of Falconbridge. By J. F. Kelley. With Illustrations,... 1 75
Modern Chivalry. By Judge Breckenridge. Two vols., each....... 1 75
Neal's Charcoal Sketches. By Joseph C. Neal. 21 Illustrations,... 2 50

☞ Above Books will be sent, postage paid, on receipt of Retail Price by T. B. Peterson & Brothers, Philadelphia, Pa.

NEW AND GOOD BOOKS BY BEST AUTHORS.

Beautiful Snow, and Other Poems. *New Illustrated Edition.* By J. W. Watson. With Illustrations by E. L. Henry. One volume, morocco cloth, black and gold, gilt top, side, and back, price $2.00; or in maroon morocco cloth, full gilt edges, full gilt back, full gilt sides, $3 00
The Outcast, and Other Poems. By J. W. Watson. One volume, green morocco cloth, gilt top, side and back, price $2.00; or in maroon morocco cloth, full gilt edges, full gilt back, full gilt sides,... 3 00
The Young Magdalen; and Other Poems. By Francis S. Smith, editor of "The New York Weekly." With a portrait of the author. Complete in one large volume of 300 pages, bound in green morocco cloth, gilt top, side, and back, price $3.00; or in full gilt,.... 4 00
Hans Breitmann's Ballads. By Charles G. Leland. *Containing the "First," "Second," "Third," "Fourth," and "Fifth Series" of Hans Breitmann's Ballads.* Complete in one large volume, bound in morocco cloth, gilt side, gilt top, and full gilt back, with beveled boards. With a full and complete Glossary to the whole work,...... 4 00
Meister Karl's Sketch Book. By Charles G. Leland. (Hans Breitmann.) Complete in one volume, green morocco cloth, gilt side, gilt top, gilt back, with beveled boards, price $2.50, or in maroon morocco cloth, full gilt edges, full gilt back, full gilt sides, etc.,....... 3 50
The Ladies' Guide to True Politeness and Perfect Manners. By Miss Leslie. Every lady should have it. Cloth, full gilt back,.... 1 75
The Ladies' Complete Guide to Needlework and Embroidery. With 113 illustrations. By Miss Lambert. Cloth, full gilt back,.......... 1 75
The Ladies' Work Table Book. With 27 illustrations. Cloth, gilt,. 1 50
Cyrilla; or the Mysterious Engagement. By author of "Initials," 1 00
The Miser's Daughter. By William Harrison Ainsworth, cloth,...... 1 75
John Jasper's Secret. A Sequel to Charles Dickens' "Mystery of Edwin Drood." With 18 Illustrations. Bound in cloth,............. 2 00
Across the Atlantic. Letters from France, Switzerland, Germany, Italy, and England. By C. H. Haeseler, M.D. Bound in cloth,... 2 00
Popery Exposed. An Exposition of Popery as it was and is,.......... 1 75
The Story of Elizabeth. By Miss Thackeray, paper $1.00, or cloth,... 1 50
Dow's Short Patent Sermons. By Dow, Jr. In 4 vols., cloth, each.... 1 50
Wild Oats Sown Abroad. A Spicy Book. By T. B. Witmer, cloth,... 1 50
Aunt Patty's Scrap Bag. By Mrs. Caroline Lee Hentz. Illustrated, 1 50
Historical Sketches of Plymouth, Luzerne Co., Penna. By Hendrick B. Wright, of Wilkesbarre. With Twenty-five Photographs,....... 4 00

HARRY COCKTON'S BEST WORKS.

Valentine Vox, Ventriloquist,.. 75
Valentine Vox, cloth,............. 2 00
Sylvester Sound, ... 75
The Love Match, ... 75
The Fatal Marriages,............. 75
The Steward,........................ 75
Percy Effingham, ... 75
The Prince,........................... 75

☞ Above Books will be sent, postage paid, on receipt of Retail Price, by T. B. Peterson & Brothers, Philadelphia, Pa.

12 T. B. PETERSON & BROTHERS' PUBLICATIONS.

NEW AND GOOD BOOKS BY BEST AUTHORS.

Consuelo. By George Sand. One volume, 12mo., bound in cloth,...$1 50
The Countess of Rudolstadt. Sequel to "Consuelo." 12mo., cloth,.. 1 50
Rose Foster. By George W. M. Reynolds, Esq., cloth,.................. 1 75
Lord Montagu's Page. By G. P. R. James, author of "Cavalier,"... 1 75
Corinne; or, Italy. A Love Story. By Madame de Stael, cloth,..... 1 00
Treason at Home. A Novel. By Mrs. Greenough, cloth,............... 1 75
Letters from Europe. By Colonel John W. Forney. Bound in cloth, 1 75
Frank Fairlegh. By author of "Lewis Arundel," cloth,................. 1 75
Lewis Arundel. By author of "Frank Fairlegh," cloth,................. 1 75
Harry Racket Scapegrace. By the author of " Frank Fairlegh," cloth, 1 75
Tom Racquet. By author of " Frank Fairlegh," cloth,................. 1 75
La Gaviota; the Sea-Gull. By Fernan Caballero, cloth,............... 1 50
Monsieur Antoine. By George Sand. Illustrated. One vol., cloth, 1 75
Aurora Floyd. By Miss Braddon. One vol., paper 75 cents, cloth,... 1 00
The Life of Charles Dickens. By R. Shelton Mackenzie, cloth, ... 2 00
The Laws and Practice of the Game of Euchre, as adopted by the
  Euchre Club of Washington, D. C. Bound in cloth,.................. 1 00
Poetical Works of Sir Walter Scott. One 8vo. volume, fine binding, 5 00
Life of Sir Walter Scott. By John G. Lockhart. With Portrait,..... 2 50
The Shakspeare Novels. Complete in one large octavo volume, cloth, 4 00
Miss Pardoe's Choice Novels. In one large octavo volume, cloth,... 4 00
Life, Speeches and Martyrdom of Abraham Lincoln. Illustrated,... 1 75
Rome and the Papacy. A History of the Men, Manners and Tempo-
  ral Government of Rome in the Nineteenth Century, cloth,......... 1 75
The French, German, Spanish, Latin and Italian Languages Without
  a Master. Whereby any one of these Languages can be learned
  without a Teacher. By A. H. Monteith. One volume, cloth,...... 2 00
Liebig's Complete Works on Chemistry. By Baron Justus Liebig... 2 00
Life and Adventures of Don Quixote and his Squire Sancho Panza, 1 75
Tan-go-ru-a. An Historical Drama, in Prose. By Mr. Moorhead,.... 1 00
The Impeachment Trial of President Andrew Johnson. Cloth,...... 1 50
Trial of the Assassins for the Murder of Abraham Lincoln. Cloth,... 1 50
Lives of Jack Sheppard and Guy Fawkes. Illustrated. One vol., cloth, 1 75
Christy and White's Complete Ethiopian Melodies, bound in cloth,... 1 00
Dr. Hollick's great work on the Anatomy and Physiology of the
  Human Figure, with colored dissected plates of the Human Figure, 2 00
Comstock's Colored Chart. Being a perfect Alphabet of the Eng-
  lish Language, Graphic and Typic, with exercises in Pitch, Force
  and Gesture, and Sixty-Eight colored figures, representing the va-
  rious postures and different attitudes to be used in declamation.
  On a large Roller. Every School should have a copy of it,......... 5 00
Riddell's Model Architect. With 22 large full page colored illustrations, and 44 plates of ground plans, with plans, specifications,
  costs of building, etc. One large quarto volume, bound,............ 15 00

☞ Above Books will be sent, postage paid, on receipt of Retail Price,
by T. B. Peterson & Brothers, Philadelphia, Pa.

14 T. B. PETERSON & BROTHERS' PUBLICATIONS.

WORKS BY THE VERY BEST AUTHORS.

The Conscript; or, the Days of Napoleon 1st. By Alex. Dumas,.....$1 75
Cousin Harry. By Mrs. Grey, author of "The Gambler's Wife," etc. 1 75
Married at Last. A Love Story. By Annie Thomas,..................... 1 75
Shoulder Straps. By Henry Morford, author of "Days of Shoddy," 1 75
Days of Shoddy. By Henry Morford, author of "Shoulder Straps," 1 75
The Coward. By Henry Morford, author of "Shoulder Straps,"...... 1 75
Above books are each in cloth, or each one is in paper cover, at $1.50 each.
Harry Lorrequer. *With His Confessions.* By Charles Lever. *Four different editions:* one at 75 cents in paper cover, and three bound in cloth, viz.: Sterling Series, at $1.00, Peoples' Edition, at $1.50, and Library Edition, at $2.00.
Charles O'Malley, the Irish Dragoon. *Four different editions:* one at 75 cents in paper cover, and three bound in cloth, viz.: Sterling Series, at $1.00, Peoples' Edition, at $1.50, and Library Edition, at $2.00.

WORKS IN SETS BY THE BEST AUTHORS.

Mrs. Emma D. E. N. Southworth's Popular Novels. 43 vols. in all, 75 25
Mrs. Ann S. Stephens' Celebrated Novels. 23 volumes in all,......... 40 25
Miss Eliza A. Dupuy's Works. Fourteen volumes in all,............... 24 50
Mrs. Caroline Lee Hentz's Novels. Twelve volumes in all,............ 21 00
Mrs. C. A. Warfield's Novels. Nine volumes in all,...................... 15 75
Frederika Bremer's Novels. Six volumes in all,........................... 10 50
T. Adolphus Trollope's Works. Seven volumes in all,.................. 12 25
James A. Maitland's Novels. Seven volumes in all,..................... 12 25
Charles Lever's Works. Ten volumes in all,............................... 20 00
Alexander Dumas' Works. Twenty-one volumes in all, ... 36 75
George W. M. Reynolds' Works. Eighteen volumes in all,......... 31 50
Frank Fairlegh's Works. Six volumes in all,............................... 10 50
Q. K. Philander Doesticks' Novels. Four volumes in all,............. 7 00
Cook Books. The best in the world. Eleven volumes in all,........ 19 25
Henry Morford's Novels. Three volumes in all,.......................... 5 25
Mrs. Henry Wood's Novels. Seventeen volumes in all,............... 29 75
Emerson Bennett's Novels. Seven volumes in all,...................... 12 25
Green's Works on Gambling. Four volumes in all,..................... 7 00
American Humorous Works. Illustrated. Twelve volumes in all, 21 00
Eugene Sue's Best Works. Three volumes in all,....................... 6 00
George Sand's Works. Consuelo, etc. Five volumes in all,.......... 7 50
George Lippard's Works. Five volumes in all,............................ 10 00
Dow's Short Patent Sermons. Four volumes in all,..................... 6 00
The Waverley Novels. *National Edition.* Five large 8vo. vols., cloth, 15 00
Charles Dickens' Works. *People's 12mo. Edition.* 22 vols., cloth, 34 00
Charles Dickens' Works. *Green Cloth 12mo. Edition.* 22 vols., cloth, 44 00
Charles Dickens' Works. *Illustrated 12mo. Edition.* 36 vols., cloth, 55 00
Charles Dickens' Works. *Illustrated 8vo. Edition.* 18 vols., cloth, 31 50
Charles Dickens' Works. *New National Edition.* 7 volumes, cloth, 20 00

☞ Above Books will be sent, postage paid, on receipt of Retail Price, by T. B. Peterson & Brothers, Philadelphia, Pa.

CHARLES DICKENS' WORKS.
☞ GREAT REDUCTION IN THEIR PRICES. ☜

CHEAP PAPER COVER EDITION OF DICKENS' WORKS.
Each book being complete in one large octavo volume.

Pickwick Papers,	50	Bleak House,	50
Nicholas Nickleby,	50	Little Dorrit,	50
Dombey and Son,	50	Christmas Stories,	50
Our Mutual Friend,	50	Barnaby Rudge,	50
David Copperfield,	50	Sketches by "Boz,"	50
Martin Chuzzlewit,	50	Great Expectations,	50
Old Curiosity Shop,	50	Joseph Grimaldi,	50
Oliver Twist,	50	The Pic-Nic Papers,	50
American Notes,	25	The Haunted House,	25
Hard Times,	25	Uncommercial Traveller,	25
A Tale of Two Cities,	25	A House to Let,	25
Somebody's Luggage,	25	Perils of English Prisoners,	25
Mrs. Lirriper's Lodgings,	25	Wreck of the Golden Mary,	25
Mrs. Lirriper's Legacy,	25	Tom Tiddler's Ground,	25
Mugby Junction,	25	Dickens' New Stories,	25
Dr. Marigold's Prescriptions,	25	Lazy Tour of Idle Apprentices,	25
Mystery of Edwin Drood,	25	The Holly-Tree Inn,	25
Message from the Sea,	25	No Thoroughfare,	25
Hunted Down; and Other Reprinted Pieces,			50

PEOPLE'S DUODECIMO EDITION. ILLUSTRATED.
Reduced in price from $2.50 to $1.50 a volume.
This edition is printed on fine paper, from large, clear type, leaded, that all can read, containing Two Hundred Illustrations on tinted paper.

Our Mutual Friend, Cloth,	$1.50	Little Dorrit, Cloth,	$1.50
Pickwick Papers, Cloth,	1.50	Dombey and Son, Cloth,	1.50
Nicholas Nickleby, Cloth,	1.50	Christmas Stories, Cloth,	1.50
Great Expectations, Cloth,	1.50	Sketches by "Boz," Cloth,	1.50
David Copperfield, Cloth,	1.50	Barnaby Rudge, Cloth,	1.50
Oliver Twist, Cloth,	1.50	Martin Chuzzlewit, Cloth,	1.50
Bleak House, Cloth,	1.50	Old Curiosity Shop, Cloth,	1.50
A Tale of Two Cities, Cloth,	1.50	Dickens' New Stories, Cloth,	1.50
Mystery of Edwin Drood; and Master Humphrey's Clock, Cloth,			1.50
American Notes; and the Uncommercial Traveller, Cloth,			1.50
Hunted Down; and other Reprinted Pieces, Cloth,			1.50
The Holly-Tree Inn; and other Stories, Cloth,			1.50
The Life and Writings of Charles Dickens, Cloth,			2.00
John Jasper's Secret. Sequel to Mystery of Edwin Drood, Cloth,			2.00
Price of a set, in Black cloth, in twenty-two volumes,			$34.00
" " Full sheep, Library style,			45.00
" " Half calf, sprinkled edges,			56.00
" " Half calf, marbled edges,			61.00
" " Half calf, antique, or half calf, full gilt backs, etc.			66.00

☞ Above Books will be sent, postage paid, on receipt of Retail Price, by T. B. Peterson & Brothers, Philadelphia, Pa. (15)

CHARLES DICKENS' WORKS.
☞ GREAT REDUCTION IN THEIR PRICES. ☜

ILLUSTRATED OCTAVO EDITION.
Reduced in price from $2.50 to $1.75 a volume.

This edition is printed from large type, double column, octavo page, each book being complete in one volume, the whole containing near Six Hundred Illustrations, by Cruikshank, Phiz, Browne, Maclise, and other artists.

Our Mutual Friend,.....Cloth,	$1.75	David Copperfield,.......Cloth,	$1.75
Pickwick Papers,..........Cloth,	1.75	Barnaby Rudge,..........Cloth,	1.75
Nicholas Nickleby,......Cloth,	1.75	Martin Chuzzlewit,......Cloth,	1.75
Great Expectations,......Cloth,	1.75	Old Curiosity Shop,......Cloth,	1.75
Lamplighter's Story,....Cloth,	1.75	Christmas Stories,.......Cloth,	1.75
Oliver Twist,..............Cloth,	1.75	Dickens' New Stories,...Cloth,	1.75
Bleak House,..............Cloth,	1.75	A Tale of Two Cities,...Cloth,	1.75
Little Dorrit,...............Cloth,	1.75	American Notes and	
Dombey and Son,......Cloth,	1.75	Pic-Nic Papers,........Cloth,	1.75
Sketches by "Boz,"....Cloth,	1.75		

Price of a set, in Black cloth, in eighteen volumes,.................................$31.50
" " Full sheep, Library style,....................................... 40.00
" " Half calf, sprinkled edges,.. 48.00
" " Half calf, marbled edges,.. 54.00
" " Half calf, antique, or Half calf, full gilt backs,... 60.00

"NEW NATIONAL EDITION" OF DICKENS' WORKS.
This is the cheapest bound edition of the entire works of Charles Dickens ever published, *all* his writings being contained in *seven large* octavo volumes, with a portrait of Charles Dickens, and other illustrations.
Price of a set, in Black cloth, in seven volumes,.......................$20.00
" " Full sheep, Library style,............................. 25.00
" " Half calf, antique, or Half calf, full gilt backs,... 30.00

GREEN MOROCCO CLOTH, DUODECIMO EDITION.
This is the "People's Duodecimo Edition" in a new style of Binding, in Green Morocco Cloth, Bevelled Boards, Full Gilt descriptive back, and Medallion Portrait on sides in gilt, in Twenty-two handy volumes, 12mo., fine paper, large clear type, and Two Hundred Illustrations on tinted paper. Price $44 a set, and each set put up in a neat and strong box. This is the handsomest and best edition ever published for the price.

THE LIFE AND WRITINGS OF CHARLES DICKENS.
THE LIFE OF CHARLES DICKENS. By *Dr. R. Shelton Mackenzie*, containing a full history of his Life, his Uncollected Pieces, in Prose and Verse; Personal Recollections and Anecdotes; His Last Will in full; and Letters from Mr. Dickens never before published. With a Portrait and Autograph of Charles Dickens. Price $2.00.

☞Above books will be sent, postage paid, on receipt of Retail Price,
(16) by T. B. Peterson & Brothers, Philadelphia, Pa.

CHARLES DICKENS' WORKS.
GREAT REDUCTION IN THEIR PRICES.

ILLUSTRATED DUODECIMO EDITION.
Reduced in price from $2.00 to $1.50 a volume.

This edition is printed on the finest paper, from large, clear type, leaded, that all can read, containing Six Hundred full page Illustrations, on tinted paper, from designs by Cruikshank, Phiz, Browne, Maclise, McLenan, and other artists. This is the only edition published that contains all the original illustrations, as selected by Mr. Charles Dickens.

The following are each contained in two volumes.

Our Mutual Friend,......Cloth,	$3.00	Bleak House,..............Cloth,	$3 00
Pickwick Papers,..........Cloth,	3.00	Sketches by "Boz,"......Cloth,	3.00
Tale of Two Cities,........Cloth,	3.00	Barnaby Rudge,..........Cloth,	3.00
Nicholas Nickleby,........Cloth,	3.00	Martin Chuzzlewit,......Cloth,	3.00
David Copperfield,........Cloth,	3.00	Old Curiosity Shop,.....Cloth,	3.00
Oliver Twist,................Cloth,	3.00	Little Dorrit,..............Cloth,	3.00
Christmas Stories,.........Cloth,	3.00	Dombey and Son,.......Cloth,	3.00

The following are each complete in one volume.

Great Expectations.................$1.50 | Dickens' New Stories,...Cloth, $1.50
Mystery of Edwin Drood; and Master Humphrey's Clock,....Cloth, 1.50
American Notes; and the Uncommercial Traveller,..............Cloth, 1.50
Hunted Down: and other Reprinted Pieces,........................Cloth, 1.50
The Holly-Tree Inn; and other Stories,...............................Cloth, 1.50
The Life and Writings of Charles Dickens,.........................Cloth, 2.00
John Jasper's Secret. Sequel to Mystery of Edwin Drood,...Cloth, 2.00
Price of a set, in thirty-six volumes, bound in cloth,................. $55.00
    "   "   Full sheep, Library style,........................ 76 00
    "   "   Half calf, antique, or half calf, full gilt backs, etc. 108.00

FRANK FAIRLEGH'S WORKS.

Frank Fairlegh,.....................	75	Harry Racket Scapegrace,.....	75
Lewis Arundel,.....................	1 00	Tom Racquet,.....................	75

Finer editions of the above are also issued in cloth, at $1.75 each

Harry Coverdale's Courtship,	1 50	Lorrimer Littlegood,............	50

The above are each in paper cover, or in cloth, price $1.75 each.

The Colville Family. By author of "Frank Fairlegh,"................... 50

MRS. C. J. NEWBY'S WORKS.

Sunshine and Shadow,...........	50	Trodden Down,.....................	50
Kate Kennedy,.....................	50	Married,...............................	50
Wondrous Strange.................	50	Common Sense,...................	50
Margaret Hamilton,...............	50	Only Temper,.......................	50
Right and Left,.....................	50		

☞ Above Books will be sent, postage paid, on receipt of Retail Price, by T. B. Peterson & Brothers, Philadelphia, Pa. (17)

18 T. B. PETERSON & BROTHERS' PUBLICATIONS.

HUMOROUS AMERICAN WORKS.

With Illuminated Covers, and beautifully Illustrated by Felix O. C. Darley.

Major Jones's Courtship. With Illustrations by Darley,.............	75
Major Jones's Sketches of Travels. Full of Illustrations.............	75
The Adventures of Captain Simon Suggs. Illustrated,............	75
Major Jones's Chronicles of Pineville. Illustrated,.....................	75
Polly Peablossom's Wedding. With Illustrations,.....................	75
Widow Rugby's Husband. Full of Illustrations,.....................	75
The Big Bear of Arkansas. Illustrated by Darley,.....................	75
Western Scenes; or, Life on the Prairie. Illustrated,.....................	75
Streaks of Squatter Life and Far West Scenes. Illustrated,...........	75
Pickings from the New Orleans Picayune. Illustrated,.............	75
Stray Subjects Arrested and Bound Over. Illustrated,............	75
The Louisiana Swamp Doctor. Full of Illustrations,..................	75
Charcoal Sketches. By Joseph C. Neal. Illustrated,..................	75
Peter Faber's Misfortunes. By Joseph C. Neal. Illustrated,..........	75
Peter Ploddy and other Oddities. By Joseph C. Neal,...............	75
Yankee Among the Mermaids. By William E. Burton................	75
The Drama in Pokerville. By J. M. Field. Illustrated,..............	75
New Orleans Sketch Book. With Illustrations by Darley,.............	75
The Deer Stalkers. By Frank Forrester. Illustrated,..................	75
The Quorndon Hounds. By Frank Forrester. Illustrated,............	75
My Shooting Box. By Frank Forrester. Illustrated,.....................	75
The Warwick Woodlands. By Frank Forrester. Illustrated,.........	75
Adventures of Captain Farrago. By H. H. Brackenridge,.............	75
Adventures of Major O'Regan. By H. H. Brackenridge, ...	75
Sol Smith's Theatrical Apprenticeship. Illustrated,.....................	75
Sol Smith's Theatrical Journey-Work. Illustrated,.....................	75
Quarter Race in Kentucky. With Illustrations by Darley,............	75
The Mysteries of the Backwoods. By T. B. Thorpe,.....................	75
Percival Mayberry's Adventures. By J. H. Ingraham,.................	75
Sam Slick's Yankee Yarns and Yankee Letters,.............................	75
Adventures of Fudge Fumble; or, Love Scrapes of his Life,............	75
Aunt Patty's Scrap Bag. By Mrs. Caroline Lee Hentz,..................	75
Following the Drum. By Mrs. Gen. Viele,................................	50
The American Joe Miller. With 100 Engravings,........................	50

SAMUEL WARREN'S BEST BOOKS.

Ten Thousand a Year, paper,$1 50	
Ten Thousand a Year, cloth,.. 2 00	The Diary of a Medical Student,................................. 75

WILLIAM H. MAXWELL'S WORKS.

Wild Sports of the West,.......	75	Brian O'Lynn,.....................	75
Stories of Waterloo,...............	75	Life of Grace O'Malley,.........	50

☞ Above Books will be sent, postage paid, on receipt of Retail Price, by T. B. Peterson & Brothers, Philadelphia, Pa.

T. B. PETERSON & BROTHERS' PUBLICATIONS. 19

MISS PARDOE'S POPULAR WORKS.

Confessions of a Pretty Woman,	75	The Rival Beauties,...............	75
The Wife's Trials,...............	75	Romance of the Harem,.........	75
The Jealous Wife,...............	75		

Each of the above five books are also bound in cloth, at $1.00 each.
The Adopted Heir.   One volume, paper, $1.50; or in cloth,..........$1 75
The Earl's Secret.   One volume, paper, $1.50; or in cloth, ... 1 75

T. S. ARTHUR'S HOUSEHOLD NOVELS.

The Lost Bride,......................	50	The Divorced Wife,...............	50
The Two Brides,....................	50	Mary Moreton,......................	50
Love in a Cottage,.................	50	Pride and Prudence,..	50
Love in High Life,.................	50	Agnes; or, the Possessed,......	50
Year after Marriage,..............	50	Lucy Sandford......................	50
The Lady at Home,................	50	The Banker's Wife,...............	50
Cecelia Howard,....................	50	The Two Merchants,.............	50
Orphan Children,...................	50	Trial and Triumph,...............	50
Debtor's Daughter,.................	50	The Iron Rule,......................	50
Insubordination; or, the Shoemaker's Daughters,........................			50
The Latimer Family; or, The Bottle and the Pledge. Illustrated,....			50

Six Nights with the Washingtonians; and other Temperance Tales.
By T. S. Arthur. With original Illustrations, by George Cruikshank. One large octavo volume, bound in beveled boards, $3.50;
red roan, full gilt back, $4.50; or full Turkey morocco, full gilt,... 6 00
Lizzy Glenn; or, the Trials of a Seamstress. Cloth $1.75; or paper, 1 50

MRS. GREY'S CELEBRATED NOVELS.

Cousin Harry,.....................$1 50   The Little Beauty,..............$1 50
The above are each in paper cover, or in cloth, price $1.75 each.

A Marriage in High Life,........	50	The Baronet's Daughters,........	50
Gipsy's Daughter,.................	50	Young Prima Donna,.............	50
Old Dower House,.................	50	Hyacinthe,...........................	25
Belle of the Family,...............	50	Alice Seymour,.....................	25
Duke and Cousin,.................	50	Mary Seaham.......................	75
The Little Wife,....................	50	Passion and Principle,..........	75
Lena Cameron,.....................	50	The Flirt,.............................	75
Sybil Lennard......................	50	Good Society,......................	75
Manœuvring Mother	50	Lion-Hearted,......................	75

G. P. R. JAMES'S BEST BOOKS.

Lord Montague's Page. Paper cover, $1.50, or in cloth,...............$1 75
The Cavalier. By the author of "Lord Montague's Page," cloth,.... 1 00

The Man in Black,...............	75	Arrah Neil,.........................	75
Mary of Burgundy,..............	75	Eva St. Clair,......................	50

☞ Above Books will be sent, postage paid, on receipt of Retail Price, by T. B. Peterson & Brothers, Philadelphia, Pa.

HUMOROUS AMERICAN WORKS,

Full of Illustrations by Darley, and each Book in Illuminated Covers.

The Books on this page are the Funniest Books in the world, and are for sale by all Booksellers, and by the Publishers,

T. B. PETERSON & BROTHERS, PHILADELPHIA.

THE FOLLOWING BOOKS ARE SEVENTY-FIVE CENTS EACH.

MAJOR JONES'S COURTSHIP. With Illustrations by Darley.
MAJOR JONES'S SKETCHES OF TRAVEL. Full of Illustrations.
MAJOR JONES'S CHRONICLES OF PINEVILLE. Illustrated.
THE ADVENTURES OF CAPTAIN SIMON SUGGS. Illustrated.
POLLY PEABLOSSOM'S WEDDING. With Illustrations.
WIDOW RUGBY'S HUSBAND. Full of Illustrations.
THE BIG BEAR OF ARKANSAS. Illustrated by Darley.
WESTERN SCENES; or, LIFE ON THE PRAIRIE. Illustrated.
STREAKS OF SQUATTER LIFE AND FAR WESTERN SCENES. Illustrated
PICKINGS FROM THE NEW ORLEANS PICAYUNE. Illustrated.
STRAY SUBJECTS ARRESTED AND BOUND OVER. Illustrated.
THE LOUISIANA SWAMP DOCTOR. Full of Illustrations.
CHARCOAL SKETCHES. By Joseph C. Neal. Illustrated.
PETER FABER'S MISFORTUNES. By Joseph C. Neal. Illustrated.
PETER PLODDY AND OTHER ODDITIES. By Joseph C. Neal.
YANKEE AMONG THE MERMAIDS. By William E. Burton.
THE DRAMA IN POKERVILLE. By J. M. Field. Illustrated.
NEW ORLEANS SKETCH BOOK. With Illustrations by Darley.
THE DEER STALKERS. By Frank Forrester. Illustrated.
THE QUORNDON HOUNDS. By Frank Forrester. Illustrated.
MY SHOOTING BOX. By Frank Forrester. Illustrated.
THE WARWICK WOODLANDS. By Frank Forrester. Illustrated.
ADVENTURES OF CAPTAIN FARRAGO. By H. H. Brackenridge.
ADVENTURES OF MAJOR O'REGAN. By H. H. Brackenridge.
SOL SMITH'S THEATRICAL APPRENTICESHIP. Illustrated.
SOL SMITH'S THEATRICAL JOURNEY-WORK. Illustrated.
QUARTER RACE IN KENTUCKY. With Illustrations by Darley.
THE MYSTERIES OF THE BACKWOODS. By T. B. Thorpe.
PERCIVAL MAYBERRY'S ADVENTURES. By J. H. Ingraham.
SAM SLICK'S YANKEE YARNS AND YANKEE LETTERS.
ADVENTURES OF FUDGE FUMBLE; or, LOVE SCRAPES OF HIS LIFE.
AUNT PATTY'S SCRAP BAG. By Mrs. Caroline Lee Hentz.

ABOVE BOOKS ARE SEVENTY-FIVE CENTS EACH.

RANCY COTTEM'S COURTSHIP. By author of "Major Jones's Courtship," "Major Jones's Sketches of Travel," etc. Illustrated. Price 50 cents.
FOLLOWING THE DRUM. By Mrs. Gen. Viele. Price 50 cents.
THE AMERICAN JOE MILLER. With 100 Engravings. Price 50 cents.

☞ *The above works will be found for sale by all Booksellers and News Agents.*
☞ *Copies of any one, or more, or all of the above works, will be sent to any place at once, post-paid, on remitting the price of the ones wanted to the Publishers,*

T. B. PETERSON & BROTHERS, Philadelphia, Pa.

Émile Zola's New Books.

The Greatest Novels Ever Printed.

NANA! The Sequel to "L'Assommoir." *By Émile Zola.* Complete in one large square duodecimo volume, price 75 cents in paper cover, or One Dollar in Morocco Cloth, Black and Gold.

L'ASSOMMOIR. *By Émile Zola.* "L'Assommoir" and "Nana" are the most Popular Novels ever published. They have already attained a sale in Paris of over Two Hundred Thousand Copies. Complete in one large square duodecimo volume, price 75 cents in paper cover, or One Dollar in Morocco Cloth, Black and Gold.

HIS EXCELLENCY EUGENE ROUGON. *By Émile Zola,* author of "L'Assommoir." One large volume, price 75 cents in paper cover, or $1.25 in Morocco Cloth, Black and Gold.

THE CONQUEST OF PLASSANS; or, LA CONQUÉTE DE PLASSANS. *A Tale of Provincial Life. By Émile Zola.* Price 75 cents in paper cover, or $1.25 in Morocco Cloth.

THE MARKETS OF PARIS; or, LE VENTRE DE PARIS. *By Émile Zola.* Price 75 cents in paper cover, or $1.25 in Morocco Cloth, Black and Gold.

THE ROUGON-MACQUART FAMILY; or, LA FORTUNE DES ROUGON. *By Émile Zola.* Price 75 cents in paper cover, or $1.25 in Morocco Cloth, Black and Gold.

HÉLÈNE; A LOVE EPISODE; or, UNE PAGE D'AMOUR. *By Émile Zola.* Price 75 cents in paper cover, or $1.25 in Morocco Cloth, Black and Gold.

THE ABBÉ'S TEMPTATION; or, LA FAUTE DE L'ABBE MOURET. *By Émile Zola.* Price 75 cents in paper cover, or $1.25 in Morocco Cloth, Black and Gold.

☞ *Above Books are for sale by all Booksellers and News Agents, or copies of any one, or all of them, will be sent to any one, to any place, at once, per return of mail, postpaid, on remitting the price of the ones wanted, to the Publishers,*

T. B. PETERSON & BROTHERS,
306 Chestnut Street, Philadelphia, Pa.

GEORGE W. M. REYNOLDS' WORKS.
NEW AND BEAUTIFUL EDITIONS, JUST READY.
Each Work is complete and unabridged, in one large volume.
All or any will be sent free of postage, everywhere, to all, on receipt of remittances.

Mysteries of the Court of London; being THE MYSTERIES OF THE COURT OF GEORGE THE THIRD, *with the Life and Times of the* PRINCE OF WALES, *afterward GEORGE THE FOURTH.* Complete in one large volume, bound in cloth, price $1.75; or in paper cover, price $1.00.
Rose Foster; or, the "Second Series of the Mysteries of the Court of London." Complete in one large volume, bound in cloth, price $1.75; or in paper cover, price $1.50.
Caroline of Brunswick; or, the "Third Series of the Mysteries of the Court of London. Complete in one large volume, bound in cloth, price $1.75; or in paper cover, price $1.00.
Venetia Trelawney; being the "Fourth Series or final conclusion of the Mysteries of the Court of London." Complete in one large volume, bound in cloth, price $1.75; or in paper cover, price $1.00.
Lord Saxondale; or, The Court of Queen Victoria. Complete in one large volume, bound in cloth, price $1.75; or in paper cover, price $1.00.
Count Christoval. The "Sequel to Lord Saxondale." Complete in one large volume, bound in cloth, price $1.75; or in paper cover, price $1.00.
Rosa Lambert; or, The Memoirs of an Unfortunate Woman. Complete in one large volume, bound in cloth, price $1.75; or in paper cover, price $1.00.
Joseph Wilmot; or, The Memoirs of a Man Servant. Complete in one large volume, bound in cloth, price $1.75; or in paper cover, price $1.00.
The Banker's Daughter. A Sequel to "Joseph Wilmot." Complete in one large volume, bound in cloth, price $1.75; or in paper cover, price $1.00.
The Rye-House Plot; or, Ruth, the Conspirator's Daughter. Complete in one large volume, bound in cloth, price $1.75; or in paper cover, price $1.00.
The Necromancer. Being the Mysteries of the Court of Henry the Eighth. Complete in one large volume, bound in cloth, price $1.75; or in paper cover, price $1.00.
Mary Price; or, The Adventures of a Servant Maid. One vol., cloth, price $1.75; or in paper, $1.00.
Eustace Quentin. A "Sequel to Mary Price." One vol., cloth, price $1.75; or in paper, $1.00.
The Mysteries of the Court of Naples. Price $1.00 in paper cover; or $1.75 in cloth.
Kenneth. A Romance of the Highlands. One vol., cloth, price $1.75; or in paper cover, $1.00.
Wallace: the Hero of Scotland. Illustrated with 38 plates. Paper, $1.00; cloth, $1.75.
The Gipsy Chief. Beautifully Illustrated. Price $1.00 in paper cover, or $1.75 in cloth.
Robert Bruce; the Hero King of Scotland. Illustrated. Paper, $1.00; cloth. $1.75.
The Opera Dancer; or, The Mysteries of London Life. Price 75 cents.
Isabella Vincent; or, The Two Orphans. One large octavo volume. Price 75 cents.
Vivian Bertram; or, A Wife's Honor. A Sequel to "Isabella Vincent." Price 75 cents.
The Countess of Lascelles. The Continuation to "Vivian Bertram." Price 75 cents.
Duke of Marchmont. Being the Conclusion of "The Countess of Lascelles." Price 75 cents.
The Child of Waterloo; or, The Horrors of the Little Field. Price 75 cents.
Pickwick Abroad. A Companion to the "Pickwick Papers," by "Boz." Price 75 cents.
The Countess and the Page. One large octavo volume. Price 75 cents.
Mary Stuart, Queen of Scots. Complete in one large octavo volume. Price 75 cents.
The Soldier's Wife. Illustrated. One large octavo volume. Price 75 cents.
May Middleton; or, The History of a Fortune. In one large octavo volume. Price 75 cent
The Loves of the Harem. One large octavo volume. Price 75 cents.
Ellen Percy; or, The Memoirs of an Actress. One large octavo volume. Price 75 cents.
The Discarded Queen. One large octavo volume. Price 75 cents.
Agnes Evelyn; or, Beauty and Pleasure. One large octavo volume. Price 75 cents.
The Massacre of Glencoe. One large octavo volume. Price 75 cents.
The Parricide; or, Youth's Career in Crime. Beautifully Illustrated. Price 75 cents.
Ciprina; or, The Secrets of a Picture Gallery. One volume. Price 50 cents.
The Ruined Gamester. With Illustrations. One large octavo volume. Price 50 cents.
Life in Paris. Handsomely illustrated. One large octavo volume. Price 50 cents.
Clifford and the Actress. One large octavo volume. Price 50 cents.
Edgar Montrose. One large octavo volume. Price 50 cents.

☞ *The above works will be found for sale by all Booksellers and News Agents.*
☞ *Copies of any one, or more, or all of Reynolds' works, will be sent to any place at once, post-paid, on remitting price of ones wanted to the Publishers,*

T. B. PETERSON & BROTHERS, Philadelphia, Pa.

Rancy Cottem's Courtship.
WITH EIGHT FULL PAGE ILLUSTRATIONS.
BY MAJOR JOSEPH JONES.
(OF PINEVILLE, GEORGIA.)

"Rancy pulled his chair a little closer, and caught hold of the thread, while she went on knittin."

ONE VOLUME, SQUARE 12mo., PAPER COVER. PRICE 50 CENTS.

☞ *Rancy Cottem's Courtship* is for sale by all Booksellers and News Agents, or copies of it will be sent at once, post-paid, on remitting Fifty cents in a letter to the publishers,

T. B. PETERSON & BROTHERS, Philadelphia, Pa.

ALEXANDER DUMAS' GREAT WORKS.

All or any will be sent free of postage, everywhere, to all, on receipt of remittances.

The Count of Monte-Cristo. With elegant illustrations, and portraits of Edmond Dantes, Mercedes, and Fernand. Price $1.50 in paper cover; or $1.75 in cloth.
Edmond Dantes. A Sequel to the "Count of Monte-Cristo." In one large octavo volume. Price 75 cents in paper cover, or a finer edition, bound in cloth, for $1.75.
The Countess of Monte-Cristo. With a portrait of the "Countess of Monte-Cristo" on the cover. One large octavo volume, paper cover, price $1.00; or bound in cloth, for $1.75.
The Three Guardsmen; or, The Three Mousquetaires. In one large octavo volume. Price 75 cents in paper cover, or a finer edition in cloth, for $1.75.
Twenty Years After. A Sequel to the "Three Guardsmen." In one large octavo volume. Price 75 cents in paper cover, or a finer edition, in one volume, cloth, for $1.75.
Bragelonne; the Son of Athos. Being the continuation of "Twenty Years After." In one large octavo volume. Price 75 cents in paper cover, or a finer edition in cloth, for $1.75.
The Iron Mask. Being the continuation of the "Three Guardsmen," "Twenty Years After," and "Bragelonne." In one large octavo volume. Paper cover, $1.00; or in cloth, for $1.75.
Louise La Valliere; or, the Second Series of the "Iron Mask," and end of "The Three Guardsmen" series. In one large octavo volume. Paper cover, $1.00; or in cloth, for $1.75.
The Memoirs of a Physician; or, The Secret History of the Court of Louis the Fifteenth. Beautifully Illustrated. In one large octavo volume. Paper cover, $1.00; or in cloth, for $1.75.
The Queen's Necklace; or, The "Second Series of the Memoirs of a Physician." In one large octavo volume. Paper cover, price $1.00; or in one volume, cloth, for $1.75.
Six Years Later; or, Taking of the Bastile. Being the "Third Series of the Memoirs of a Physician." In one large octavo volume. Paper cover, $1.00; or in cloth, for $1.75.
Countess of Charny; or, The Fall of the French Monarchy. Being the "Fourth Series of the Memoirs of a Physician." In one large octavo volume. Paper cover, $1.00; or in cloth, for $1.75.
Andree de Taverney. Being the "Fifth Series of the Memoirs of a Physician." In one large octavo volume. Paper cover, $1.00; or in one volume, cloth, for $1.75.
The Chevalier; or, the "Sixth Series and final conclusion of the Memoirs of a Physician Series." In one large octavo volume. Price $1.00 in paper cover; or $1.75 in cloth.
Joseph Balsamo. Dumas' greatest work, from which the play of "Joseph Balsamo" was dramatized, by his son, Alexander Dumas, Jr. Price $1.00 in paper cover, or $1.50 in cloth.
The Conscript; or, The Days of the First Napoleon. An Historical Novel. In one large duodecimo volume. Price $1.50 in paper cover; or in cloth, for $1.75.
Camille; or, The Fate of a Coquette. ("La Dame aux Camelias.") This is the only true and complete translation of "Camille," and it is from this translation that the Play of "Camille," and the Opera of "La Traviata" was adapted to the Stage. Paper cover, price $1.50; or in cloth, $1.75.
Love and Liberty; or, A Man of the People. (Rene Besson.) A Thrilling Story of the French Revolution of 1792-93. In one large duodecimo volume, paper cover, $1.50; cloth, $1.75.
The Adventures of a Marquis. Paper cover, $1.00; or in one volume, cloth, for $1.75.
The Forty-Five Guardsmen. Paper cover, $1.00; or in one volume, cloth, for $1.75.
Diana of Meridor. Paper cover, $1.00; or in one volume, cloth, for $1.75.
The Iron Hand. Price $1.00 in paper cover, or in one volume, cloth, for $1.75.
Isabel of Bavaria, Queen of France. In one large octavo volume. Price 75 cents.
Annette; or, The Lady of the Pearls. A Companion to "Camille." Price 75 cents.
The Fallen Angel. A Story of Love and Life in Paris. One large volume. Price 75 cents.
The Mohicans of Paris. In one large octavo volume. Price 75 cents.
The Horrors of Paris. In one large octavo volume. Price 75 cents.
The Man with Five Wives. In one large octavo volume. Price 75 cents.
Sketches in France. In one large octavo volume. Price 75 cents.
Felina de Chambure; or, The Female Fiend. Price 75 cents.
The Twin Lieutenants; or, The Soldier's Bride. Price 75 cents.
Madame de Chamblay. In one large octavo volume. Price 50 cents.
The Black Tulip. In one large octavo volume. Price 50 cents.
The Corsican Brothers. In one large octavo volume. Price 50 cents.
George; or, The Planter of the Isle of France. Price 50 cents.
The Count of Moret. In one large octavo volume. Price 50 cents.
The Marriage Verdict. In one large octavo volume. Price 50 cents.
Buried Alive. In one large octavo volume. Price 25 cents.

☞ *Above books are for sale by all Booksellers and News Agents, or copies of any one or more, will be sent to any one, post-paid, on remitting price to the Publishers,*

T. B. PETERSON & BROTHERS, Philadelphia, Pa.

MAJOR JONES'S GEORGIA SCENES.
By Author of 'Major Jones's Courtship.'

"'Silence, fellers, silence!' bawled out over a dozen at one time. When they had become somewhat quiet, Major Jones mounted a chair, and read out in a full round tone, and right off, the whole bill, from 'Great Attraction,' to 'Performances to commence at half-past seven precisely.'"—Page 12.

ONE VOLUME, SQUARE 12mo., PAPER COVER. PRICE 75 CENTS.

☞ *Major Jones's Georgia Scenes* is for sale by all Booksellers and News Agents, or copies will be sent at once, post-paid, on remitting Seventy-Five cents in a letter to the publishers,

T. B. PETERSON & BROTHERS, Philadelphia, Pa.

PETERSONS' DOLLAR SERIES
OF GOOD AND NEW NOVELS, ARE THE BEST, LARGEST, AND
CHEAPEST BOOKS IN THE WORLD.
Price One Dollar Each, in Cloth, Black and Gold.

A WOMAN'S THOUGHTS ABOUT WOMEN. By Miss Mulock. Every Lady wants it
TWO WAYS TO MATRIMONY; or, Is It Love, or, False Pride?
THE STORY OF "ELIZABETH." By Miss Thackeray, daughter of W. M. Thackeray
FLIRTATIONS IN FASHIONABLE LIFE. By Catharine Sinclair.
THE MATCHMAKER. A Society Novel. By Beatrice Reynolds. Full of freshness and truth.
ROSE DOUGLAS, The Bonnie Scotch Lass. A companion to "Family Pride."
THE EARL'S SECRET. A Charming and Sentimental Love Story. By Miss Pardoe.
FAMILY SECRETS. A companion to "Family Pride," and a very fascinating work.
A LONELY LIFE. A Thrilling Novel in Real Life.
THE MACDERMOTS OF BALLYCLORAN. An Exciting Novel by Anthony Trollope.
THE FAMILY SAVE-ALL. With Economical Receipts for Breakfast, Dinner and Tea.
SELF-SACRIFICE. A Charming and Exciting work. By author of "Margaret Maitland."
THE PRIDE OF LIFE. A Love Story. By Lady Jane Scott.
THE RIVAL BELLES; or, Life in Washington. By author "Wild Western Scenes."
THE CLYFFARDS OF CLYFFE. By James Payn, author of "Lost Sir Massingberd."
THE ORPHAN'S TRIALS; or, Alone in a Great City. By Emerson Bennett.
THE HEIRESS OF SWEETWATER. A Love Story, abounding with exciting scenes.
THE REFUGEE. A delightful book, full of food for laughter, and sterling information.
LOST SIR MASSINGBERD. A Love Story. By author of "The Clyffards of Clyffe."
CORA BELMONT; or, THE SINCERE LOVER. A True Story of the Heart.
THE LOVER'S TRIALS; or, The Days Before the Revolution. By Mrs. Denison.
MY SON'S WIFE. A strong, bright, interesting, and charming Novel. By author of "Caste."
AUNT PATTY'S SCRAP BAG. By Mrs. Caroline Lee Hentz, author of "Linda," "Rena."
SARATOGA! AND THE FAMOUS SPRINGS. An Indian Tale of Frontier Life.
COUNTRY QUARTERS. A Charming Love Story. By the Countess of Blessington.
SELF-LOVE. A Book for Young Ladies, with their prospects in Single and Married Life contrasted.
LOVE AND DUTY. A Charming Love Story. By Mrs. Hubback.
THE DEVOTED BRIDE; or, FAITH AND FIDELITY. A Love Story.
THE HEIRESS IN THE FAMILY. By author of "Marrying for Money."
COLLEY CIBBER'S LIFE OF EDWIN FORREST, with Reminiscences.
THE MAN OF THE WORLD. This is full of style, elegance of diction, and force of thought.
OUT OF THE DEPTHS. A Woman's Story and a Woman's Book, the Story of a Woman's Life
THE QUEEN'S FAVORITE; or, The Price of a Crown. A Romance of Don Juan.
THE CAVALIER. A Novel. By G. P. R. James, author of "Lord Montagu's Page."
THE RECTOR'S WIFE; or, THE VALLEY OF A HUNDRED FIRES.
THE COQUETTE; or, LIFE AND LETTERS OF ELIZA WHARTON.
WOMAN'S WRONG. A Book for Women. By Mrs. Elloart. A Novel of great power.
HAREM LIFE IN EGYPT AND CONSTANTINOPLE. By Emmeline Lott.
THE OLD PATROON; or, THE GREAT VAN BROEK PROPERTY.
THE BEAUTIFUL WIDOW.   TREASON AT HOME.   PANOLA!

☞ *The above Books are all issued in "Petersons' Dollar Series," and they will be found for sale by all Booksellers, News Agents, and on all Railroad trains, at One Dollar each, or copies of any one, or more, will be sent to any place, at once, post-paid, on remitting the price of the ones wanted in a letter, to*

T. B. PETERSON & BROTHERS, Philadelphia.

MAJOR JONES'S TRAVELS.
By Author of "Major Jones's Courtship."

"Says she to Major Jones, I'm a poor woman, my husban's sick, won't you hold this bundle for me till I go in the drug-store for some medicin'. I did so, got tired of waiting, and walked down to the lamp-post to see what it was. 'It was a live baby,' and the sweat poured out of me, I tell you, in a stream."—*Page* 111.

ONE VOLUME, SQUARE 12mo., PAPER COVER. PRICE 75 CENTS.

☞ *Major Jones's Travels* is for sale by all *Booksellers* and *News Agents*, or copies of it will be sent at once, post-paid, on remitting *Seventy-five cents* in a letter to the publishers,

T. B. PETERSON & BROTHERS, Philadelphia, Pa.

MAJOR JONES'S COURTSHIP

AND OTHER BOOKS BY MAJOR JONES, JUST PUBLISHED AND FOR SALE BY

T. B. PETERSON & BROTHERS, PHILADELPHIA.

Major Jones's Courtship.

MAJOR JONES'S COURTSHIP. Detailed, with Humorous Scenes, Incidents, and Adventures. By Major Joseph Jones, author of "Rancy Cottem's Courtship," "Major Jones's Travels," "Major Jones's Georgia Scenes," etc. Revised and Enlarged. With Twenty-One Full Page Illustrations on Tinted Plate Paper, by Darley and Cary. One volume, 12mo., uniform with this volume, price 75 cents.

Major Jones's Travels.

MAJOR JONES'S TRAVELS. Detailing his Adventures, Humorous Scenes, and Incidents, in each town he passed through, while on his tour from Georgia to Canada. By Major Joseph Jones, author of "Major Jones's Courtship," "Rancy Cottem's Courtship," "Major Jones's Georgia Scenes," etc. With Eight Full Page Illustrations on Tinted Paper, by Darley. One volume, 12mo., uniform with this volume, price 75 cents.

Major Jones's Georgia Scenes.

MAJOR JONES'S GEORGIA SCENES. Comprising his celebrated Sketches of Georgia Scenes, with their Incidents and Characters. By Major Joseph Jones, author of "Major Jones's Courtship," "Rancy Cottem's Courtship," "Major Jones's Travels," etc. With Twelve Full Page Illustrations on Tinted Plate Paper, by Darley. One volume, 12mo., uniform with this volume, price 75 cents.

Rancy Cottem's Courtship.

RANCY COTTEM'S COURTSHIP. With Other Humorous Stories. By Major Joseph Jones, author of "Major Jones's Courtship," "Major Jones's Travels," "Major Jones's Georgia Scenes," etc. With Eight Full Page Illustrations on Tinted Plate Paper, by Cary. One volume, 12mo., uniform with this volume, price 50 cents.

☞ *Above Books by Major Jones, are for sale by all Booksellers and News Agents, or copies of any one or all of them, will be sent to any one, to any place, at once, post-paid, on remitting the price of the ones wanted, to the publishers,*

T. B. PETERSON & BROTHERS, Philadelphia, Pa.

Major Jones's Courtship.
WITH 21 FULL PAGE ILLUSTRATIONS.
BY MAJOR JOSEPH JONES.
(OF PINEVILLE, GEORGIA.)

"By this time the galls was holt of my coat-tail, hollerin as hard as they could."

ONE VOLUME, SQUARE 12mo., PAPER COVER. PRICE 75 CENTS

☞ *Major Jones's Courtship is for sale by all Booksellers and News Agents, or copies of it will be sent at once, post-paid, on remitting Seventy-five cents in a letter to the publishers,*

T. B. PETERSON & BROTHERS, Philadelphia, Pa.

MRS. SOUTHWORTH'S WORKS,

EACH IS IN ONE LARGE DUODECIMO VOLUME, MOROCCO CLOTH, GILT BACK, PRICE $1.75 EACH.

All or any will be sent free of postage, everywhere, to all, on receipt of remittances.

ISHMAEL; or, IN THE DEPTHS. (Being "Self-Made; or, Out of Depths."
SELF-RAISED; or, From the Depths. The Sequel to "Ishmael."
THE PHANTOM WEDDING; or, the Fall of the House of Flint.
THE "MOTHER-IN-LAW;" or, MARRIED IN HASTE.
THE MISSING BRIDE; or, MIRIAM, THE AVENGER.
VICTOR'S TRIUMPH. The Sequel to "A Beautiful Fiend."
A BEAUTIFUL FIEND; or, THROUGH THE FIRE.
THE LADY OF THE ISLE; or, THE ISLAND PRINCESS.
FAIR PLAY; or, BRITOMARTE, THE MAN-HATER.
HOW HE WON HER. The Sequel to "Fair Play."
THE CHANGED BRIDES; or, Winning Her Way.
THE BRIDE'S FATE. The Sequel to "The Changed Brides."
CRUEL AS THE GRAVE; or, Hallow Eve Mystery.
TRIED FOR HER LIFE. The Sequel to "Cruel as the Grave."
THE CHRISTMAS GUEST; or, The Crime and the Curse.
THE LOST HEIR OF LINLITHGOW; or, The Brothers.
A NOBLE LORD. The Sequel to "The Lost Heir of Linlithgow."
THE FAMILY DOOM; or, THE SIN OF A COUNTESS.
THE MAIDEN WIDOW. The Sequel to "The Family Doom."
THE GIPSY'S PROPHECY; or, The Bride of an Evening.
THE FORTUNE SEEKER; or, Astrea, The Bridal Day.
THE THREE BEAUTIES; or, SHANNONDALE.
FALLEN PRIDE; or, THE MOUNTAIN GIRL'S LOVE.
THE DISCARDED DAUGHTER; or, The Children of the Isle.
THE PRINCE OF DARKNESS; or, HICKORY HALL.
THE TWO SISTERS; or, Virginia and Magdalene.
THE FATAL MARRIAGE; or, ORVILLE DEVILLE.
INDIA; or, THE PEARL OF PEARL RIVER.
THE WIDOW'S SON; or, LEFT ALONE.
THE MYSTERY OF DARK HOLLOW.
ALLWORTH ABBEY; or, EUDORA.
THE BRIDAL EVE; or, ROSE ELMER.
VIVIA; or, THE SECRET OF POWER.
THE HAUNTED HOMESTEAD.
BRIDE OF LLEWELLYN.   THE DESERTED WIFE.
THE CURSE OF CLIFTON
THE WIFE'S VICTORY
THE SPECTRE LOVER.
THE ARTIST'S LOVE.
THE FATAL SECRET.
LOVE'S LABOR WON.
THE LOST HEIRESS.
RETRIBUTION

☞ Mrs. Southworth's works will be found for sale by all Booksellers.
☞ Copies of any one, or more of Mrs. Southworth's works, will be sent to any place, at once, per mail, post-paid, on remitting price of ones wanted to the Publishers,

T. B. PETERSON & BROTHERS, Philadelphia, Pa.

MAJOR JONES'S GEORGIA SCENES.

By Author of 'Major Jones's Courtship.'

"'Silence, fellers, silence!' bawled out over a dozen at one time. When they had become somewhat quiet, Major Jones mounted a chair, and read out in a full round tone, and right off, without spelling a word, the whole bill, from 'Great Attraction,' to 'Performances to commence at half-past seven precisely.'"—Page 1⸺.

ONE VOLUME, SQUARE 12mo., PAPER COVER. PRICE 75 CENTS.

☞ *Major Jones's Georgia Scenes is for sale by all Booksellers and News Agents, or copies will be sent at once, post-paid, on remitting Seventy-Five cents in a letter to the publishers,*

T. B. PETERSON & BROTHERS, Philadelphia, Pa.

www.ingramcontent.com/pod-product-compliance
Lightning Source LLC
Chambersburg PA
CBHW031746230426
43669CB00007B/503